JAPAN BEHIND THE FAN

By the same author

Poetry

THE DROWNED SAILOR
THE SUBMERGED VILLAGE
A CORRECT COMPASSION
A SPRING JOURNEY
THE DESCENT INTO THE CAVE
THE PRODIGAL SON
REFUSAL TO CONFORM
JAPAN MARINE: A POEM SEQUENCE
PAPER WINDOWS
JAPAN PHYSICAL (Kenkyusha, Tokyo)
WHITE SHADOWS, BLACK SHADOWS

Autobiography

THE ONLY CHILD
SORROWS, PASSIONS AND ALARMS

Travel

TOKYO
THESE HORNED ISLANDS: A JOURNAL OF JAPAN
TROPIC TEMPER: A MEMOIR OF MALAYA
BANGKOK
FILIPINESCAS: TRAVEL IN THE PHILIPPINES TODAY
ONE MAN'S RUSSIA
STREETS OF ASIA
HONG KONG

Novel

THE LOVE OF OTHERS

Drama

THE TRUE MISTERY OF THE NATIVITY
THE TRUE MISTERY OF THE PASSION
MOTHER COURAGE (Brecht)
THE PHYSICISTS (Dürrenmatt)
THE PRINCE OF HOMBURG (Kleist)

Translations

THE DARK CHILD (Camara Laye)
THE RADIANCE OF THE KING (Camara Laye)
MEMOIRS OF A DUTIFUL DAUGHTER (Simone de Beauvoir)
THE HEAVENLY MANDATE (Erwin Wickert)
THE TALES OF HOFFMAN
THE LITTLE MAN (Erich Kastner)
DAILY LIFE OF THE ETRUSCANS (Jacques Heurgon)
DAILY LIFE IN THE FRENCH REVOLUTION (Jean Robiquet)
etc. etc.

JAPAN BEHIND THE FAN

James Kirkup

WITH TWENTY-FOUR PAGES OF PLATES
AND ONE MAP

LONDON
J. M. DENT & SONS LTD

First published 1970

Made in Great Britain
at the
Aldine Press · Letchworth · Herts
for
J. M. DENT & SONS LTD
Aldine House · Bedford Street · London

SBN: 460 03887 7

Contents

Illustrations

Everything you know merely by hearsay is different when you actually get to see it.

(*Yoshida Kenko*)

The Japanese people have loved nature so passionately that they have interwoven her life and their own into one continuous drama of the art of pure living.

(*Fenollosa*)

It is always wrong to explain the phenomena of a country simply by reference to the character of its inhabitants.

(*Musil*)

Zeno replied, in answer to the question whether anything was at rest: Yes, the flying arrow is at rest.

(*Kafka*)

Foreword

LIFE IN Japan made a new person of me. I learned here, sometimes painfully, how to live and how to write. Japan has taught me to have the courage to be myself, to be an individual and solitary in a civilization where conformity is the rule and solitude the exception. Yet however peculiar and lonely I may appear here, I do not feel an outcast, as I do in England. Nor can I think of myself as an expatriate, for I feel at home everywhere in the East as I never do in Europe. Beyond the pettiness of much of Japanese life, and beneath much that is ugly on the surface, there is a profound, vast, resonant affirmation of life, a sense of ultimate quiet and eternity in everything, a mythological unity. These things perpetually comfort and enfold me, as in the strong arms of a giant god: I feel touched by them continually, as by the long smile of Buddha, that smile that is no smile.

I believe that nearly everything in my book reposes on this fundamental feeling. Its essence is a sense of the continuity of being which I have had since childhood, but was never so vividly aware of until I came to Japan.

Marcel Jouhandeau has a passage in his 'Que tout n'est qu'allusion' (*Journaliers 1960*) which expresses exactly the sense of mythological continuity I experience in Japan:

> Je surprends souvent chez moi mieux qu'une enfance, des surprises de nouveau-né. Le monde est devant mes yeux, comme si je sortais du sein de ma mère sans autres souvenirs qu'antidiluviens ou préhistoriques.

It is easy enough to say that if I were a Japanese things would be different. Of course they would. I am spiritually an Oriental, but I am not Japanese; I am a European and so my fate is different. This must be accepted, as I do accept it: it is my difference that makes me see things in a way no one else can see them. Like all races, the Japanese have their faults: the inability to see things except in conventional terms is one of them, and one which is completely at variance with my own way of looking at life. I do not mind these faults; it is the virtues I am interested in. Moreover I find things much more interesting than people, and Japan is above all else a land of things.

In this book, I portray everyday life as it is in Japan now and, in parts, as it was. Even in the short space of the last five years Japan has changed considerably, and not always for the better. Today I find appalling Japan's lack of common public morality, her increasing materialism and heedless search for immediate satisfactions, her totally uncritical absorption of many of the worst features of American and European life, her inane crazes for motoring, American musicals, golf, bowling, James Bond and American English conversation lessons.

I feel these things most strongly of course because I have been living in the gigantic cities of Osaka and Tokyo, and Osaka and Tokyo are not Japan. It is when I leave the cities and travel to my favourite places—Matsue, Yagi, Kanazawa, Yokote, Kōyasan, Kochi, Kumamoto or Kagoshima—or when I wander alone into the temple silences of the northern mountains or the southern islands, that I feel the true Japan will never die, and that her real, native spirit, at present under some evil enchantment, is asleep only for a short time.

Sooner or later, the best Japan, which is the Japan of the Japanese, not the Japan of the Westerner, will flourish again with all its vital traditions, its long mythologies and fundamental ceremonies.

Acknowledgments

Grateful thanks for permission to reprint material in this book which first appeared, in a slightly different form, in the following books or periodicals: the *Guardian*, *Orient/West*, *Japan Quarterly*, the *New Yorker*, *Japan Industrial* (vols. I and II), *Peace News*, the *New York Times*, *Réalités*, *Venture*.

Some of the material was also broadcast on the Overseas Services of Japan's national radio network, N.H.K., to South America, U.S.A. and Europe.

Most of this book has already appeared in Japanese translation in various Japanese magazines, and in two books, *Nippon no Insho* and *Ogi wo Suteta Nippon*, both issued in Japan by Nan 'Un Do Publishing Company, Tokyo. Many chapters have been used in textbooks for Japanese students: *Japan Now* (Eichosha, Tokyo), *Return to Japan* (Nan 'Un Do, Tokyo) and *The Way I See Japan* (Kinseido, Tokyo).

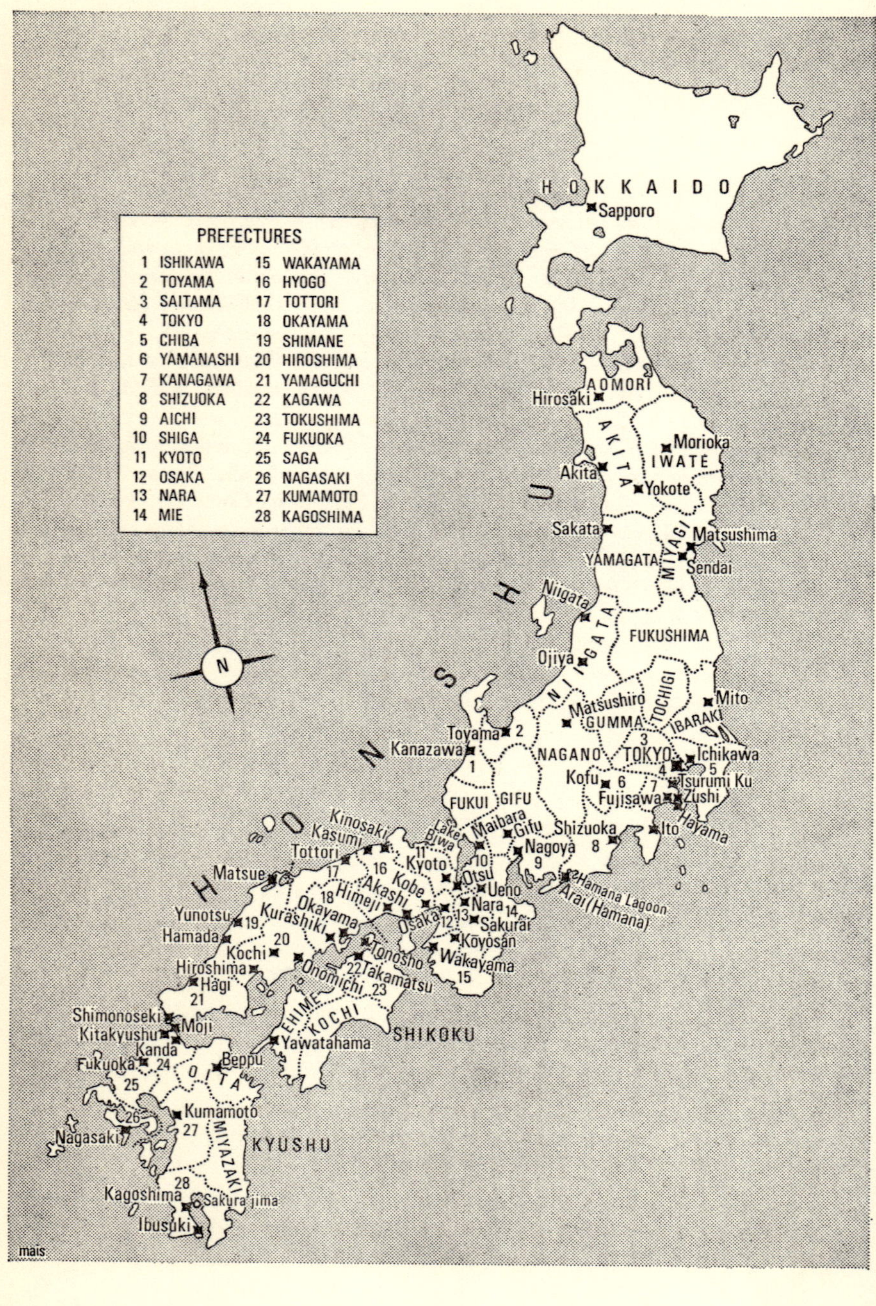

PREFECTURES
1 ISHIKAWA
2 TOYAMA
3 SAITAMA
4 TOKYO
5 CHIBA
6 YAMANASHI
7 KANAGAWA
8 SHIZUOKA
9 AICHI
10 SHIGA
11 KYOTO
12 OSAKA
13 NARA
14 MIE
15 WAKAYAMA
16 HYOGO
17 TOTTORI
18 OKAYAMA
19 SHIMANE
20 HIROSHIMA
21 YAMAGUCHI
22 KAGAWA
23 TOKUSHIMA
24 FUKUOKA
25 SAGA
26 NAGASAKI
27 KUMAMOTO
28 KAGOSHIMA
N
HOKKAIDO
Sapporo
AOMORI
Hirosaki
AKITA
Akita
IWATE
Morioka
Yokote
Sakata
MIYAGI
Matsushima
Sendai
YAMAGATA
HONSHU
Niigata
NIIGATA
FUKUSHIMA
Ojiya
TOCHIGI
Mito
Matsushiro
GUMMA
IBARAKI
Toyama
Kanazawa
NAGANO
TOKYO
Ichikawa
Kofu
Tsurumi Ku
Fujisawa
Zushi
Hayama
FUKUI
GIFU
Kinosaki
Kasumi
Lake Biwa
Maibara
Gifu
Shizuoka
Ito
Tottori
Kyoto
Nagoya
Matsue
Kobe
Otsu
Akashi
Himeji
Ueno
Nara
Hamana Lagoon
Arai (Hamana)
Okayama
Yunotsu
Kurashiki
Osaka
Sakurai
Hamada
Koyosan
Kochi
Tonosho
Wakayama
Hiroshima
Takamatsu
Onomichi
Hagi
EHIME
KOCHI
Shimonoseki
Moji
Kitakyushu
Yawatahama
SHIKOKU
Kanda
Fukuoka
Beppu
OITA
Kumamoto
Nagasaki
MIYAZAKI
KYUSHU
Kagoshima
Sakura jima
Ibusuki
mais

PART ONE

WINTER

I

RETURN TO JAPAN

As soon as we docked in Kōbe on that early winter morning I was at the rails, waiting impatiently to get off. While I queued for the Health and Immigration inspection I gazed upon Kōbe harbour with its semicircle of green mountains, some touched with snow in the distance, and at the lively port workers on ships and quays. It gave me an almost unbearable thrill to be so close to Japan again, to hear phrases of Japanese shouted by the dock labourers in their winter clothes and slit-toed, dark blue sock-shoes called *jikatabi* which give them such an agile walk.

When I was eventually allowed to land I said goodbye to no one, but just shoved my bag and *furoshiki*, or cloth-wrapped bundle, into a taxi and made straight for Sannomiya station. I had nowhere to go and no one to meet, but all that mattered was that I was back in Japan. It was better to be alone, to be unmet. The morning air sparkled with sun and cold on the frosted, grey-tiled roofs and I was radiantly happy.

Where should I go? Kōbe is nice enough, but a little too British for my liking. There are two fascinating museums in the city: the Hakutsuru Art Museum on a lovely site by the Sumiyoshi River, high in a ravine of the Rokko Mountains behind Kōbe, and the Kōbe Museum of Nanban Art.

Apart from these museums, the only places I really like in Kōbe are the Toritentoji Temple, that seems suspended on waterfalls of steps on top of Mount Maya, and some of the low bars and strip shows in Fukuhara. But it was only 8 a.m., a little too early for a strip show, even in Japan, and too late for the Toritentoji Temple, which should be visited at sunrise before the hordes of Japanese school children on conducted tours begin tearing through it. There would be time later to visit Kōbe again.

So I struggled aboard a packed slow train to Osaka. I should of course have waited for a more comfortable and quicker express, but all I wanted was to be on my way in Japan, so I caught the first available train. I stood looking out of the window at the industrial landscapes between Kōbe and Osaka, those visions of a charming hell under a pall of pastel-tinted smoke, of ugly factories transformed by the grace and energy of their workers into palaces of grim delight on a background of distant green-grey, snowy mountains. In between the factories were bare paddy-fields, an occasional hill with small wooden houses and little gardens whose only blossom, just then, was variegated washing and crimson *futon* or mattresses hanging out to air in the sun. We reached Osaka in just under an hour, and I found a room at the very drab Y.M.C.A. It was cold too, but I didn't mind: I was back in Japan.

In the streets of Osaka, that seem to move as relentlessly as assembly lines, I always felt I was the one person walking in the opposite direction to that taken by the massed millions of office workers. At times I thought I was going to be pitilessly trampled underfoot, so insistent and undeviating were the pressures of those morning and evening masses. Yet humanity was always there, softening for me the terrors of an automated society; amid the regimented throngs there would be children playing and running like the wind, slipping nimbly through the serried ranks of people waiting obediently at traffic lights. Here and there would appear a blue-jeaned boy on a bicycle, holding a tray of steaming soup or noodle bowls in one hand above his towel-wreathed head, or, more often, carrying his dishes suspended behind him in metal containers on dashpot springs. (This was the first new thing I noticed in Japan; it is of course much safer for boys delivering hot food to apartments and offices to have both hands on the handlebars. But there are still many boys who use the old method.)

When the impenetrable throngs of people seemed as if they were really going to surge silently right over me, I took refuge on a peaceful building site behind some wooden boards on a main street. I joined there a group of workers working on one of the many splendid modern office buildings and hotels being erected all over Osaka in the shadow of a complex network of overhead highways. The men were just loafing about, standing in their baggy pantaloons and dark blue *jikatabi* round a huge bonfire of wood shavings, warming their patched backsides. It was a very frosty day, and I observed that they kept turning round and warming the other side also. They welcomed me to the comparative quiet of their building-site bonfire with smiles and greetings of 'Oss!' (This is short for '*Ohayi gozaymasu*' or 'Good morning'.) These were the first smiles I had seen that morning in the tense-faced Osaka crowds.

I knew at last, as I walked the winter streets of Osaka, that I was back in Japan, because of the peculiarly delightful fragrance of the air. Just as one knows one is in France from the smells of Gitanes, coffee, chestnuts, beer and garlic, so one knows one is in Japan from the mingled aromas of bath-fumes, woodsmoke, Peace and Ikoi cigarettes, hot soy sauce, dried fish, pickles and seaweed. But the most typical fragrance of all, and one uniquely Japanese, is that of pomade: the crisp, clear air of winter was drugged with the scent of rich, black, pomaded hair. It is spiced too with the clean, fresh smell of Japanese bodies, savoury with the breath of peppery rice crackers wrapped in seaweed, laced with hot saké and the sweet tang of boot polish rising from the rows of shoe-shiners kneeling on bits of old *tatami* matting along the edges of the pavements, where their little tin braziers were odorous with burning *sushi* (fish) and *o-bento* boxes—the disposable wood-shaving lunchboxes of Japan. All this had haunted my nostrils ever since I had left Japan just over a year ago, and now came back to me like a remembered dream perfectly realized. At every step I was wafted along on waves of this delicious mixture of erotic aromas.

Despite their worried early morning faces, Osaka people are among the cheeriest in Japan, and they are also the most money conscious. The usual greeting in Osaka is not 'How are you?' but 'How much money are you making?'

Early February: a curious festival is observed at many shrines, temples and women's schools round about this period. It is called Hari Kuyo. During the ceremonies, prayers are said for women participating in the ritual so that they may become skilled seamstresses. At the ceremony prayers are also said for the repose and salvation of the souls of broken needles. I remembered this when I passed a small sweatshop in a narrow lane in the Namba district of Osaka, where six young girls sat at whirring sewing-machines, shoulder to shoulder, running up cheap shirts and blouses.

Memorial services for broken needles are especially interesting at the Sensoji Temple in Asakusa, Tokyo, where huge lumps of *tofu* (white bean-curd) and *konyaku* (devil's tongue jelly) are placed on lacquered and brocaded stands in front of the Awashima Hall in the temple compound. Housewives and students of dressmaking wearing formal kimono come to stick their broken needles into the big cubes of *tofu* and *konyaku*, all the time chanting 'Namu amida butsu' in invocation to the Buddha Amitabha: 'May broken needles rest in peace!' At the end of the day the lumps of *tofu* and *konyaku* containing thousands of broken needles and even some broken thimbles (Japanese thimbles are in the form of rings) are solemnly buried in a section of the temple compound.

I discovered a good Western-style restaurant in Namba, the great entertainment district of Osaka. It is the Restaurant Wakakusa, and it serves fine steaks and mixed fish grills with well-chilled Guinness or any other brand of European beer you care to mention. It is rather expensive, so I could only go there once; it is situated in Minami Sennichimae, Dotombori. In this area of covered arcades of shops there are also many good native-style and Chinese restaurants. The famed 'Alaska' restaurants—one on top of the Hanshin department store, the other, outrageously expensive, on the roof of the Asahi Shimbun building right opposite the Osaka Festival Hall—I cannot recommend, though both give magnificent views of Osaka, the former of the Osaka station area, the latter (which has the noisiest kitchens in Japan) of the river and the maze of overhead highways.

More to my liking are the simple ordinary Japanese restaurants where one eats very well and very cheaply: *yakitori* stands selling bamboo skewers of roasted bits of chicken and liver, and the *sushi* joints serving delicious raw fish with rice rolls. Osaka is particularly famous for its *saba-zushi*, made from strips of delicious pickled mackerel on small slabs of rice.

I like the little curtain that hangs over the entrance to many small restaurants. It is an oblong of cloth, generally blue with white characters, giving the name of the establishment and its speciality; it is split into three segments or crenellations. It usually hangs by tapes from a bamboo stick, and is curiously difficult to describe because we have nothing like it in Europe. The nearest English word for this *noren* would perhaps be 'pelmet', though the French *lambrequin* conveys the idea more accurately. Loti, with typical precision, calls it a *tendelet*.

Osaka is the Manchester of Japan, but it proudly describes itself as 'the Venice of the Orient' because of its many canals and bridges. Most of the canals are little used nowadays, and are gradually being filled in to provide new motorways for Osaka's dense traffic. The canal that runs along the main entertainment street of Namba, called Dotombori, is very smelly sometimes and not very attractive by day; but at night, when it reflects the lights of eating-houses and floating oyster restaurants and the rutilant colours of neon signs, it is enchanting; a good view can be obtained from the restaurant of the Kirin Beer Hall. The many bridges are always packed with strolling throngs, and the *k-tin k-tan* sound of wooden-soled sandals clitter-clattering over the road is something so authentically Japanese that one's whole being is flooded with nostalgia for the seventeenth century of paper lanterns, oiled paper umbrellas, fans and noble *samurai*.

Today large numbers of barges can still be seen on the canals of Osaka. Whole families live all their lives on these rather drab craft, which are always garlanded with washing. There are special municipal dormitories for the children of the barge owners; the children are sent to school with other 'land children' after a brief training at the dormitory in the disciplines of land society, something with which most barge children and their parents are not familiar.

The fine castle in Osaka was originally built by Toyotomi Hideyoshi in 1584, but was reconstructed in 1931. The donjon is 157 feet high, and, as in most newly constructed castles in Japan, the ascent can be made by lift. It contains an interesting museum with various articles of historic interest connected with the city. Parts of the original walls still stand, and these are remarkable for the colossal stones, granite blocks of immense size, which were shipped across from the island named Shodoshima in the Inland Sea. The broad moat always seemed to be dry whenever I visited the castle, which is best viewed in April when the cherry trees are in bloom. I was amused to find in the castle park a special 'Toilet for Foreigners'. (There is another in Osaka station: obtain the key at the locker-room, and one can enjoy an hour's peaceful reading quite undisturbed, right at the busy heart of Osaka, a city where foreigners are rare.)

Perhaps the best place to appreciate Osaka's 'Venetian' quality is on the small island of Nakanoshima, situated between the Dojima and Tosabori rivers. It is the civic centre of the city, and there are many important public buildings here. At one end of the island is a small park which is a pleasant place on fine evenings. Here lantern-lit rowing boats may be hired and one can have a saké drinking party on the water. (Take your own saké.)

Special Osaka versions of Kabuki historical drama, considered by connoisseurs to be superior in many ways to the Tokyo style, can be seen at the fine new theatre, with its white walls, balconies and temple-like roofs constructed in Momoyama period style, which is situated just opposite the Takashimaya department store in Namba.

But the real reason for going to Osaka is to see the Bunraku or puppet plays. Unfortunately these are now not very well supported by a television-minded public, though there is a fine modern theatre for the puppets in Dotombori. Each time I visited Osaka I went straight to the Bunrakuza, but nearly always found it closed, or occupied by some variety show or Shimpa Kabuki troupe. Indeed the basement seems to have been turned into a bowling centre, and in the darkened foyer there are only two dolls on display, looking sad and forlorn. Previously the Bunraku troupes had been financed by the Shochiku film company, but recently they have been sponsored by a semi-government organization called Bunraku Kyokai, and the two main troupes of doll-handlers have been reunited. The name of the Bunraku theatre in Dotombori has been changed to the Asahiza, where popular dramas and modern comedies drawn from television series are also shown when the dolls are not playing. The name has been changed in order to avoid giving the wrong impression that the theatre is used exclusively for puppet shows, which will still be staged there at regular intervals between tours of the main cities of Japan. It was therefore usually in Tokyo that I was able to see regularly the Bunraku performances I had so often enjoyed in Osaka. Recent visits by the troupe to the United States and Europe were tremendous successes, for the Western public displayed an enthusiasm for this traditional Japanese theatre such as can never be found among the modern Japanese.

One of my favourite shops in Dotombori is one selling Karatsu earthenware, perhaps the finest of its kind in Japan. In A.D. 291, in the era of Jingu Kogo the Great, three sons of the Korean emperor visited Japan. One of them, Korei Kojiro Kaja, founded an ancient pottery at Karatsu and presented its products to Jingu Kogo. This is considered to be the origin of Karatsu earthenware, which reached the peak of its perfection in the reign of Toyotomi Hideyoshi—the

Japanese like to think of him as their Napoleon—at the end of the sixteenth century. It is still a remarkably beautiful product, well-designed, with fine texture and colour. In the era of the Tokugawa feudal government (seventeenth century) the general use of Karatsu ware was prohibited, and it therefore became the symbol of noble and elegant distinction. The Korean influence, the elegance, the distinction still remain, though now the earthenware is available for anyone who can afford it. I like this type of earthenware better than any other produced in Japan. The tea bowls are much sought after by devotees of the tea ceremony.

It is lovely to be in a truly civilized community again, to meet again with inborn good breeding and courtesy: to be handed, with a smile and a bow, hot, steaming, lilac-scented towels in a dim underground bar lit mainly by glaucous aquaria and the gold casing on Mama-san's eye-tooth. The girls are restful and attractive: I feasted my eyes on their calm faces with their dark-thatched, sleepily tilted lids, their full lips warm with undiscovered kisses, brilliant with smiles of frankly admitted pleasure. I felt myself responding again willingly to a sweetness of nature that is so admirable and uncloying because it hides so much steel. I was glad to return to this land where beauty and behaviour are based on rules that give conventionality and tradition new dimensions.

Yet I knew my attitude towards the Japanese had changed, as I myself had changed. During my two years in Sendai, in northern Japan, living with the kindest people of all in a kind land, I had idolized my fellow citizens. But now I felt curiously detached and calm, able to love the Japanese in a more rational way, as ordinary human beings, not as strange creatures in an almost supernatural world.

This new attitude helped me to see the Japanese in a different light. I now felt about them something I had never fully appreciated before: their great differences in personality are nearly always masked by a desire to be like everyone else, by a similarity of behaviour and appearance and dress that sometimes makes them appear to be a race of dolls—but very subtle, wonderfully articulated and highly intelligent dolls.

2

SNOW COUNTRIES

MORE than half of Japan is immobilized every year under tons of snow. Great damage is caused, and many lives are lost, but very inadequate steps are taken to prevent a recurrence of the annual disasters with their attendant floods, landslides, epidemic diseases, food shortages and other calamities. The northern parts of Japan—particularly Niigata, Toyama and Akita—are naturally the worst affected snow areas. This region of Japan is called 'the snow country', a phrase which has given the title to a famous novel about a country geisha by today's leading Japanese novelist, Yasunari Kawabata.

Snow is one of the great themes of Japanese painting and literature. Wood-block print artists used very skilfully the unprinted whitenesses of their paper, sometimes with faint embossings to suggest drifts (as in the case of Harunobu's snow prints), to give the impression of snow under moonlight or lamplight. Yasunari Kawabata's exquisite novel, *Snow Country*, is one of the supreme examples of the literature of snow in modern Japan. Snow is naturally often the subject of poetry, both classical and contemporary, as in this lovely *haiku* or seventeen-syllable poem by the famous Meiji Era poet and essayist Shiki (1867–1902), whose life began with the Meiji period and ended only ten years before its close in 1912:

> A mountain village—
> Underneath the drifting snow
> A murmuring stream.
> (*Yama-zato ya*
> *yuki tsumu shita no*
> *mizu no oto*.)

In this poem the very sounds of *yama* (mountain), *yuki* (snow) and *mizu* (water) seem to give a frozen feeling, and to evoke infinite distances of whiteness and cold.

Here is a modern poem by a little-known woman poet, Takako

Sawaki, which expresses very well the Japanese feelings both for snow and for one's 'native place':

WINTER

The snow falls softly on the earth.
My little music-box, O my native village,
When I shake you, you always whisper
Your subtle secrets, soft as an infant's dream. . . .
How could I expect the rumour of my love
Would travel so far?
O how could I expect to find the echo there,
Around the hearth of my old home,
Sprinkling icily, ceaselessly?
Whitely, obediently, and so quietly,
The snow lies thick on my native village.

But snow in Japan is also an occasion for festivities and solemn ceremonies. In remote northern Nagano Prefecture there is a unique snow festival which is fundamentally a prayer to the gods for a heavy fall of snow, which is thought to portend a good harvest. I once saw a local amateur performance of Kabuki drama at a small village near Sakata. The audience sat on straw mats on the snow, and the stage itself was composed of hard-packed snow and ice. If snow began to fall during the performances the spectators did not take shelter; they simply put up their oiled paper umbrellas, or *bangasa*, or covered their heads with old bits of *tatami* matting.

In Niigata the small town of Ojiya produces a special kind of textile that is bleached by being laid out on the snow. At Yokote the children build snow houses, or *kamakura*, which they furnish with mats and a small altar adorned with candles and offerings of fruit, rice cakes and sweet rice wine; these altars are dedicated to the gods of snow, who bring water to flood the ricefields and thus produce a rich harvest.

The most extraordinary snow festival takes place at Sapporo in the northernmost island of Hokkaido, a place which spends about five months of the year buried in snow. In the city's central Odori Park gigantic snow statues and models of buildings are set up. Some of the statues are of traditional Japanese deities like Hotei, the pot-bellied god of luck; but unfortunately an increasing number of statues are of television heroes like Batman and Robin or the movie monsters that have taken such a firm and horrible hold on the imagination of Japanese school children. These television and movie monsters have monstrous names, like Ultraman, Godzilla, Mothra and Gamera, and the fascination Japanese children feel for these sub-human, usually moronic, beasts seems to me highly sinister. Famous buildings are also constructed in snow. Most of the donkey-work in this tremendous, useless and unbeautiful display is done by Self-Defence Forces from the big Makomanai Base. They create, in curiously lumpy, ugly pop-art style, Westminster Abbey, Noah's Ark, the Sphinx, the Statue of Liberty and the Taj Mahal. It is curious to see these edifices cheek by jowl in the park. The display is considered 'educational', and hordes of school children get time off from their lessons to go and visit it. In the winter of 1966 the theme of the snow festival in Sapporo was 'Make the 1972 Winter Olympics a Big Success'.

The highly emotional attitude of the Japanese towards snow is partly responsible for their inability to deal with it in a practical way. They can make snow sculptures of hideous banality, but they cannot keep their railways clear, and sometimes roads even in Tokyo become impassable. This affects the livelihood of farmers in the snowbound areas. For example, in the town of Tsunan dairy produce workers were compelled to throw milk away into the snow because transportation could not get through to take it away. Now the farmers are beginning to feel they were better off in the old days—dairy farming is something comparatively new in Japan—when they would spend their snowbound winter months sitting round their hearths making folk-toys or simple and beautiful handicrafts, all of which are now dying out.

This example of cataclysm in winter is equalled in summer time, when, during the month of June, the rainy season hurls itself mainly at the southern parts of Japan, again creating widespread damage and loss of lives on southern Honshu and the islands of Shikoku and Kyushu. The world thinks of Japan as a land of earthquakes, and though in fact earthquakes do rock the islands almost daily they are minor affairs and do no damage; after one has lived a while in Japan they pass unnoticed. But the region round the town of Matsushiro in northern Nagano Prefecture suffers so badly from tremors that the school children and other inhabitants have their special earthquake drills. Here the cataclysm is to some extent prepared for, though if a major quake comes to Japan—any day now, the experts predict—our puny human precautions will be practically useless.

I have already mentioned the sacrifices of young human lives to the mountains. Skiing also has its inexperienced victims. Winter in

Japan means skiing and skating for almost every young person. The stations are crammed with people, carrying skiing and skating equipment and loaded with huge rucksacks, who are waiting to get on trains to take them to the various skiing resorts. They sit and sleep for hours, in long, regimented rows, on the station platforms and even in the streets approaching the stations, patiently waiting for extra trains to be put on to take them for a day or two's skiing. Sometimes they wait all night, and are too exhausted to ski—or to learn to ski—when they eventually reach their destinations. Certainly many of them have serious accidents on the crowded slopes due to inexperience and fatigue, and at stations one also sees a number of returning casualties, limping along on crutches, their feet and arms and sometimes their necks rigid in icing-sugar plaster. This rush to the mountains and the snow reminds me of nothing so much as the suicidal frenzy of the Gadarene swine. The seasons of summer and winter: the seasons of cataclysm in Japan.

Whenever there is a particularly cold spell—the *taikan* or 'coldest season' officially starts on 21st January—I see curious manifestations of the almost mystical devotion expressed towards snow and ice by the Japanese. Once I happened to be at Ito, in Shizuoka Prefecture, on 7th January, when a strange ceremony is held on the sea coast at Araihama. On that day scores of young men, clad only in exiguous white cotton breech-clouts, and carrying on their naked shoulders a heavy portable shrine, richly gilded and decorated, plunge into the freezing sea with their sacred burden. They are led and encouraged by an older man wearing a crested ceremonial robe and waving an ancient Japanese sword. This event is part of the annual Arai Shrine festival programme, and its origins are religious. It is part of the general prayers that are offered to the sea-deities of the shrine for big catches of fish and safe voyages by the fishing fleet. The fisherboys make a remarkable sight as they splash and push their way with the shrine into the bitingly cold billows. They go right up to their necks in the water, but appear to be in a kind of trance of manly effort, a trance probably maintained by their ceaseless, hoarse, rhythmical chanting and shoving. They say they never feel the sting of the icy sea on their naked bodies, and never catch cold, for their efforts are looked upon with benevolence by the deities they serve.

The little town of Arai is situated on the Imagire Inlet of the Hamana Lagoon, which I consider to be the most fascinating example of scenic beauty on the new Tokaido line. The shrine festivities are very popular and are attended by thousands of worshippers. This traditional event, the carrying of the *mikoshi*, or portable shrine, into the sea is held every other year. An interesting place near by which gives fine views of the wintry Pacific is Shiomizaka, literally 'sea-current-viewing-slope'.

I saw a similar festival in mid winter at Goshogawara, in Aomori Prefecture, in the far north on Honshu. This festival, called 'Hadaka Matsuri', is usually held on 8th February, which according to the old lunar calendar is officially the end of the year. It is something of an endurance feat for the scantily clad youths with white cotton towels rolled round their cropped heads. They bathe in big bamboo-bound cedar vats of bitterly cold water in which float chunks of ice, while their mates toss wooden tubs of 'ice broth'—water thick with shaved ice—over their backs and chests. This is also a ceremony with religious connotations, and is held in the local shrine courtyard. It is supposed to bring bumper rice crops and preserve the community from disease. Youths who do not go through this ceremony are not considered fully fledged men.

Another endurance test in icy water is undergone by judo and karate trainees in the Asahigawa River that runs through Akita City, also in the far north of Japan. Wearing judo garb, the trainees wade chest-deep through the ice-laden river as part of their *kangyo* or mid-winter training designed to toughen them both physically and spiritually. A similar cold-water ceremony, in which youths in breech-clouts are doused with icy water, can also be seen in the south, e.g. at Shitennoji Temple's *doya-doya* festival in Osaka.

I have also witnessed several ceremonies of this type in Tokyo itself, where *kan-geiki*, or cold-weather training, takes many forms in many places. In the Kanda district young apprentices (and sometimes their masters) dressed only in white cotton breech-clouts with white towels rolled like fillets round their shaven polls throw pinewood buckets of icy water over themselves in the courtyard of the Kanda Myojin Shrine, and accentuate the freezing cold by having huge standing fans creating an arctic gale.

Ascetic practices are carried out by trainee monks and by priests who stand in an attitude of meditation under a plunging waterfall at Meguro Fudo Temple or under the Biwa Falls at Mount Takao, just west of Tokyo. At Onju-in Temple in Ichikawa, near Tokyo, the temple abbots chant sutras and dash icy water over themselves seven times a day, starting at 3 a.m., during the 100-day period of religious training.

This temple is known as Japan's leading *dojo*, or training hall. The ascetic training, which begins on 1st November and lasts until 10th February, is severer here than anywhere else in Japan; the participants read prayers, copy sutra texts and listen to Buddhist lectures. During the entire period they wear only a thin white cotton breech-clout and subsist on watered rice-gruel. When the training period is over the trainees are given the rank of *suho-fukyoshi*, which gives them the authority to conduct certain rites for Buddhist believers.

I spent a day in genteel Kōbe. I had wanted to visit the famous landscape garden called Sorakuen, but was disappointed to find when I got there that it is open only twice a year—16th April to 31st May for the display of azaleas, and 1st October to 23rd November for chrysanthemum viewing. But I paid my respects to the gaudily painted (mostly bright orange) Ikuta Shrine, and at the Suma Temple, one of the oldest Buddhist temples in Japan, I thought of a prayer. In the temple's park there are many varieties of cherry, but these still showed no blossom. However, there were some very frail white early plum flowers on one sheltered tree. (The Japanese 'plum', with the white blooms, is actually a kind of small apricot. The real plum has pink blossom, and flowers somewhat later, about the same time as the cherry. The white blossom seems like a symbol of winter, just touched with the promise of spring.) Then came a sudden pelting shower of sleet, stacking the brown and green and grey mountains at the ends of Kōbe's steep streets in fading, ascending ranks of whiteness whose shapes seemed to be suspended in the freezing mist of clouds.

I jumped on a bus to Fukuhara, which was less animated than usual. In a little noodle shop I warmed my soaking toes and numbed fingers at the *hibachi*, a blue earthenware bowl of mammoth proportions in which lumps of charcoal were glowing with a rosy, comforting warmth and a rather sour smell that gives a headache if one lingers over it too long. A hot, steaming towel thawed out my frozen face; the boiling hot, pale green tea and a bowl of *soba* (buckwheat noodle) soup warmed my inside. There is nothing like a bowl of Japanese noodles for cheering one up in cold weather: *soba* really puts heart into one, and it 'sticks to the ribs'.

Despite the lack of real blossom, the streets around the stations in Kōbe and the miles-long shopping arcades of Motomachi were already sprigged with fluorescent pink plastic sprays, from which dangled tiny lanterns. But the spacious streets of Kōbe, not really crowded at the best of times, now were curiously lifeless; people were too busy keeping warm to want to go strolling and shopping. But the swelteringly overheated department stores were thronged. In those places too the plastic blossom was out, as it was in the vast underground shopping centres around Sannomiya station.

Kōbe is famous for its beer-fed cattle that are cut up into luscious steaks, extremely expensive. I do not care for this sort of food, but it is well cooked and served at the Ikariya Restaurant on the north side of Ikutashinmichi, which also serves good pork and fish in Japanese style; the place can be recognized by the blue anchor (*ikari*) hanging outside.

When in Kōbe my preference is for a small Okinawan restaurant called Naha, behind the Sannomiya shrine and just across from the Daimaru department store. It is decorated with very phallic folk-craft objects, and the 'hormone' menu is largely composed of potent snake dishes (in the summer season)—cobra, vipers in stew and snake wines—but at other times it is possible to regale oneself with pork, lamb, tongue, duck, liver, kidneys which one broils on a hotplate at one's own table. And it is surprisingly cheap: about ten shillings (50*p*). But vipers and cobras are expensive. The hotel restaurants are not recommended: poor service and high taxes. Another moderately priced little restaurant is the Escargot in Sannomiya, where the service is with a smile and the food appetizing and very varied.

Back in Osaka it was cold, but there were only occasional flurries of snow through which the massed office workers appeared less grim, less substantial, like ghosts of business people in clothes woven of darkness, air and light. Among them there would sometimes appear a lady in winter kimono, her shoulders shrouded in a fluffy pastel-tinted stole, on her feet red velvet *tabi* (ankle-socks) and wooden pattens or *geta* that looked warm and practical. Other kimono-clad women wore the conventional white *tabi* and gave the impression that they were freezing. When it rains or snows, women tie plastic toe-caps to the front of their wooden pattens, a very practical way of keeping spotlessly clean the *tabi* that are easily soiled by dust and mud and sullied by trampling feet in crowded trains and streets.

Some women were wearing a semi-Western-style coat of synthetic fur—blue, green, pink—over their kimono: these coats are half-length, with short 'penguin' sleeves, wide at the armholes, narrow-cuffed. Sometimes a woman could be seen trotting along on her *geta*, toes neatly turned in (this helps to keep the thong securely held in the *tabi*'s split between the great toe and the next) and hands drawn up inside the narrow cuffs of the wide, short sleeves, giving an amputated look.

At least half the population seemed to be wearing square white gauze masks, ostensibly to protect them from smog or germs. But many Japanese, especially girls, who are self-conscious about their snub noses (they admire Westerners' big noses, which they call 'high noses') use winter as an opportunity to hide what they consider to be an ignoble feature; few of them seem to realize how charming these little button-noses are in their cat-faces. When suffering from eye infections, the Japanese wear oblong white eye-patches, not the eye-fitting black patches of the West. Once, when I had conjunctivitis, I used a black eye-patch from Europe, and everyone looked at me with mingled terror and amusement, for in Japan a black eye-patch is the sign of a wicked *samurai*, and is often used in movies and on television to denote evil. (Characters wearing dark glasses are always gangsters.)

As for the men, and the *soba* and *sushi* boys careering along on their loaded bikes, a little blue and white cotton towel flying over their shoulders from clenched teeth, I believe they wear these germ masks simply to keep their noses warm in the biting winds from the Japan Alps.

I noticed that more boys and young men are now wearing their hair long, possibly in order to help them keep warm; there are hair styles that come right down over the collar in a kind of duck's tail, thick and glossy but still carefully combed and pomaded, taking their shape from the neat little skulls beneath them. The extreme styles of the Western pop groups are also seen: the Japanese haircut is too standardized, without much individuality. But the barbers are still the best in the world, though the price of a haircut, shampoo and shave (massage given free) has doubled from 150 yen to 300 yen (about six shillings, or thirty new pennies) and is still going up.

Tramcar fares have also gone up, from thirteen to fifteen yen. Public bath-house charges have risen from ten yen to twenty-five yen. The price of food and drink is sky-rocketing. Prices of vegetables, meat and fish have trebled. Cups of coffee, once fifty yen, are now eighty or a hundred yen. The prices of seats in cinemas and theatres and sports auditoriums have also shot up during my year's absence. People are earning more, but to no purpose, as the price of everything is jumping. The whole of Japan seems inflated like a big advertisement balloon that might go pop at any moment, and people seem to be holding their breath in the rarefied monetary atmosphere.

Tourists are also hard hit. A few weeks after my arrival, I was handed this notice at my hotel:

> Effective from 11th April 1962. The Management regrets very deeply that Foreign Tourists who have hitherto being [*sic*] exempted from the regular 10% tax on room, meals and drinks, will no longer be exempted as of the 11th April 1962, due to a change in the Japanese law. Thank you for your co-operation. The Management.

Our co-operation could hardly be avoided, and at very short notice too. Our co-operation in Japanese hotels includes, as well as the 10 per cent tax, a 10 or 15 per cent service charge. (One's bill, plus 10 per cent, is increased by 10 or 15 per cent of that total, a quite iniquitous arrangement.) The money derived from the service charge is supposed to be shared out among the staff in the place of gratuities, but it has recently been revealed that it all goes straight into the management's pockets. One doesn't mind paying extra for good service—this has suddenly become almost non-existent—but it galls one to think that those who have given it are not rewarded. No wonder the service in all hotels and restaurants is rapidly deteriorating.

Thinking about the dire inflation of the Japanese economy one early winter morning, I was cheered by the lovely sight of the symbol I have just used to describe this inflation: there were fleets of pink-and-white-striped advertisement balloons trailing long wire ladders of red and blue transparent characters, shot through by the sharp sun over the Hankyu building, one of the biggest department stores in Osaka. There was a strange figure standing outside Osaka station—was it a man or a woman?—shrouded in what appeared to be white butter muslin that flapped in the freezing wind. The face was mysteriously shrouded; I was told that it was a begging nun. She was beating a parchment gong or tambourine with a curved stick. She stood with bent head, never acknowledging the few coins that were placed in her pouch.

The winter *sumo* or Japanese wrestling tournament is under way at the vast stadium in Namba. Between bouts, the huge, stout wrestlers were easing their corpulences through the admiring crowds of fans in the busy streets. The wrestlers—some of them unusually tall for Japanese—wore dark kimono, and strolled with their big bare feet in plain wooden *geta* in a leisurely, splay-footed walk. Their plump little hands were tucked away inside their kimono's pagoda sleeves, and their neat top-knots of hair, carefully pomaded and brushed and rolled back in a sort of stiff crest on top of their heads, glistened like polished lacquer in shafts of snowy sun. They moved with great pride and nobility; though immensely strong and heavy, they are the gentlest and most good-natured of people.

Tall *sushi*-shop boys kept skittering crazily through the showers of sleet on six-inch-high *geta*, laughing and singing wildly. One of the two six-inch teeth snapped off one boy's *geta*, and he went sprawling in the slush. He had to be supported by two heartily laughing friends while he shoved the wooden tooth back into the groove underneath the wooden sole and banged it firmly into place. Then off they all dashed, pell-mell, helter-skelter, clitter-clash, throwing out their feet and their absurd footwear in all directions. Their long, sturdy legs in their tight faded blue jeans were vaguely reminiscent of the garb of seventeenth-century Japanese retainers.

The icy wind at my trouser-leg runs sniffing like an ill-trained dog about to bite my ankles. In extremes of weather Japan is at her most beautiful; but cold and rain make Osaka the most melancholy and lonely place on earth. Outside a department store Pacific War casualties, wearing regulation white, their maimed stumps of arms and legs extended into cold steel and leather artificial hands and limbs, play a sad air on their battered instruments as they beg for money, kneeling on the icy pavement with bowed heads. I once took a very unwilling picture of a group of such derelicts in Sendai: the camera shop refused to print it, but gave no reason. None was needed. One of the men, horribly scarred, has a face as frightening as an eroded statue's. No one takes any notice of them in the driving rain and sleet. No one gives them money.

After such a sight, I am almost ashamed to enter a bar for a little warmth. The place is hardly bigger than a large wardrobe, and filled with the overpowering stink of gas from the broken elements of a small gas fire. (The gas in Japan is deliberately given a particularly nauseating smell to warn people of escapes and to discourage suicides.) On the counter, vivid alcohols in gay glasses rimmed with the green radiance of an aquarium of neurotic tropical fish that are always savagely chasing one another. The grumbling music of Edith Piaf in in a lugubrious French *chanson*. A bar girl comes running in with a bag of hot chestnuts and a few twigs of very early cherry blossom, sent from Sakurajima in the far south, and which she proceeds to arrange in a whisky bottle: a few deft, firm touches—glancing at me all the time out of the corner of her eye—and the spiky pink flower arrangement takes on new dimensions, becomes a small work of art that puts the glossy nude on the calendar to shame. The bar girl has dyed ginger hair but a radiant smile, with perfect, pure white teeth in palest coral lips; fairy ears and dark, sparkling eyes, like the hearts of anemones, drowned in lavender eye-shadow and sooty mascara. I had forgotten how rare smiles are in these parts. The cities of Japan are losing their smiles as prices rise. Only in Tohoku and other remote country districts is one still suddenly rewarded with quite unasked-for beams from healthy, honest faces. Tohoku lingers in my memory as a land radiant with smiles. I often return to Sendai and Matsushima, Morioka and Hiraizumi, Yokote and Akita, Hirosaki and Aomori.

At the Osaka Central Post Office the clerks frank letters by hitting the stamp a smart tap with a small mallet in the head of which is an adjustable date stamp. Japanese post offices are tedious places. There is an unnecessary division of labour in the larger ones: here, for example, one cannot have letters weighed at the stamp counter. One has to go to the end counter where the clerk, after weighing the letter, scribbles the amount of stamps required in the corner of the envelope, in pencil that could easily be rubbed out. (One might write in a lesser figure oneself, but this kind of mean dishonesty would never occur to a Japanese.) Then one takes the letter back to the stamp counter where the clerk gives one stamps to the correct amount. The same procedure must be adopted for parcels. There is a special counter selling day-of-issue stamps and neatly date-stamped envelopes, which are often delightfully designed. Cigarettes are also obtainable from this counter. There are always a few workmen sleeping on the seats. To obtain a letter from the poste restante (you must call it General Delivery or you will not be understood) no proof of one's identity is asked. The clerk merely asks one to write one's name on a little piece of paper, and then only if one's name is difficult, like mine. (In Tokyo Central Post Office, however, I was asked for my passport; I didn't have it, so they accepted the evidence of an old letter I had on my person.)

Osaka people are said to spend all their money on food, while Kyoto people spend all theirs on finery. The cheap Osaka restaurants are always packed. One of the best in the station area is the Kirin Beer Hall. Strangers bow and smile, even if they are women, when joining a foreigner's table. Orders are given, and the waitress always asks if one would 'lice' or 'bled'. Pint bottles of Kirin beer are brought, but one is given only tiny tumblers to drink it out of. (However, the excellent draught beer (*nama-biiru*) is served in big jugs.)

A 'two-kind' plate which I ordered in a tiny workmen's café was composed of three oysters (delicately fried) and a slab of roast beef, artistically arranged on the pretty plate with a spoonful of potato salad, a handful of coleslaw and one-sixteenth of a small tomato. A big, ribbed 'shape' of gluey rice with some gouts of red pickle: it was warm and filling. The Japanese workmen in baggy pantaloons and *jikatabi* were eating the parsley garnish with relish after dousing it with soy sauce, so I ate mine that way too.

Every restaurant window displays the entire menu in the form of imitation dishes, called 'samples', all most cunningly contrived to look real. In fact, the artistry of these wax imitations is so high that I cannot believe they are not real. The way fried eggs and diced carrots, prawns and fried oysters, sliced tomatoes and green peas, as well as a host of Japanese and Chinese dishes are counterfeited in these riotously coloured window displays is simply incredible. I used to feel sure that it must be real food which somehow had been miraculously preserved by spraying with transparent lacquer. But no, it is all artificial. Even the sprigs of parsley, which look so authentic, and the bowls of Japanese rice soup called *miso-shiru* are artificial. Artificial too are the plates of bread, toast and rice.

There are special factories in Osaka and Tokyo where this sort of false food is concocted. It always looks better than the real thing, because whenever a new restaurant is about to open the chefs prepare all these dishes in their best style; they are then taken to the factories, where everything is carefully moulded, exactly as it is on the plates, and reproduced in wax which is then skilfully coloured and tinted to give an appearance of the utmost naturalism. The workers at these factories must be perpetually watering at the mouth at the sight of the waxen delicacies they are preparing, and I imagine that when they are presented with real food for actual consumption they wonder whether it is really real, or just wax. The factories also hire sets of standard dishes to smaller and less ambitious restaurants, so one sees the same food reproduced in thousands of small cafés, snack shops and coffee bars. I once saw some waiters taking these wax dishes out of a showcase, dusting them, washing them in soapy water and polishing them up with shammy leather. It was strange to see dishes of curried rice or lacquer boxes of *tempura* (fried fish and vegetables) being handled in this way, like ornaments or kitchen utensils.

Liquids, including glasses of draught beer with foaming tops, and a bewildering variety of ice-cream floats and sweets, are also artfully represented, but a cup of hot coffee is usually a cup filled with roasted coffee beans; I was sure these beans were real, but when the waiters, to their great amusement, allowed me to examine them I discovered that these too were false. The sugar lump and the tiny jug of cream going with the coffee are also artificial.

'How often do you clean these samples?' I asked, stroking with wonder a hamburger with a fried egg on top of it.

'Once a year,' the waiters replied, 'when we clean up everything for the New Year.'

It is one of the most fascinating sights in Japan, one I often stop to gaze and wonder at.

Outside every tobacco kiosk, and on every shop, restaurant and coffee-shop counter, there is a vivid scarlet telephone for public use. These notes of brilliant scarlet in sometimes drab streets are delightful. The phones on the streets are constantly in use, for the Japanese have an awful telephone mania and it is often necessary to walk for a few blocks before one finds a free one. The price of a local call, only ten yen, is one of the few things that have not gone up.

After prim and proper Malaysia I was struck once again by the dirt and dust of Japan, the broken roads, even in the centre of Osaka, the continual digging up of pavements and highways, the jammed traffic's tedious slowness, stink and noise, the proliferation of vast new office buildings in the course of frenzied and often apparently haphazard construction, the fairly new-looking blocks already being torn down to make way for even bigger and more modern ones. Everywhere there is this hell of construction, and the air is filled with confusion and banging. Huge yellow girder-lifting, pile-driving and earth-moving machines throng the deep-dug sites of new buildings which are now always constructed with two basements of shops and arcades: one of the most extraordinary examples of this is the vast underground shopping centre called Santica Town in the bowels of the earth near Sannomiya station in Kōbe. Osaka too has immense congeries of underground shops, cinemas, cafés and quick-snack stalls.

Enormous concrete overpass and express highway pylons stand like the trunks of ruined statues all over the centres of Osaka; on some of them, vivid orange or pale mauve girders, some of which finish dizzily in mid air, have already been laid to carry the lanes of traffic. Women in dark bloomers with white cotton towels over their heads push barrows of stones or earth.

As I felt in Hong Kong's New Territories, this construction mania cannot be an expression of faith in the future: rather the opposite, as most of the buildings have a plain, shoddy, temporary look, a built-in obsolescence which makes one feel terribly uneasy; it seems the expression of the universal desire to get into the thermal current of inflation and make a fast buck before money loses all value whatsoever. One hates to think what such buildings would be like in an earthquake, though all are built on rafts of concrete and are said to be earthquake-proof. However, the dreadful earthquake in Niigata showed that even well-constructed modern apartment blocks can tilt over at alarming angles in a big shake. And the underground warrens, swarming with people, would surely be death traps for those unfortunate enough to be caught inside them by an earthquake, a flood or an outbreak of fire.

Mid March: now we are right in the middle of the annual travel hysteria, the season when Japanese tourists and the first batches of foreign visitors fill the long-distance trains. The school holidays have begun, and there are long crocodiles of black-uniformed schoolboys and sailor-suited schoolgirls at the stations, in the streets and department stores and at every 'famous' place in Japan, where they all have group photographs taken, and buy up the cheap frippery and tasteless rubbish of souvenir shops.

Kyoto and Nara are unbearable at these times. The tranquil old gardens of moss and stones and fine-raked sand are desecrated by hordes of rowdy, giggling children, by saké-drinking parties with transistor radios. One cannot see the ancient temples for the people, and the litter strewn about at beauty-spots and under the cherry trees in blossom is disgusting. Most Japanese seem to have no sense of public responsibility in this respect. Waste-paper baskets are set up, but are soon full to overflowing, and no one comes to empty them. In any case, there are not enough of these receptacles. There are some public-spirited children and adults who periodically take it upon themselves to clean up the mountains of trash left on the slopes and sacred summit of Mount Fuji. Groups of women can be seen going to the parks in the evenings to sweep up the litter and make it into great bonfires, so that the grass under the flowering cherries is clean the next morning for an hour or so. But one feels this is a superhuman task, a cleaning of the Augean stables which could only be properly undertaken if the whole nation developed a conscience about the mess it makes. In towns and cities the pavements are piled with trash, the streets are awash with paper; at evening small bonfires sometimes burn in the gutters outside shops. The disgrace of the filthy streets flows over into parks, shrines and holy places. The simple answer is for each traveller to carry every bit of his own rubbish away with him and burn it at home.

There are pushing and struggling crowds of middle-aged men and women on the annual trip from the country scrambling into the already overcrowded subways and trams and buses of Osaka and Kyoto. There are huge queues at all the ticket offices, and at the taxi-ranks outside Osaka station one sometimes has to wait half an hour for a cab. Hotel rooms are hard to get. Restaurants are packed all day. There is really not much pleasure in visiting Japan at cherry-blossom time. The rough behaviour, the pandemonium and the noise are just overwhelming. Autumn and winter are by far the best seasons in Japan, and the crowds that flock to view maples and chrysanthemums always seem more orderly than those attacked by cherry-blossom hysteria. After a first quick look cherry blossom sickens the sight: a candy-floss nausea turns the stomach and the eyeballs.

All the papers are full of photographs of early cherry blossom at Yugawara, an attractive spa on the Fujiki River in Kanagawa, about sixty miles from Tokyo, where the first cherry blossom of the spring has appeared almost overnight. The place's two lovely waterfalls, Fudo-no-taki and Godan-no-taki, are even lovelier in the mists of white and pale pink blossoms, but the hordes of riotous saké-drinkers bathed in the rosy flower light under the trees in Yugawara Park are flushed a deeper pink round the eyes.

According to the traditional lunar calendar, spring in Japan begins on 4th February. But the entire country is still in the process of stirring out of its wintry lethargy. Spring does not really begin until mid March.

I couldn't get near the ticket office at Osaka station to buy a ticket to Okayama. But a kind railway official saw my plight, and obtained one for me and put me on the right train. He even carried my bag for me. So often I meet with these small, unexpected kindnesses, performed so willingly and pleasantly. The people who do perform them seem to be becoming rarer; but undoubtedly it is often one kind person doing some casual good deed to a stranger who makes memorable a certain place that might otherwise not be noteworthy. When I meet such people I am ashamed of my criticisms of the Japanese: I am sure all Japanese are kind at heart, but are now so confused and embarrassed and awkward and provincial that they cannot conceive of themselves helping others; all their energies are directed towards the desperate task of helping themselves in a land of almost panic confusion where it is everyone for himself. Japanese courtesy and refinement and tranquillity are high ideals which can be achieved only at rare moments.

Thinking this over, I came to the conclusion that my feelings this time in Japan are very much like what a 'coloured' person might feel in England: there is no resentment shown towards me, and indeed I am often offered proofs of regard and affection. But there is always the sense of being, in more ways than one, 'other' than they are. I try not to forget what I was told by a priest at the Temma Tenjin shrine in Osaka:

'We are all brothers because we all eat the earth's food.'

I am off on my wanderings again. A stranger in a Kyoto bar wrote out for me in Japanese and English a *waka* poem by a nineteenth-century poet, Wakayama Bokusui. I quote his translation here, because it typifies my life:

I go beyond many mountains and streams.
I travel through the country
Where there is an endless loneliness.

3
OKAYAMA AND KURASHIKI

THE train from Osaka to Okayama provides a scenic ride that is never far from the sea. The views of the pine-dotted beaches at Suma and Maiko, just past Kōbe, are entrancing, and from Akashi one has a glimpse of the island of Awaji lying across the Akashi Strait. The famous cherry trees of Suma in the precincts of Sumadera, a Buddhist temple with many historical associations, were still not in bloom of course, but a light scattering of snow gave them a floscular candour. The snow lay in thick, broad pads of whiteness on the low, yearning branches of the pine grove, gnarled and fantastic, along the seashore at Maiko, where my eye has always been caught by the curious Western-style house, formerly owned by Baron Sumitomo, and now a hotel, known as Maiko Villa. The sea, blue-grey, was heavy with foreign ships. Just past Kōbe I saw the beginnings of the great bridge that is to link Honshu, Awaji and Shikoku. One of the big luxury inter-island steamers was ploughing through rough waves on its daily voyage between Kōbe and Takamatsu on Shikoku. Towards Shioya the Inland Sea is fringed with artificial embankments made of concrete tetrapods that look like primitive sex images, their stocky thighs roughly clad in loose snow.

I look for the 'White Heron' castle of Himeji. This superb structure has now been restored to its original splendour, and its wide, white wings really do make it look like this beloved Japanese bird settling on a nest. It also makes me think of an ancient pine tree spreading dark, drooping branches, snow-laden, that sweep up at the ends, bearing fans and finials and fardels of black foliage with frondiferous grace against a pure white sky. Unlike the grandiloquent castles of the West, Himeji is grandiose without megalomania, a fortress, like the Japanese soul, so clad in the consciousness of its own inner strength that it requires and conveys no outward show of aggressive force.

However one sees this structure, a monument to Japan's brilliant feudal past, it cannot fail to impress one with its bold dignity and noble simplicity, a simplicity that unifies and exalts the extraordinary complexities of its construction and design. This calm balance between simplicity and complexity is symbolic of Japan and the Japanese character: simplicity so pure that it becomes a priceless and perfect luxury, complexity so profound that it becomes a mute and unconscious intelligence, both qualities operating together to produce the world's most sensitive and ingenious race.

Today, beyond the castle, in the surrounding hills, one sees other, newer landmarks: a towering memorial to the city's dead whose lives and homes were destroyed in the Second World War, and the fairy-tale towers and monuments of the fantastically pretty Central Park, to my mind the most attractive modern park in all Japan. From the heights of this park reproductions of Rhineland gothic towers and an elegant pagoda can be viewed, with delicious incongruity, against the prospect of the castle in the plain below. Most moving is the memorial to the civilian war dead: it represents a sword whose hilt is partly buried in the earth, and whose tip points towards the sky, a mighty symbol of peace and reconciliation.

The town of Himeji, dominated by the fuming smoke-stacks of the Fuji Iron and Steel Company, one of the largest and most fascinating steel factories in the East, is an attractive and friendly place, one which I always enjoy visiting.

The fairy tinkle-bells chime and chime again as the train draws out of Himeji's fine modern station *en route* to Okayama. The tune is an old song about Japan's first railway linking Shimbashi in Tokyo and Yokohama. It is charmingly childlike at first hearing, but becomes almost unbearably irritating when played time and time again before and after the conductor's broadcasts of utterly useless and trivial information.

The train turns slightly inland, and the countryside's pointed hills suggest a former islanded sea, as does some of the landscape between Nagoya and Kyoto. The last time I came to Okayama was in the damp heats of June, when vendors on the platform were selling big baskets of huge Okayama peaches, very cheap and very juicy. All round Okayama there are the low, stunted trees of espaliered peach orchards, now candied with snow. The region is famous for its fine rushes (called *i*—how simple!—in Japanese) which are woven into the high-quality rush matting for *tatami* known as *i-mushiro*. The rushes, both in their natural colour, bleached or dyed in violent hues, are also woven into all kinds of tourist souvenirs—table mats, handbags, purses, screens, fans and slippers. Unfortunately, like most Japanese folk-art today, the designs are mechanical and the quality of tourist souvenirs in particular is extremely poor. A little more attractive is the *bizen-yaki* porcelain for which Okayama is also celebrated. This is made into bizarrely shaped figures of gods, birds, insects and beasts.

As it was sleeting heavily when the train drew into Okayama station —wonderfully described in Henri Michaux's *Un Barbare en Asie*—I decided to remain on the train and go on to Kurashiki, the next stop, about half an hour's ride. The name of this ancient town means 'seat of the granaries', because in the seventeenth century Kurashiki was a thriving port for the shipment of rice produced in the great plains round this area. Many of the ancient rice granaries, beautifully restored, remain in the centre of the town, and some of them have been made into charming historical and folk-craft museums. The Ohara Art Museum is well worth a visit.

The area round the station, as in most Japanese towns, is awfully sordid and unattractive, but about ten minutes' walk down the main street opposite the station I came to the beautiful old part of the town, centred round the river and the canals crossed by hump-backed bridges. The old rice granaries are square and dignified, pure white walls criss-crossed with black lattice-work broken by a few small, deep windows. Most wonderful are the grey-tiled roofs of the region, reminiscent of the roofs of Himeji Castle: I like especially the white courtyard walls topped with long, narrow roofs and eaves of tiles. I received a sudden strong memory of the *patios* of Cordoba and Seville and Granada as the clouds of snow suddenly cleared for a few moments and a strong shaft of sunlight illuminated a group of these fine old warehouses arranged round a central court. The only thing lacking was a fountain.

I went to ask for a room at the Kurashiki Kokusai Hotel, a modern monstrosity which has tried, unsuccessfully, to combine traditional and contemporary styles of architecture. The exterior is positively elephantine, and the place seems to be something of a white elephant. I was the only guest. At the reception desk I asked for a single room (there are eighteen singles) and was told they were all occupied. This is the standard technique today adopted by all Western-style hotels during the off-season. They shut up all the single, cheaper rooms and force single visitors to take expensive double bedrooms. When I asked the hotel clerk why I couldn't have a single room he blandly lied that they were all occupied by permanent guests. A likely tale, and one that was patently untrue. I was the only guest, the only diner in the dining-room, where lunch was excellent and reasonable. Down in the bowels of the hotel a dark, empty bar and a desolate coffee shop. The interiors were all decorated with pointless luxury, with that ghastly good taste, common to all modern hotels, that turns the most *shibui* atmosphere into something expensive and pretentious. (The Shin-Hankyu Hotel near Osaka station is one of the few exceptions to this criticism.) A souvenir stall paraded dull rush matting and handbags and horrible dolls.

I escaped to the Ohara Art Gallery, beautifully housed in a converted or adapted rice warehouse. As is usual in Japanese collections of Western art there is much that is second and third rate; the usual Rodin copies—a striding torso, John the Baptist and one of the Burghers of Calais—seemed to be battling through the sleet round the entrance. Inside there was the inevitable Renoir—the Puritan basis of the Japanese character stands in awe of nudes, always female, for the Japanese do not seem to be interested in male nudes. The Renoir, gaped at reverently by the Japanese, was a blurred mish-mash of pinks and browns, revoltingly fleshy and shapeless: I do not like pictures with women in them.

But there is an exquisite Forain backstage scene at the ballet, a good Braque, a good Matisse and a goodish Picasso. The chief pride of the gallery is an El Greco 'Annunciation' which looks to me like a pupil's copy of the much larger one in the Prado or in Toledo.

Even more interesting is the Archaeological and Folk-Art Museum across the canal. It is also housed in an adapted warehouse, from whose odd, narrow windows on the creaking, ancient wood staircases I had lovely views of curving roofs on houses and courtyard walls and of a curious urinal like a *vespasienne*. The exhibits, splendidly displayed, include rare Haniwa and Jomon figures and tumulus relics from the seventh and eighth centuries A.D. There were some Han Dynasty small Buddha heads with profiles of such purity they reminded me curiously of classical Greek sculpture.

I made a racing tour of the park, high on a bluff overlooking the town. It is centred round a shrine, and, as at nearly all Shinto shrines in Japan, there are swings and roundabouts for children, but in the driving sleet they were deserted. All the time I was up there I saw only one student, in tracksuit, soaking with snow and sweat, doggedly over-exerting himself in training for a marathon. There is a dejected little zoo containing a few dark cages of monkeys, deer, sacred cranes, all looking miserably lonely and bored. From this eminence I got another view of Kurashiki—not the ancient seventeenth-century show-place, but a modern industrial city ringed with factories and smoke-stacks: the principal industry is the making of cotton yarn. In the far distance the Inland Sea glimmered like a sheet of dirty pewter. I felt a surge of depression and rushed to pull the bell hanging in front of the shrine: after giving it a good rattle, throwing some coins into the box and praying to whatever deity there might be enshrined there, I felt better, and ran downhill with streaming hair.

Back down in the town again, people looked at me strangely. In Japan *everyone* but policemen and postmen carries an umbrella when it is raining. I was looked upon as an eccentric. To get out of the sleet I went wandering along a big shopping arcade and eventually found myself back at the station, where I was just in time to catch an express to Okayama.

Okayama is famous for its Korakuen Park, which is said to be one of the three most perfect parks in Japan, the other two being the Kairakuen in Mito and the Kenrokuen[1] in Kanazawa. The Korakuen Park, covering about twenty-five acres, was laid out late in the eighteenth century by Lord Ikeda, the *daimyo* or feudal lord of the province. It is a magnificent example of elegant and varied landscaping, with pavilions, lakes, ponds, cascades, imitation mountains, rice-fields, tea plantations and palm and apricot groves. The maples, cherries and apricots are lovely in season. I saw the place in a strange season, on a day of sleet and rain: it was beautiful, but wintry—desolate, like a glorified waterworks. I trudged through the drenching sleet under a pretty rose-red umbrella hired from the office for only twenty yen. The plum blossom, both white and pink, was out here, starring the darkness of the waning afternoon with brightness. Camellia bushes were trimmed into huge cube shapes, and there were rows of tea bushes, neatly clipped, pretending to be a 'sea'. Everywhere I looked there were new vistas of artificial islands, hills, streams and waterfalls, groves of bamboo, their airy gracefulness bowed with the weight of wet and sleet, stepping-stones, a bridge over a pond from which rose, on lank stems, dead brown lotus leaves, and a stream crossed picturesquely by eight planks laid zigzag across its stony waters. In the distance a castle tower. There is an excellent restaurant or tea house by the lake,

[1] One of the ornaments of this park is a large and interesting stone phallus.

but this was closed. However, several souvenir stalls and cake shops serving green tea were open, and in one of these I warmed my frozen hands and nose while sipping boiling hot, pale green tea from a rustic brown handleless cup.

I managed to get a taxi at the main gate, and, crossing the big Tsurumi Bridge, reached another park, known as Higashiyama-koen or Kairakuen, from which I had a chilling view of Kojima Bay. I rode back to the station, about two miles, and found the Japan Travel Bureau not far away in the Temmaya department store. For a wonder, there was an efficient clerk who could speak English, and he gave me all the information on how to get to Saidaiji to see the Naked Festival. Buses would be running all night until six o'clock the next morning from the Temmaya department store; the trip to Saidaiji takes about half an hour. The real fun does not start until late evening, so I spent the next few hours enjoying my favourite hobby, wandering round the streets of a new town. Okayama has canals running through the centre of the shopping district, and these were lined with trees in winter overcoats of straw. A few heavenly white flowers of the Japanese apricot were out. I had a fortifying dinner in the restaurant of a Western-style hotel overlooking the busy station plaza: a huge rice omelette with mushroom soup in a little red lacquer bowl, and tomato salad.

4
PHALLIC RITES

SAIDAIJI is the name of a Buddhist temple (very ancient and dedicated to Kannon) as well as being the name of the small port town clustered round the sacred place.

On 14th February every year, at the coldest time, a very curious festival is celebrated here. The festival is over five hundred years old and is known as the Eyo Matsuri. After nightfall thousands of near-naked youths dash through the temple grounds, uttering strange cries, and run up the altar steps to pray for the divine mercy of Kannon. A priest throws a pair of sacred wands called *shingi*, about one inch in diameter and seven inches long—they are actually phallic symbols—into the masses of youths who scramble and fight for possession of these trophies. Anyone who captures one or both of the wands 'will attain lifelong happiness, it is said' (according to the Official Guide to Japan published by the Japan Travel Bureau).

It is a curious event, because there is a mixture of many elements—pagan, phallic, religious and commercial. From the religious point of view it seems to be essentially a purification rite, an act of homage to Buddha, Kannon and the gods of Japan, and a test of physical and spiritual endurance. This kind of test is common in Japan, not only in winter as I have already pointed out, but also in the hot season. At the height of Japan's terrible summer heat men bundle themselves up in as much clothing as they can get on, cover themselves with rugs and blankets and quilts and squat round roaring bonfires, drinking quantities of hot saké. It is a kind of jovial defiance of the elements, a contest against heat and cold using these extremes of temperature themselves as weapons to subdue them. Japanese devil-may-care high spirits come out well in such wild contests.

There are many 'naked' or phallic festivals during the Japanese winter: those in Fukushima and the northern parts of Japan are particularly vigorous and uninhibited. The participants are not actually naked, unless, as often happens, they lose the breech-clout in the *mêlée*. Round their loins they wear this breech-clout, which is known by the wonderfully evocative name of *fundoshi*, a long strip of cotton which passes tightly through the cleft of the buttocks, through the crotch and then, loosely covering the private parts, is firmly knotted round the lower hips, after being wound round the waist. Occasionally a black material is used, but the *fundoshi* is nearly always white. Sometimes a brightly coloured ribbed woollen belly-band called a *haramaki* is also worn, but some men tie a dark kimono sash round the waist. It is an extremely manly attire, and shows off the good points of the male body to perfection.

Generally speaking, only young men participate in the festival, which was originally a celebration of the attainment of manhood. The jostling can be very rough, and quarrels break out between gangs of youths for the possession of the sacred sticks. The festival, however, is sometimes joined by older men, young boys with their fathers and even by women, mostly middle aged.

Buses were leaving the Temmaya department store in Okayama every few minutes. The last bus back to Okayama from the festival would be at 6 a.m., for this is an all-night affair. I did not have to queue long to get a seat on one of the packed buses. Most of the passengers were young men, and all of them belonged to some small group of friends or fellow workers (in Japan, the two are synonymous, for few Japanese have personal friends in the sense we know friendship in the West). With these 'company friends' they would run naked, linked by arms round shoulders, through the streets of Saidaiji. In Japan no one goes to a festival alone, except me. Loneliness on such occasions is considered eccentric.

Among the passengers were also some grey-haired grannies in sober, snuff-coloured kimono, chattering animatedly about the excitements in store. I was the only foreigner, and all through that long night at Saidaiji I saw no other foreigners, though the papers reported next day, with typical Japanese self-satisfaction, that 'many foreigners' had attended this festival. Today so many Japanese seem confused and uncertain about the value of their culture, and it is regrettable that they look for the presence of Westerners at their festivals and theatres and art exhibitions as a kind of final proof of the excellence of these native Japanese institutions, whose beauty and uniqueness require no such artificially absolute standards of judgment. I saw no foreigners: perhaps they were stuck up in the borings official stand above the *mêlée*—'far from the madding crowd' indeed. It is quite fatal to enjoyment, whether one is a Japanese or a Westerner, to attend any festival as an official guest. One is shepherded away from the scene of the action, and therefore from the vivid, panting reality of the event, which is observed primly from the chilly altitude of official boxes. The Japanese seem afraid that foreigners, usually much bigger and stronger than the Japanese, will get trampled underfoot or see something they ought not to see. Especially at a 'naked' festival, one must get down on the ground and mingle freely with the participants in the rites, to get the feel of the thing.

When my bus arrived at Saidaiji it was about 8 p.m. I did not know which way to go, but just set off walking along a narrow street of brightly lit shops open to the cold air of night. It was sleeting again. Small groups of youths in Western clothes were assembling in doorways of shops and bath-houses; others in wine shops were downing tumblers of hot saké. In a couple of hours, rosy with wine, they would strip in the public halls and bath-houses opened for their convenience, and start racing in groups through the town, giving ceaseless rhythmical shouts of 'washo! washo! washo! washo!'

The climax of the spectacle, when priests would throw the two sacred sticks into the throng, would not be reached until after midnight, so I strolled across a bridge and spent the next hour or so wandering around a very queer fairground. One part of it was entirely taken up with displays of farm machinery, mostly small mechanical hand ploughs for ricefields, threshing machines and so on. Also on display was a new type of solar home-heating apparatus that can now often be seen on the roofs of houses in Japan: it is an oblong frame containing tubes that gather the heat of the sun, store it and transform it for household use.

There were also many stalls selling cakes, fruit, pickles, rice crackers, candy-floss and souvenirs. There was a small shooting gallery and, in a small tent, a very frank strip show in which the good-natured, good-looking girls really divested themselves of every stitch of clothing, to the delighted applause of the mainly male audience. The atmosphere was good-tempered, innocent, natural, easy. The girls did not appear to me disgusting or shocking in any way. They performed with professional abandon, and every pose they struck was dignified by the beauty and youth of their bodies. They would smile affectionately at the men, as if the girls appreciated the vigour of the feelings they were arousing. It was a fascinating show, non-stop. It went on all night, getting wilder and wilder towards the break of day. Only two hundred yen, about four shillings, and see the show through as many times as you liked. There used to be frank sex shows like this in dark tents along the main street in Fukuhara, but unfortunately these have been severely cleaned up by the Kōbe municipal authorities —who have also put into force a police regulation forbidding urinating in the streets, the first of its kind in the history of Japan, because of complaints from foreign lady tourists and Christian missionaries. Despite their piety, Christian missionaries in Japan do not seem to recognize innocence when they see it: for these strip shows, however uninhibited, are childlike in their candour and of a totally inoffensive absurdity.

There were other, cheaper sideshows, admission only fifty yen, standing room only: a haunted house in which real rats ran over one's feet, and windy tents where one could watch cobras and pythons, doped with opium, being fondly handled by naked ladies; or small, worried, baffled dogs and melancholy inattentive monkeys abstractedly doing unnatural tricks; a young lady with understandably soot-caked front teeth eating or swallowing fire; and a middle-aged semi-geisha with deformed feet of a kind I had never seen before—they were forked, with only two large toes, the nails brilliantly lacquered. For a small extra fee, one was allowed to feel them: they were icy cold. From time to time she would hang, swinging slightly, on a grubby silken rope, lifting first one foot, then the other, in a pathetic kind of dance. She was unable to walk: as dawn was breaking I saw her being carried to a car by her young male assistants.

The standing audiences that slowly shuffled through these cheaper sideshows were composed mainly of country lads, schoolboys and small children: the young men shouting non-stop explanations of these gruesome sights kept declaring that they were 'educational'. Outside the tents barkers kept up a continuous frenzy of comment and invitation, speaking through small mikes fixed right in front of their mouths. The din outside and inside these neon-lit, flare-lit shows was appalling.

When I emerged, in something of a tizzy, from the haunted house, in which I had been briefly felt by a 'secret hand' (which I seized and found to be a real human hand belonging to someone concealed behind a piece of canvas) and bashed gently over the head by floppy white long-haired 'ghosts' with big, bruised mouths and eyes wide with horror, I found the rain and sleet had stopped and the muddy lane between the booths jammed with sauntering bands of saké-flushed revellers.

I groped my way into the dark car park between the booths and a small river or canal, and there, in company with scores of others, both men and women, relieved nature in the open air, a time-honoured Japanese custom that gives no offence, because of the purity of the Japanese mind; they see nothing wrong in it; indeed, they simply do not see it. It is not a question of averting their eyes from such sights: for them the sights do not exist. This ability to overlook what in our censorious Western society would be construed as a misdemeanour is one of the most engaging characteristics of Japanese life, though recently, under the puritanical influence of the Tokyo Olympics and the large increase of tourists from America and Europe, the Japanese are losing this admirable detachment, becoming miserably self-conscious and prim.

I sat down on a wet stone in the dark among dead weeds, watching the lantern-lighted *shoji* or paper sliding windows of small wooden houses on the other bank reflected in the flowing water. It was like a scene from a seventeenth-century wood-block print. I sipped a small bottle of saké, then another. I was in a mood of picturesque melancholy and enjoyed my romantic solitude. I sang Japanese folk songs to myself, very softly and beautifully, feeling at home and enchanted with my own company. The bridge across the water, adorned with lights and lanterns, was packed with people in winter kimono. The smells of roasting dried fish and hot soy sauce and grilled cubes of bean-curd paste scented the cold air. I felt at peace.

But in the near distance there were increasing shouts, panting cries of 'washo! washo!' and frantic blowings of police-whistles—*peep-peep! peep-peep! peep-peep! peep-peep!* The whistles had exactly the same double rhythm as that used by bus girls guiding a backing coach and calling at the same time 'awry! awry!' (all right! all right!) to the driver.

I squeezed through the crowds in the lane and elbowed my way across the bridge to the temple compound. On my right was a brightly lit Buddhist altar, covered with candles, fruit, incense, vegetables and rice-cakes, housed in a plain but elegant wooden building at the top of a short flight of steps. As at all Buddhist temples, there was a small shop to one side of the main altar, and here I bought from the smiling attendants some cotton towels printed with an animated horde of naked young men, all pressed tightly together in their battle for the sacred sticks. I also bought a small amulet of crimson and gold brocade shaped like a scrotum, and some candles and incense sticks. Surrounded by the jostling worshippers I lit my candles, stuck them drunkenly on the spikes of the plain metal candelabra in front of the altar, clapped my hands, bowed my head and prayed to Buddha that during the coming year I might lead a potent and uninhibited sex life. All around me men and women and children were praying the same prayer. The chant of our voices rose with the clouds of incense to all-compassionate Buddha. Lost somewhere in the incense-misted dimness beyond the acres of *tatami*, on which groups of celebrants were sitting, drinking wine, eating and playing cards, the image of whatever it was on the altar seemed to send out shooting rays of joy and power and virile affirmation.

My meditations and intercessions were interrupted by the breathless arrival, at a jog-trot, of a dozen naked youths, their rosy, peachy bodies glistening with snow and sweat, their shouting faces abstracted in a kind of supernatural ecstasy as they staggered, arms encircling each other's bare shoulders, towards the scintillating altar. They were being guided, in their seemingly tranced exhaustion, by two older men in civilian clothes blowing their two-blast whistles with needlessly hysterical urgency to clear the way for the phallus-worshippers. These broke formation at the bottom of the wooden steps and ran up them to the barrier in front of the altar. Some of them were too tired to run; they just walked up, very painfully. But once at the top of the steps they resumed their dignity, clapped their hands, bowed their heads and murmured a brief prayer. Then, turning and laying their arms about each other's shoulders once more, they again took up their rhythmical chant of 'washo! washo!', ran down the steps and tore away in a mad rout into the lantern-hung darkness beyond the temple, there to imbibe fresh pots of hot rice wine.

They seemed to have gathered fresh strength, because even those who had barely been able to totter up the steps now trotted along with their mates in a lively and vigorous way. It was as if they were all suffused with some common magic or spirit or power extending from the divine source, a power that was transmitted to the stronger ones and mystically transferred to the weakest and weariest of the band, who immediately were re-created and restored by contact with their more vital fellows. Once the physical contact was dropped, however, the group lost its mass strength. The trance of the reunited bodies was a good one, for whenever a youth stumbled on the steps or tripped over in the road he was sustained in the enfolding arms of his brothers, and was unhurt.

In another group—a fresh group was arriving now at the altar every minute or so—a young man slipped and tobogganed painfully all the way down the steps on his bottom, an accident which caused his exiguous breech-clout to become undone. His nakedness was exposed to all the spectators, who saw without looking or commenting; the Japanese are accustomed to seeing each other naked. The youth, only about sixteen, was unhurt, and seemed to be strengthened by the support and ministrations of his friends, who all took a hand in putting him to rights. In a few minutes he was gaily trotting off with the rest of the band, shouting and jigging with the best of them.

Among the groups was a handsome father of three small sons. He came, dressed in a black *fundoshi*, bearing the youngest, about five, astride his naked shoulders, while he held the other two, about eight and nine, by the hand. A murmur of admiration went up from the crowd at the sight of this fortunate male who had fathered three sons; daughters are considered of little value in a Japanese family. The importance attached to sons can be judged by the disparaging pride with which a father will refer to his boy as 'my pig son'. The little boys' plump faces were flushed—they had probably been given sips of rice wine—their naked limbs rosy, their lips parted in dazed smiles, their dark eyes shining with excitement. Unafraid, they shoved their way among the naked, sweating thighs of the youths and men all round them, and by some miracle were not trampled underfoot. It was touching to see them pray beside their father, a fine figure of a man, displaying the utmost gravity as they clapped their hands and bowed their heads. When the father bowed his head, the little boy on his shoulder, finding himself thus inclined towards the altar, also instinctively dipped his shaven pate. Then, as if renewed, the boys turned, dashed down the steps with *Father-san* and began their steady trotting, jigging and piping of 'washo! washo!'

I was being pushed and shoved about unmercifully, but these contacts with the crowd and with the hot, slippery bodies of the participants in the rite are part of the fun and galvanize the watchers with electric currents of zest and mysteriously transmitted energy. I could feel my batteries being replenished, minute by minute.

Then two stout middle-aged ladies, with linked arms, wearing white knickers and wide white cotton swaddling bands, which suppressed their chests into some semblance of manly flatness, came pluckily and determinedly running. They were soaked in sweat, and long, matted tendrils of black hair hung down their napes from the twisted white towels knotted round their heads. Even their eye-glasses were streaming with sweat, but they were both bravely smiling. More and more women began to appear, always in pairs, never in groups. Only the women wore towels round their heads: all the men were bare-headed. I could not help admiring the courage of these women, but felt they were out of place at this male celebration: to my mind, their presence had a weakening effect. But Japan is nothing if not all-inclusive, so, in true Japanese and Buddhist fashion, I compassionately accepted their rather unwelcome intrusion into these male rites.

I thought the presence of women at such a predominantly male festival must be yet another of those assertions of female equality which are becoming so widespread in Japan. But in fact, I later learned, women have taken a small part in this type of festival from the earliest times. In order to be quite certain that the women are not unclean in any way, they are compelled to live for one month in the seclusion of a monastery, enduring rigid training, eating special vegetarian food and spending their time in prayer and meditation. They are not allowed to take part with the men in the fierce tussle for the luck-bringing sacred wands.

Young men are seemingly considered clean by nature, for they are required to undergo no such penance. At most, they refrain from all forms of sexual pleasure the night before the festival, and of course on the night of the festival itself prepare themselves in the usual Japanese fashion by taking long, hot, purifying baths and warming up with hot rice wine. It is believed that if a young man attends a festival immediately after performing some sexual act his penis will drop off or some other great misfortune will befall him. No one has ever lost more than his breech-clout, but there are stories of 'unclean' boys who were injured in the battle for the sacred wands or crushed to death by *mikoshi*, or heavy, ornate, portable shrines, falling on them.

Now the groups of steaming youths were collecting on a big, wooden-pillared, high-roofed stage. More and more of them came running up the steps and packed themselves into the throng. In the end, late arrivals could get in only by hurling themselves from their mates' shoulders into the boiling mass of naked bodies. Some climbed up the pillars and, with loud yells, jumped into the seething ocean of manhood. Others clambered up on the high beams below the tiled roof and gazed down on the frenzied pushing and thrusting down below, or yelled encouragingly to friends trying to screw their way in through the press of bodies.

Some brought great tubs of icy water and sloshed them over the excited youths, causing huge clouds of steam to rise from their heated flesh. The spectators screamed at the sight of the steam, but the youths were apparently unaware of the chill pounce of the water on their backs and heads. Again and again they were doused, and again and again the steam rose to the rafters, where now many boys, more agile than the rest, were crouching and clinging like hordes of bats. Soon not one inch of woodwork was visible: it was all covered by naked bodies. Thc pillars looked extraordinary, like carved medieval masterpieces illustrating some hilarious inferno. From time to time someone would slip and fall heavily into the dense throng, but no one ever seemed to be hurt. However, a number of fist fights started breaking out, their cause unknown.

Then the priests appeared at an opening high in the roof, bearing the two sacred wands in their hands. The naked throng's excitement grew frenzied, and there was much violent pushing and shoving to get a good position. Several youths were thrust off the platform and down the steps, their feet tangled in undone loincloths.

No one interfered with the displays of uninhibited sexual symbolism, often accompanied by unmistakable movements and gestures. There was no need to interfere, because indecency is in the mind of the beholder, and there were no indecent thoughts in our minds as we witnessed these primitive pantomimes of life and creation. At the moment it all seemed quite natural. It was a deeply religious pagan carnival, and we had all become possessed by the god of procreation.

The shoving and shouting suddenly became extremely violent. The priests, having blessed the wands, cast them into the milling horde. Now real fighting started; there were terrible thuds and grunts and bloody noses were seen, backs lacerated by nails, ripped breech-clouts were flung high in the air while their hapless losers battled to recover them. The two youths who had been lucky enough to catch the wands were immediately buried under a pile of bodies: they were lying face downwards, holding the wands gripped tightly against their bellies while other men clawed at them trying to make them release their precious symbols. One boy's wand was eventually broken in two and a great shout went up from the victorious group which had managed to obtain a portion of this luck-bringing object. When they got back to work next day their employers would suitably reward them for their efforts, which one supposes promote successful business.

The lucky winners were chaired shoulder high by their cheering comrades shouting 'Banzai! Banzai! Banzai!'

Then all at once the whole thing was over and the crowds of spectators and excited participants began dispersing quietly and calmly as if nothing had happened. I have often observed this phenomenon in Japanese political or religious demonstrations: great heat is engendered while all are working together, chanting together, marching together through the streets, waving banners, posters of protest against American nuclear submarines and the war in Vietnam. But when the rally is over the temperature immediately drops, and the possessed, fanatical adherents of a cause are seen to be not possessed, not fanatical, but simply ordinary, law-abiding, nondescript, anonymous figures. Indeed I think perhaps one reason the Japanese love taking part in mass meetings and festivals is that they enjoy losing their faceless anonymity and taking on the personality and the power of a corporation or organization or movement. It takes them out of themselves for a while, and afterwards they enjoy a smoke and a glass of beer as they're cooling off.

Another winter festival of the phallus is held every March at the Shinto shrine of Tagata Jinja, not far from Nagoya. I attend this festival every year. Shinto shrine phallic festivals seem quieter and more reverent than Buddhist ones. At Tagata the worshippers crowd in adoration round a huge gilded wooden penis (testicles are never represented in Japanese phalloi) which is carried under a sacred canopy by dedicated young priests. However, there is the same fairground atmosphere as at Buddhist rites. The stalls sell souvenirs, phallus-shaped eandy and 'accessories' for both men and women containing miniature phalloi; or one can buy a brass phallus in a beautiful little wooden box lined with black velvet on which the sacred memento (called *ohmamori*) lies discreetly enveloped in white shrine paper. It is only about an inch long, but every one is different. It is beautifully made.

PART TWO

SPRING

I

TRAVELLING TO TOKYO

THE train journey by second-class coach from Osaka to Tokyo was perfectly comfortable, though rather crowded. This particular journey was made before the introduction of the new Tokaido line expresses.[1] I was able to spend much of my time in the restaurant car admiring the countryside, an ever-increasing sight in Japan. I give here, for the benefit of those unfamiliar with the geography of Honshu, a quick account of the chief sights between Osaka and Tokyo, some of which I shall return to in more detail later.

The spring was a dry one, and many of the rivers were wastes of grey stones and boulders, but here and there freshets in hillsides and cliffs sprang out, flooding the neighbouring fields of fortunate rice farmers with white water. In dark pines or in farmhouse gardens, ever and again would come the pure jet of colour from a flowering cherry or plum. These simple wild varieties of cherry are much more pleasing to the eye than the pink flocculence of lush city trees.

There were some jolly tipplers of beer and saké on my express; some of them had sprigs of flowering cherry behind their ears. However, I saw none of the rowdyism which sometimes takes place on trains at the season when the *sakura* or cherry blossom blooms.

The sun was warm and bright, and so it was strange as well as sad to read in a newspaper of five lumberjacks being killed when an

[1] See my *Tokyo* (Phoenix House).

avalanche of snow crushed their lodge in Togamura village, Toyama Prefecture, on the upper reaches of the Momosegawa River.

In the same newspaper an eighteen-year-old factory worker from Kawasaki, Yoichi Abe, had this letter exhibiting public spiritedness, remarkable in one so young, and especially in a Japanese.

> The season when picnic grounds become dirty with scattered trash and paper has come. Starting from this year, let us try to keep clean our picnic grounds by ourselves.
>
> I would like to suggest you take a vinyl *furoshiki* [1] when you go on a picnic. When you go home you can bring with you left-over foods wrapped in vinyl *furoshiki*.
>
> When it rains a vinyl *furoshiki* can serve as an umbrella. One can sit on it even on wet ground where newspapers are of no use. It also can serve as a table spread on the grass.
>
> I don't think lack of trash boxes is the sole reason for dirty picnic grounds.

Approaching Kyoto, the five-storeyed pagoda of the Toji Temple, lying on the right, the highest in Japan, seemed to swim in cherry blossom. The station at Kyoto was jammed with Japanese tourists swarming round small, harried groups of foreigners in charge of Japanese guides. There was something utterly endearing about the enthusiasm and gaiety of those crowds of school children on their annual *shugaku ryoko*, or educational and cultural excursions. They save up a long time for these trips, which are encouraged by the Ministry of Education and which often last several days. I admired the cheerfulness and patience of the teachers who accompanied them, and felt sorry that such excellent ways of extending the children's knowledge of their history and country were sometimes criticized by both Japanese and foreigners as ill-organized, too long and too apt to interfere with the enjoyment of adult tourists.

This is true, but is there really nothing to be done about it? A good idea perhaps would be to limit school excursions to certain periods of the month, leaving the rest of the time more free for adults to enjoy scenery and ancient buildings and treasures. It is a pity too that even the older children can think of nothing better to say to passing foreigners than 'Hallo' or 'Harro', usually followed by a burst of infectious giggles. Part of their preparation for such a trip, I suggest, might be some training in elementary English conversation for those

[1] A large square of cloth, or plastic, used for making bundles and carrying things.

who wish to speak to foreigners. The very most one ever gets out of them is: 'What is your name? How long stay Japan? Where is your country?' Such questions, asked by some bolder spirit in the class, usually provoke more gales of laughter in his classmates, so that the poor boy sinks into silent embarrassment and does not venture to say another word. However willing one is to converse with children and students, there comes a time when one feels one simply cannot endure another of these questions and their accompanying giggles. Japanese teachers! Please teach your children to ask some *new* questions! And help them to answer questions they may be asked. Most Japanese students are nonplussed if they are asked a question which is not in their phrase book.

Outside Kyoto we crossed the River Kamo, with Mount Hiei still snowy in the distance, and next to it Mount Hira. The valleys round these mountains are noted for the beauty of their blossom in spring, and for the maple leaves in autumn. If you must go to Kyoto in spring, it is better to view the cherries at the country villages of Yase and Ohara, at the west foot of Mount Hiei. In the latter village is the most exquisite Sanzen-in Temple with its spare, lovely halls and pictured screens and paintings of the Mandalas by Eshin. You must of course take a look at Kiyomizu Temple adrift on blossom; one stands on the projecting platform that looks over a cliff and sees below clouds upon clouds of pink florescence. But the true spirit of *sakura* is best appreciated out in the country.

We raced straight through Otsu, where the poet Basho lies buried; I have often wanted to visit his grave with the tributes of a poem and a handful of wild flowers, but it was three years later before I did so: I sent him an arrow-prayer through the dusty window. Close to the Uasu River was Omi-Fuji, so called because of its resemblance to Fuji. The vast spread of glittering blue Lake Biwa lay to the left for mile after mile until we came in sight of Hikone Castle towering whitely over the hills. After Maibara the train went through a mountainous region whose greens and browns were injected here and there with sharply pink shoots and fountains of wild cherry, and on the left Mount Ibuki's lower slopes too were shot with pink. Then came Gifu, famous for lanterns, parasols and cormorant fishing, and the River Kiso, which the Japanese, with their love of flattering comparisons, call the 'Rhine of Japan'. On to the great modern city of Nagoya, set in an immense, swivelling plain where the fields just now were bright with rape and *renge*, or Chinese milk vetch.

North of Toyohashi the train skirted the green lagoon of Bentenjima, also known as Lake Hamana, with its many acres of bamboo stakes to which are fastened nurseries for eels, carp and other kinds of fish. Round Yaizu wonderful views of the embankmented sea coast and little fishing towns are followed by even more wonderful, and extensive, views, north of Shizuoka, of Suruga Bay. I kept hoping for a sight of Mount Fuji, but unfortunately the elusive mountain was lost in cloud, as it so often is.

On to the popular seaside and hot-spring resort of Atami, with its many hotels and bathing establishments. J. M. Richards rather humorously compares this stretch of scenic coastline dotted with resorts and white hotels with Weymouth, Scarborough and Margate. Atami is, I suppose, the Japanese equivalent to Margate, though, at least to a foreigner, it is infinitely more charming. From Odawara, a pleasant old castle town steeped in history, the train moved round Sagami Bay, with more popular resorts, including perhaps the most famous one in Japan, Enoshima, and the Kamakura of the Great Buddha. Just before Ofuna station there is a large concrete statue of the goddess Kwannon standing on a cliff, imposing, but, like most of these modern monster statues, vulgar and, seen from behind, rather stupid. (Compare its vacant back with the scholarly stoop of the Great Buddha of Kamakura's shoulders.) Yokohama at night, shimmering with neon, is now almost joined to Tokyo by the sprawling industrial city of Kawasaki, though the latter is not in fact as ugly as people always say; it should be visited, for it has a fine station and a well-planned centre and an amusing entertainment district not far from the station. Shortly afterwards the echoing, swarming halls of vast Tokyo station.

I was very tired when I reached Tokyo, so I went straight to my room at the Dai Ichi Hotel and after a bath went to bed. Before falling asleep I opened the New Testament on the bedside table—*American Standard Version and Japanese Colloquial Version, Bilingual Edition*—and found myself looking at John 20, vv. 21–23:

> Jesus therefore said unto them again, Peace be unto you: as the Father hath sent me, even so send I you. And when he had said this, he breathed on them, and saith unto them, Receive ye the Holy Spirit. Whose soever sins ye forgive, they are forgiven unto them; whose soever sins ye retain, they are retained.

As so often happens when one opens the Bible at random, this passage spoke to my need. (Perhaps such occasions, however rare, are not as random as one imagines.)

But yet another passage in this book, a passage quite unauthorized, spoke even more closely to me. It was a few words written in English in a rather unformed hand on the back inside cover. The words ran: 'Dear Betty, I thank some kiss, Sugimoto Natsukawa.' I pondered long over this. The red Dai Ichi stamp was blurred—with tears? I suspected a parting between East and West, one of the most terribly rending partings there can ever be, and that marks for life. I said a thought which was not a prayer for this queer heartbreak that some Japanese man had felt compelled to commit to writing, and in what may have been to him a most sacred or a most mysterious book. It is always the one who is left behind who suffers more, and it is always the Japanese who are left behind by those from the West. We can never fully comprehend their grief at parting, a grief that refuses to allow itself to be seen even by the most beloved. To show sorrow and shed tears would be lacking in consideration and selfish in the extreme. For partings are always great public affairs, all smiles and flowers, in Japan. Those concealed heartbreaks: they combine to create something one always senses in Japan—a vast accumulation of loneliness and unspoken misery, with no one to tell it to. I hope this man found some relief by telling it to the Bible in his own sad way, in English, in a strange single room of a lonely American-style hotel. Some hotels, like the Kanko Hotel in Nagoya, now have Buddhist scriptures in English in every room instead of the Bible. And why not indeed? Christians form an infinitesimally small part of the population in this land of Buddha.

The Dai Ichi is a hotel that always reminds me of some dreamlike building out of Kafka, with its endless corridors, its identical doors, its dark, cubical courtyards of yellow brick honeycombed with square windows whose green Venetian blinds are always drawn.

I suddenly felt hungry, so I went down to the basement snack bar for a sandwich. The waiters took absolutely no notice of my entrance; or rather, one of them watched me sit down, then he turned his gaze away from me and went on watching the television with the other waiters. It was a Friday night, a night I have come to dread in Tokyo, the night when all-in wrestling or, as the Japanese call it, 'pro-wrestling', is televised. Everything simply comes to a stop for this ghastly exhibition of counterfeit but no less sickening violence, a display which hypnotizes and enraptures the Japanese so much that they forget to eat and drink; one can't get service anywhere, conversation dies in the bars as the madames and hostesses crowd round the set, taxi-drivers refuse to take customers, but sit watching their miniature transistorized sets with screens the size of postcards and will not move until the last grisly gougings and wrenchings are over. There is something horribly sinister in this absolute mania of the Japanese for watching others suffer pain and inflict it, as if it were some compensation for their own lack of power, their sense of hopeless insecurity and quite unjustified inferiority. Many of the foreign pro-wrestlers stay at the Dai Ichi Hotel, haunting the lobbies and restaurants with their lumbering bodies and grotesquely masked heads.

Finally, I had to go to the counter and beg for food and drink. The waiters expressed insolent surprise that anyone should want to eat or drink while the sacred rites of pro-wrestling were engaging their attention. I was grudgingly and slowly served by barman, sandwich-boy and waiter who kept interrupting their work to crow and shout with glee whenever one of the contestants on the screen 'broke the rules', hit the referee or did something particularly disgusting to his opponent. One Japanese gentleman in the snack bar, a youngish man who had been politely waiting at his table for service, suddenly went red and started shouting in a very loud and alarming voice at the boy attendants lolling against the bar watching the set. This was a most unusual outburst for a Japanese to make in public. One of the attendants then came and stood before him, bowing very low and most respectfully, rattling off profuse conventional forms of apology. The others took no notice at all of this interruption. I am sad to think that Japan, which only eighteen months ago was still a land where one could expect pleasantness and courtesy, should be degenerating in this way, and so swiftly. (Of course if management pockets what should be employees' tips the staff have a just grievance, but it is sad that they should take it out on the customer.)

The next evening I again went down to the snack bar. An old American war film was being shown, with the usual sergeant refusing orders, being individualistic and awfully cross with everyone. To my astonishment, one of the people watching this guff with intense admiration was one of the all-in wrestlers from the show the night before. He was wearing a strange red hood which covered his entire head except his eyes and mouth and nose. Apparently he lives in this hotel. Last night, on the television screen, all eyes had been upon him;

tonight, despite his odd get-up, no one was paying him the slightest attention. He too couldn't get service until he banged on the table, making everyone jump rather, before returning absorbedly to an irate John Wayne grousing and making the most awful faces at his wretched troops.

I couldn't sleep, so I got out of bed and dressed. I was feeling strangely uneasy and restless. Not wanting to take a sleeping capsule, I went out for a stroll. It was one of those evenings that come once or twice a month and which I have often noticed in Tokyo, when there seems to be an atmosphere of savage melancholy over everything; faces in the train to Shinjuku were drawn, unhappy, brooding. At every station there were great splodges of rice-vomit on the platforms and drunks lying full length, sound asleep on the benches. I got lost, and kept changing trains at the wrong stations. I found myself on oddly fast, non-stop trains that kept bearing me out relentlessly into drab, cold, neon-lit suburbs of tiny wooden houses towered over by new barrack-like blocks of flats and electric advertising signs. There was a curious blackness, as if the air had been steeped in Chinese ink, a haunting emptiness and sense of impermanence in everything; the many drunks seemed to be final products of this unhappy, wild and discontented ambience.

When at last I got to Shinjuku, I soon found what last summer had been an attractive quiet bar, only to discover that now all the bartenders were new, the *décor* changed for the worse; a blaring juke-box played 'The Bells of St Mary's' as a twist tune on electric Japanese guitars. Everyone at the counters looked crazed with melancholia and drink, their faces blank or fevered with a bad light of glowering mistrust. Girls everywhere, in pairs or in office groups, were soaking up highly coloured confections of virulent violet, chocolate and traffic-signal crème de menthe glutted with rich red cherries embedded in rough hunks of ice. I felt decidedly unwanted, though no one spoke to me. The barman, however, was perfectly polite, wiping the counter maddeningly after every sip I took of my weak Nikka highball. I was glad to get out.

I went next to an all-night coffee bar where I sometimes used to meet amusing people who were being determinedly degenerate in such an innocent way that my heart used to melt for them. Now it was full of mooching couples who had come to doss down for the night, very uncomfortably, on the hard upholstery of Japan. Some youths had brought their black cloth night-masks, the sort J.A.L. gives you on the Polar Flight, to help them sleep in the bar's changing lights, which were anyhow rather low. Others were stuffing their heads with ear-plugs, hired at the cashier's desk, to keep out some of the record-player's only too high fidelity. An air of dissolution, madness and totally uninventive depravity hung over the place. In a few minutes I was bored so I went away, before the slow-coach waitresses, drugged with a diet of sleeping pills and noodles, could come and take my order.

I wandered round the midnight streets of Shinjuku. Everywhere drunks, fights, people furiously running, escaping from some terror round the corner, some nightmare that was never there when I went to look. A workman was beating his head on the pavement, wiping the stones with bloody hands while groups of students sauntered by uncaringly, singing maudlin folk-songs. In a quiet lane one boy had set up a small table and was selling, quite simply, hard-boiled eggs, an activity radiantly pure in that awful miasma of despair; he handed me, with a bow and a smile, a little twist of salt in *sakura*-pink paper to sprinkle on the eggs I bought. This one person and his simplicity and goodness saved the evening for me and reasserted my faith, never very weak, in the nobility of the Japanese.

But it was extremely depressing. I took the train back to my hotel at Shimbashi. In my carriage were an elderly man, quite drunk, and a vicious young woman in kimono, probably a bar hostess, who had him firmly by the lapels, by which she dragged him into the train. She kept seizing his muffler (the Japanese use this English word) and pulling him close to her, violently and roughly, her powdered, only-just-pleasant face obviously seething with rage and temper under the mean surface. The man kept falling asleep, and at least once a minute she would give his nose a horrid sharp tweak to make him wake up. He finally tired of this and gave her face a harmless slap. They got off at Kanda and went staggering down the steps. No one took much notice of them. Obviously a bar madame and a defaulting customer or a tired lover.

I too got off at Kanda and took a taxi the rest of the way to my hotel. The driver had to make a long detour because the Ginza had suddenly been ripped up by hundreds of workmen who were rushing about with their tools and machines under batteries of arc-lamps, constructing a new subway which, like everything else in Japan at that time, had to be 'ready for the Olympics'. I stopped the taxi for two minutes to buy some fruit at a street stall; the driver insisted on being paid fifty yen extra for waiting this brief space, a meanness unheard of a year ago.

Fortunately such nights occur only about twice a month. The rest of the time, Tokyo is a reasonably pleasant place. Part of the reason for the degeneration in public life is the Government's tax system, which compels companies to just throw away large sums of money on food and drink and free entertainment for their employees at the bars and clubs and cabarets of Shinjuki, Shibuya, Akasaka and Ikebukuro. The money has to be spent so that no excess profit is shown on tax returns; this means that at least twice a month every office man goes on a roaring spree at his company's expense. The bars and cabarets are quick to take advantage of all this loose money being flung around, and send their prices sky high, so that it is now difficult to find places where one can just have a quiet, cheap drink at a bar unpestered by service and hostesses. It is not unusual for bottles of beer (small bottles—large bottles are now never served in clubs) to be charged at five thousand yen (five pounds) and whisky costs the earth. This is all right for company employees on expense accounts unlimited, but for the ordinary quiet drinker who pays for his own drink the clubs and cabarets have now priced themselves right out of his range. A man who does not pay for his own liquor loses all self-respect. Japanese business men and expense-account employees have lost theirs long ago.

A warning to foreign visitors to Japan: *never* enter an establishment called a Cabaret (often mis-spelt Cabalet), a Salon (often mis-spelt Saron) or a Club (Crab) or one with a name entirely in Japanese characters. Never enter a bar which does not display the prices outside. Never enter a place where there are girls in kimono, ballerina-length or floor-length evening dresses. Unless of course you wish to be gypped or are content to pay prices so ridiculously high, you wonder how the smiling madame has the nerve to write it on the bill and then bow you away charmingly from the door. Above all, never allow yourself to be dragged into a bar by attractive hostesses, and never listen to the recommendations of touts who say they will guide you to a nice bar. These are definite clip-joints. If you allow yourself to be taken to a bar by a tout, he will sit with you at the counter and offer you several drinks. He will offer rounds of drinks to all the girls, saying 'It's on me'. After you have consumed a certain number he will excuse himself and say he is going to the lavatory. You will never see him again, and you are left stuck with a massive bill. He gets his rake-off next day. Touts are particularly rife in the Shimbashi area.

The pleasures of bar society have declined in Japan. For a foreigner, the best thing to do is to buy your own drink and consume it in your hotel room. If you feel you must have company, take a flask to a coffee shop or patronize only those bars which are called 'Stand Bars', where there are usually no hostesses. Here one does not stand at the bar, but sits on stools. These are the best and cheapest bars in Japan, and the company is often interesting. The bartenders are first class—many of them have attended the bartenders' colleges in Shinjuku or Shibuya—and the only rather sad thing about these places is that sometimes one of the girls behind the bar will come and plant herself right in front of you and watch every mouthful you drink. She is only trying to be attentive and polite to the master-male, but it does get a bit tiresome to be watched so closely, especially if she has no conversation, whatever else she may have to recommend her.

I had intended in this book to mention some of the good bars I have found, but on second thoughts I shall not do so except in certain cases, because Japanese bars tend to disappear overnight or change their character so completely that they become unrecognizable. Unless one has a reliable Japanese or foreign friend to show one around it is best to look for oneself, keeping one's eyes peeled for any telltale signs. And once one has entered a bar, one should never hesitate to walk straight out again if one doesn't like the look of the place. (Though this is something a Japanese, concerned not to 'lose face', would never do.)

2

FLOWER FESTIVALS

SPRING time in Japan: the first, pale, delicate willow leaves ghosting the trailing boughs of weeping willow in Kyoto lanes seem to me more typical of Japanese spring time than the profusions of sickly pink cherry blossom.

In Japan the cherry blossoms are called 'the king of flowers', and they are also a kind of national emblem, though the chrysanthemum is really the national flower. Many things are named after the *sakura*, or cherry blossoms: innumerable trade marks bear this word; the new fashionable colour for lipstick or ladies' stockings or dresses is called *sakura*; *sakura* paper is pink tissue paper, a *sakura* moon is a misty vernal moon and *sakuramochi* is a kind of sweet bean-paste rice-cake wrapped in a cherry leaf. One of the most popular Japanese folk-songs, sung enchantingly everywhere at this season by little bands of primary school children on park outings, and distorted by every kind of jazz, vocal and 'singing strings' arrangement, is 'Sakura'; it is the signature tune of the season, and almost of Japan. Cherry wood is used for woodcuts, for walking-sticks and for boxes made from its bark and intended to hold green tea leaves.

Some privileged Japanese who can afford to make the trip, and can obtain the necessary permission from the Government to leave the country, are now going to Washington for their cherry-blossom viewing. They are not the only Japanese who deplore the heartless way the Japanese people are treating their once almost sacred emblem, the subject of so many of the great poems and paintings of this country's long cultural past. A housewife in Fujisawa City, Shige Ishimoto, wrote thus to the *Asahi Shimbun*:

> One recent weekend, I went to Ueno Park to see the cherry blossoms at night. The place was packed because the cherry blossoms were at their best. What surprised me most was the behaviour of the cherry viewers.
>
> At the foot of the five-storeyed pagoda were piles of rubbish, strewn as if garbage cans had been overturned. People drank, ate, shouted and sang

loudly, regardless of those about them. In the crowds were mothers with children.

I spent three years in Chicago where my husband was stationed. Even Maxwell Street, which is notorious as one of the world's dirtiest streets, was not as bad as what I saw the other day at Ueno Park.

In winter, Chicago residents stay at home. But when spring arrives, they suddenly pour out into parks and enjoy outdoor cooking, just as we do in Japan. But American picnickers do not leave food and other waste in their wake.

I told my American friends in Chicago about Japan's good points and suggested they see the country for themselves.

Now, I am not so sure of my fellow citizens. I do believe, however, that we still have outstanding capabilities and temperament.

And yet the people I see at cherry-blossom-viewing parties, on the roads and in public conveyances, are not, in my view, conducting themselves as responsible members of society.

Mrs Ishimoto's letter illustrates not only the irresponsibility that is growing in Japan, but also the deep concern with which many Japanese view this unhappy development in public morality. It is my belief that 'the cult of mediocrity', which is the bane of democratic countries, simply does not suit the Japanese who, as Mrs Ishimoto rightly and proudly declares, 'have outstanding capabilities and temperament'. What the Japanese need is some great father figure they can look up to with affection and reverence. The Emperor once supplied this basic need in Japanese psychology; but today, though he is still looked up to, he has been 'popularized' by the press and played down by the Occupation. He has been made the subject of a best-selling biography (*Hirohito*, by Leonard Mosley) and impersonated on the Japanese screen by the well-known Kabuki actor Koshiro Matsumoto in *Emperor Hirohito and a General.* On 7th April 1967 their Majesties the Emperor and Empress travelled by train to Osaka and Okayama, not in imperial solitude and invisibility, but by the regularly scheduled Hikari super-express on the new Tokaido line. The Emperor has become public property. The Japanese may now look upon his face. He is no longer a god.

Many Japanese, especially those desirous of being invited to America or Britain, have been falling over themselves in their eagerness to proclaim how democratic they are. In fact what the Japanese need and long for is a formal but benevolent paternalism, a feeling of authority exercised over them in every walk of life and influencing their behaviour in society through the examples of religion, art (including

Fisherman on the outskirts of Tokyo

Snow Festival at Sapporo City

Regional restaurant in Shinjuku

Small eating shops in the Tokyo fish market

Indoor gymnasium in Tokyo

(*Left*) The Imperial Palace moat

Olympic stadium

National Museum in Tokyo

Kyoto temple and garden

The Tōgudō and pond

Kenrokuen park

Teahouse

At the Sensoji temple in Asakusa

Kabukiza theatre

the military arts of fencing, judo, archery, *kendo* and *karate*) and other noble disciplines. The great flaw in democracy is its false assumption that everyone is equal, and its hypocritical claim that all men are free. The freedom of the individual is something that must grow inside him; it cannot simply be superimposed upon him by a state decree saying that the aim of democracy is the pursuit of freedom and happiness. Where there is no discipline there can be no personal freedom, a view best expressed by Wordsworth in his sonnet on liberty. Most Westerners have no idea what democracy means, or have completely misconstrued it. Governments too use it merely as a catch-phrase; in fact it no longer has any meaning. The Japanese, trying sincerely to be as polite as possible to America and the West, have taken up democracy wholesale, and naturally they have become imbued with all the misconceptions the West is prone to. The Japanese will continue to degenerate until they can find some sort of guided democracy which will give personal freedom some meaning and in which individual anarchy will, paradoxically, have full play. The present cult of mediocrity and the common man is making fools of the Japanese, who are by nature not mediocre at all, and not common.

The spring equinox and the autumn equinox are great national holidays in Japan. The whole nation, nearly, takes a day off, for Government offices, schools, banks and many companies are closed. Yet nearly all the shops and restaurants remain open; there is not that atmosphere of sudden death that makes public holidays in Europe so mournful.

The spring equinox: 21st March. On that day the weather was balmy; the mercury stood at 18·5° C., about five degrees higher than normal for the time of year. The Emperor, Empress and Crown Prince Akihito observed the traditional rituals of the spring equinox at the Imperial Palace Sanctuaries. The rites were officiated at by the Emperor himself and were also attended by Prince Yoshi and other members of the imperial family. There was a great exodus of people from Tokyo to mountains and seaside and hot-spring resorts. Atami, where the cherry blossom was in full glory, was packed with hundreds of thousands of vacationers, and Jukkoku Plains, between Atami and Hakone, were dense with hikers, while cars sped in an endless stream along the newly opened Izu Skyline Drive. The temples at Kamakura and Nikko were thronged with families visiting graves to pay respects to their ancestors, and excursion boats started cruising on Lake Chuzenji for the first time that year. Thousands of skiers enjoyed the last vestiges of snow on the high slopes in Oku Nikko and tens of thousands of climbers scaled the Tanzawa Ranges in Kanagawa Prefecture, where the peaks were still covered by snow that had fallen only one week previously.

Tokyo itself was crammed with country visitors, who nearly all converged upon the great cherry-blossom-viewing park at Ueno, where at night the lantern-lit blossom was exquisitely pretty. But those who customarily went every year at this time to view the cherries against the dark grey background of the Imperial Palace moat's massive leaning walls were disappointed; these trees have been removed altogether because of Olympic road construction work. Yasukuni shrine too was a favourite rendezvous: this is a great Shinto shrine in memory of the Japanese war dead, and the cherry blossom here is most beautiful, and perhaps more moving than anywhere else in Tokyo. Here one can still sense in the Japanese that traditional feeling of *mono-no-aware* or pathos for the fleetingness of the blossom, a symbol of the brevity of human life. Perhaps the Japanese appreciate the cherry blossoms most when they are falling in the spring wind and strewing the fresh green grass with drifts of white and pink petals. Cherry blossoms must be appreciated in the mass, not singly as are the lotus and the lily.

I prefer cherry viewing in the smaller parks of Tokyo, such as those along the Sumida River in Asakusa, the Inogashira Park (famous also for plum blossom and a grove of giant cedars), Shinjuku Gyoen (an old imperial garden famous also for its chrysanthemum displays in October), Kiyosumi Garden and Korakuen Garden.

My favourite is Kiyosumi Garden, a bit worn and dingy at times when there is no blossom, like a threadbare but beautiful patch on the grim working suit of industrial Tokyo. Its full name is Kiyosumi-Teien Garden. It is about twelve acres in area and stands near Kiyosu Bridge; it is one of the finest landscape gardens in the metropolitan area. It is best to visit it—as well as almost any other place in Japan—as soon as it opens, at 8 a.m., when one will have the garden to oneself. (It closes at 4 p.m.) It is most celebrated for its fine rocks in romantic arrangements that yet have a classic severity; these rocks were gathered from all over Japan by connoisseurs in the art of rock-choosing and arranging. Originally the garden belonged to Baron Iwasaki, who donated it to the municipality in 1924. There is a lovely lake with little peninsulas of twisty pine, each providing a different vista or a subtle change in mood. There is also an artificial hill where cherry and azalea are cunningly planted to give a 'typical' natural look, but one slightly enhanced by art. There are lots of interesting stepping-stones across narrow streams and round the lake as well as on grassy pathways, where they have a most charming effect. There are pleasant old summer-houses of wood and thatch where it is nice to sip a glass of saké (take your own bottle) and watch the bright kimono of ladies strolling in this authentic setting, so still and perfect amid the din of the thronged city. Baron Iwasaki also once owned the Rikugien Garden, another delightful spot, at Komagome in Tokyo.

At Rikugien I watched the old women gardeners in their baggy blue trousers, or *monpe*, their grey heads draped in the white and blue cotton towels, piling dead winter leaves with long-handled bamboo rakes, and was reminded of Morishige Hisaya singing in his fine, deep voice the fairly modern folk-song, 'Kare Susuki', which Seiji Sekino, a former colleague of mine at Sendai, kindly translated for me. Here are a few lines of his excellent version (he modestly calls it an 'improvisation'):

The cold winter blast is sweeping,
The dead pampas grasses are bending,
And I feel loneliness bitter
In the deep mountains here. . . .

The sight of blossoms here also reminded me of a brief poem by Takuboku, translated by Dr Hiroshi Takamine in his book on the poet, *A Sad Toy*, in this way:

Would that my spirit turn into spring breeze,
Passing through the flowers of cherry trees,
And reach you around your sleeves. . . .

Some of the trees in the park had little poems tied to them, celebrating in mostly conventional language and images the miracle of the cherry blossom and the sadness of its fall. I tried to think of something new to write about cherry blossom, and realized how difficult this must be for the Japanese. I finally, after hours of thought, wrote this:

The lake seems to rise
To meet the falling blossom
Whose reflections drop
Into the drowning sky.

I had just bought a remarkable Japanese fountain-pen which instead of a nib has a paint-brush shaped like a beautiful bud of an ash tree.

I inscribed the poem with this on a piece of pink paper and floated it in the lake where, slowly weighted down by falling petals, it gradually foundered.

The Rikugien Garden was first laid out in the early eighteenth century by Lord Yanagisawa Yoshiyasu, and is a typical garden of the feudal times. There is a grove of ancient trees on an artificial hill and a fine old teahouse. It is open every day all the year round.

An old woman gardener's gesture, hand to cheek, with tip of little finger on lower lip as she suddenly smiled at me, had a curious coquettish charm; there was something very distinguished about that old woman. Perhaps she had been a geisha who had fallen on evil days. Her wise old eyes had me summed up in a minute with some of the geisha's professional skill in diagnosing a client's moods and anticipating his wishes. She said one word: 'Sabishii?' I nodded, and we smiled at each other, and looked round the lonely garden. She said, nodding sagely: 'Neh?' We were alone together in that early morning solitude.

Korakuen Garden: tufts of grass like heads of hair. The weeping cherry, two hundred and fifty years old, was in full blossom, its pale pink petals delicate against dark boughs stained with moss. It was like an anchored cloud, tinted by the rose of sunrise.

The construction of this garden was started in 1629 by Yorifusa Tokugawa, feudal Lord of Mito, but he died before he saw its completion. His son, Mitsukuni, a man of learning, an amateur of things Chinese and a great lover of nature, carried out his father's last wishes in the design of the garden and hastened its completion. He was a great believer in Confucianism: therefore the garden has many traces of Chinese styles. He had Shu Shun Sui, a learned refugee from China, as his adviser in its creation. It was Shu Shun Sui who gave the garden the name Korakuen, a name taken from the teachings of Confucius and meaning 'a sage must be first in enduring hardships, and often overcoming them and bringing happiness to all, the last to seek the reward of enjoyment'.

The garden covers an area of about seventeen acres with hills and water, rocks and stones, trees and shrubs in sensitive arrangement. The outstanding feature of the garden is the harmonious and natural blending of Japanese and Chinese taste and spirit, for the Japanese in all things feel themselves very close to the Chinese. The entrance to the garden is through the Karamon, or Chinese Gate. The lake was specially designed by Iemitsu, third in the Tokugawa Shogunate; one of the lake's features is a small island with a temple to Benten, a Hindu deity, known in Japan as one of the Seven Deities of Good Luck. There is a stone bridge known as the Full Moon Bridge, as it is built in the form of a semicircle which is completed by its reflection in the water.

After the Meiji Restoration in 1868 this garden, along with the adjoining estates, came to belong to Central Government property and then went under the jurisdiction of the military with an arsenal being built on the estates. In March 1923 a law was passed for the preservation of the garden as an historical monument, but six months later it was severely damaged in the Great Earthquake. The Kantoku-tei, or Glass Teahouse, built at a time when it was unusual to use glass instead of paper for windows and doors, was completely destroyed. Today there is a small modern teahouse there bearing the same name.

In December 1936 with the removal of the arsenal the garden was placed under the supervision of the Tokyo Municipality.

Near by is the great Korakuen Amusement Park, with its funfairs, restaurants, bath-houses, ice- and roller-skating rinks, the great Korakuen baseball stadium and, most important of all, the judo hall, called Kodokan, the centre of international judo, the Japanese art of self-defence. The late afternoon sunlight was slanting through the big windows of this enormous practice hall, where hundreds of Japanese males and one or two foreigners, from the age of five upwards, were practising individual falls and throwing. One American sported a black belt. There are many Japanese with black belts. I saw one grey-haired, elderly man wearing a red one. The sun glowed through the wide cream trousers of the boys, which, suffused by the dark shadows of their limbs, flapped around their bare feet. Padded jackets, loosely swinging: the determined way they seize hold of each other's lapels before attempting a throw. Trousers and coats are monogrammed with black characters.

The smaller boys are twittering like sparrows. But when they have all been gathered into a corner to listen to a quiet talk from an instructor there is a silent intensity in the air of the hall, broken only by the sound of the older boys' bare feet slapping on the pale green, plastic-covered *tatami*, by the thud of falling bodies, by a few grunts and gasps and shouts of defiance. The boys' long black shadows wrestle also. The dispassionate embrace of the opponents, often so intimately close, grasping each other with pure and austere and passionate absorption. A dedication of youthful strength to wise and chivalrous ends: a pair of young men bow to each other ceremoniously before suddenly falling into a grim, determined clutch. The abandon, deeply controlled, however, with which they throw themselves upon one another is exciting to watch. It is the same outright and clever utilization of energy as one observes in workmen in Japan, the same rich expenditure of unstinted bodily effort, generous and warm and wild. Except that judo of course is the art of using the minimum of effort: Japanese workmen know that art too.

The young men sometimes get into very close and intimate couplings of legs and arms and torsos, but there are no heavy erotic overtones in this; the contestants are too occupied in countering the next move to have thoughts of sex, though judo, like many other manly sports, may be an expression of subconscious love for one's own sex. The spectators in the gallery include a few single women watching those grapplings with an absorption almost spiderlike in its intensity.

After watching these quite ordinary boys and men practising this noble sport, I find the Japanese remind me more than ever of the ancient Greeks. I have even greater respect and admiration for the Japanese male. This sport brings out in him a grave formality; it is the occasion for movingly reserved intimacy with other men. I feel this to be the right relationship between males; the Japanese seem to fall into it quite naturally, perhaps because of the disciplines of their great traditions which, though apparently forgotten in the spiritual waste of modern life, can never be unlearned. Perhaps Western men establish the same kind of *entente* with each other in boxing and wrestling. Certainly the American sporting the black belt seemed to have this rapport with his various Japanese opponents. It makes me wish I were a whole man. I could never empty myself of sentiment and emotion sufficiently to practise this sport. But it made me calm, though a little sad, to spend an hour or so watching judo.

Curiously the vigorous contestants reminded me at times of the two young men I saw gravely dancing a slow foxtrot together in a gay bar.

I looked on the Japanese in the streets outside with a new eye: those slender, lissom, almost girlish bodies—how much hidden strategy and age-old, instinctive skill in self-defence did they conceal? Their light-footedness, their rather dancing walk, on their toes, hips well forward—but this is caused not by judo. Rather it is the result of wearing *geta*, which compel the wearer to adopt a rather thrusting action in walking, on the balls of his feet with the heels of the *geta* hanging loosely, and sometimes trailing with a lackadaisical charm on the dust and stones of Japanese roads.

I like the fatalistic Japanese expression *shikataganai*, meaning roughly 'it can't be helped', the equivalent of a Frenchman's helpless shrug of the shoulders.

A neat cherry-blossom party observed in Mukogaokayuen Garden, on the south bank of the Tama River, where the commonest variety of cherry, and also the most fragile, is the *Somei-Yoshino*. (The *yae-zakura* or multipetal and *yama-zakura* or mountain cherry do not bloom until later in April.) The party consisted of nearly twenty people. They had brought with them two large rugs, and before sitting down on the edges of these they had all removed their shoes, a compulsive Japanese habit when the feet are to be placed on *tatami*, highly polished wood floors or any other clean surface. (A Japanese will *never* go to bed with his socks on, however cold it is.) In the centre of the rugs a vinyl tablecloth had been spread, and on it were bottles of beer, domestic whisky and also, of course, the tall, noble green bottles of rice wine with their boldly charactered labels. The members of the party were eating *sushi* and cold *tempura* (which is delicious at a picnic). They were enjoying themselves, but were perfectly well-behaved and indeed impressive in their neatness and fastidiousness. The Japanese call this kind of picnic under the cherry blossoms *hana yori dango*, a quaint expression meaning literally 'better to eat dumplings than to view cherry blossoms'. I cite this instance of an attractive cherry-viewing party, one of the many I noticed during the four cherry seasons I have known in Japan, lest it be thought that all cherry viewers are rowdy louts and unprincipled litterbugs. The Japanese one sees behaving in this refined, formal but perfectly natural way make one love Japan.

A more religious type of flower festival, called *hana matsuri*, is held on Buddha's birthday, 8th April, which is just when cherry blossom is at its peak of full-blown loveliness. Every Buddhist temple observes the *Kambutsu-e* ceremony, when a small statue of Buddha, enshrined in a miniature temporary flower-decorated altar called *Hana-mido* (flowery altar), has sweet tea poured over it by believers using tiny ladles, from which they then sip the tea. This ceremony is particularly fine at the Asakusa Kannon Temple (Sensoji); but I prefer attending that at Gokokuji, a great temple near my house in Mejiro. Here there is also a gorgeous procession of local residents in resplendent historical costumes. The occasion is a most joyous one, and a demonstration of community effort producing something artistic, dignified and very charming in the celebration of a religious festival. The cherry blossom at Gokokuji Temple is ravishingly pretty.

I prefer plum-blossom viewing to cherry-blossom viewing, and maple-leaf and chrysanthemum and full-moon-in-September viewing better than either. It was spring, and so I went to Mito early in the season to renew my acquaintance with the lovely apricot gardens and their delicate white flowerings of 'Japanese plum', or *ume*. The best time to view these is in early March, but I heard that the first blossoms had appeared in the last week of February, so I went to see them then.

My emotions were very mixed as once again, after nearly two years, I took a very early train northwards from Ueno. It was going on to Taira and Sendai; it was a trip I had made so many times before, during my two years in the north of Honshu. It was lovely to ride again on this north coastline with its rivers and bridges and timber-yards: that curious virulent green weedlike stuff is still spread on the river bank a few miles north of Tokyo, on the right-hand side. I often wondered what it was, but no one could ever tell me. There were lots of *futon* (mattresses) hanging outside in the cold sun of that Sunday morning: some of them bright scarlet, others patchworked or chequered like Malay male sarong material. Some had borders of black velvet, others were hemmed with an unusual croceate colour. In the train was the really exquisite Japan Travel Bureau poster advertising the plum blossom in Mito's Kairakuen Garden: a formal, almost espaliered, black plum tree with dusky white blossoms sparkling on a gold-leaf background. Red lettering completed the colours of the Holy Roman Empire.

Pale, shining skeletons of new buildings, wood-frame houses with clumps of tiles set like the squares of a chequer-board on the airy roof, ready for the tilers. On river banks old winter grass was being burned, while already there were many men and boys hopefully fishing in the rocky rivers. There was even a golf-course laid out on a dried-up river bed. (In the fabled past, Noh plays used to be performed where now the golf-course lies.) Farther on there were netted driving-ranges for golfers wishing to practise the accuracy of their swing: black-and-white ringed targets stood out with primitive boldness against the wind-woven netting. The golf-course was very busy, and every target on the driving-range had its dedicated, golf-mad Japanese business man in Bermuda culottes feverishly swiping at ball after ball. The caddies on the golf-courses in Japan are always girls; they carry the Japanese golfer's highly expensive and complicated equipment in smart, gadgetty crimson or yellow leather golf-bags. The earnestness with which the Japanese have taken up this 'goroff', as they call it, is as appalling as their passion for bowling and pro-wrestling; there is something hideous in this very American determination to be one up on everybody else.

In the dining-car the smell of rice wine and beer; the fragrance of Japanese cigarettes, one brand of which has the revoltingly analphabet name 'Hilite', a typically Western corruption of language, is as individual and nostalgic as French Gauloises or Spanish Bisontes. Many Japanese smokers hold filter-tip cigarettes—Hilite or Hope—clenched between their teeth, with parted lips, and this gives them a singularly fearsome aspect.

Little back-garden-sized horseshoes of ribbed paddy-fields, looking brown and withered (for this is an unusually dry spring, with just the trace of a glint of rare water here and there) in small valleys near the railway. These small terraced dales look carefully and deeply cultivated; they look like ancient cultural treasures, so finely worked are neat embankments and irrigation ditches, ghosted with dead, pale grasses and wintry bamboo, with white egrets looking forlorn in their fruitless search for fish.

Mito is only about an hour's ride by express from Tokyo. It was once a great feudal stronghold of the Mito branch of the House of Tokugawa, and is now the administrative centre of Ibaragi Prefecture. The road from the station lies along the bed of the old moat of the castle buildings, which were nearly all destroyed during the Meiji Restoration and during American air raids in 1945. But one can still enjoy a fine view of the surrounding countryside by entering the castle grounds through the Ninomaru or intermediate enclosure. Some distance away, in the third enclosure or Sannomaru, is Mito Park, otherwise known as Kôdôkan-kôen, which contains a very beautiful building, the Kobuntei, meaning literally 'pleasure-culture house'. The Kobuntei was so called because of the many kinds of cultural entertainments that were once held there, including the making of ink-pictures, the writing of Chinese and Japanese poems and the composition of fine works of calligraphy.

This great artistic treasure house was completely destroyed during the war by American bombs. It was rebuilt between 1955 and 1958 in all its original detail, a patient labour of love and restoration which has resulted in one of the finest reproductions of an old-style Japanese manor house in existence. (The original house was built in 1842 by Nariaki Tokugawa, ninth Lord of Mito, who used to hold meetings there with men of letters for the composition of poems and other works of literature.) The dwelling, classic but modern, has two parts, the Kobuntei and O-rugoten or 'Rear Place', and they are connected by a corridor. The O-rugoten has ten fine rooms, including the exquisite Matsu no Ma or Pine Tree Room, which was the private apartment of the lord's wife when she visited there with her *gotenjochu* or court ladies. Other rooms, decorated with agreeably attributive names, are Momiji no Ma or Maple Room, Hagi no Ma or Bush Clover Room, Sakura no Ma or Cherry Blossom Room, Tsutsuji no Ma or Azalea Room, Momo no Ma or Peach Blossom Room and Kiku no Ma or Chrysanthemum Room. These were originally all ante-rooms for the *gotenjochu*.

From 1869 to 1874 the O-rugoten became the temporary residence of the late Yoshiko, widow of Nariaki. In those days the Ume no Ma or Plum Blossom Room was her servants' quarters. Two wooden-floored rooms on the ground floor of the Kobuntei were where the famous literary meetings were held.

The third floor of the Kobuntei was designed by Prince Nariaki himself for his pleasure parties. This progressive prince installed a lift to bring up food and drink from the ground floor-kitchen. There is now a very steep, narrow, high-rising, slippery wooden staircase in the house; two dense queues of people were ascending and descending it, and this seemed highly dangerous to me—if someone had slipped and fallen all the visitors on that treacherous stairway would have been knocked flying. I should have liked to see the house under less crowded conditions—it would be wonderful to hold a literary meeting there under the full moon of September—but it was worth the struggle and the apprehension to see those perfect rooms and the view of the white plum blossom from their sliding windows.

At Mito I spent a long time walking under the blossom. Here and there lay still a stretch of old snow, but these relics of winter were slowly melting in the fairly warm sun of noon that was bringing out the blossom with almost audible pops. (Japanese mystics or Zen Buddhists in contemplation say they can hear the opening of a cherry-blossom bud!) The plum was just beginning to flower, and this is perhaps the most exquisite moment of its exquisitely brief life. The unopened buds are pinky brown; the few opened flowers are an ethereal white on the dark, twisty boughs against a blue sky full of moving, pale grey snow-clouds. Plum blossom makes an unforgettable impression of delicacy and rarity when it first comes out.

There were many stalls and sideshows in the park. Some stalls were selling celluloid masks and *kokeshi*, others pink and white candy-floss ready-wrapped in polythene bags that were blowing and bouncing like balloons in the wind. Some wonderful fruit, vegetable and fish stalls, others with trays of local sweets and marine delicacies from Isohama, Oarai, Minato, Isosaki and Otsuko. (These are all pleasant seaside resorts; at the latter Rabindranath Tagore resided for a short time during his visit to Japan in 1924.) One such stall is selling small fresh crabs that are very sweet-savoured. A helicopter and a tiny plane keep taking off from a field near a lake or lagoon, where boating is popular; I joined the queue and after half an hour was able to take a five-minute flip round the plum garden; there were grand views of the city and of the Pacific. It was nice to be up there away from all the crowds and the miles upon miles of cars.

I watched on an improvised stage in the park a display of graceful dances by girls in kimono, grand, gold-embroidered *obi* (belt) and black-lacquered *katsura*, or wig. They carried sprays of artificial blossom and big, heavy fans. There was also a large crowd watching a tea ceremony being performed out of doors, on a big sheet of crimson cloth, by the young lady pupils of a rather formidable-looking old dame in dark kimono who watched their every movement out of the corner of her hawklike eye; she was a real tyrant. Woe betide the poor girls if they made a mistake in the presentation and serving of the tea to the three soberly clad old women sitting at a table covered with red cloth! They would never hear the last of it! Though the young girls' hands were red with cold and, I thought, trembled slightly, their movements were subdued and correct, and they whisked up the green tea powder with their bamboo whisks most elegantly, displaying an indescribable charm in their kneeling, with bent napes, before the iron kettle, the bamboo ladle and the other simple but beautifully made implements of this highly sophisticated ceremonial. Behind the grand old dame with the fearsome demeanour of an ancient court lady was a small tent of red-and-white striped material in which the other pupils watched their fellow students' performances with bated breath, and awaited their turn to display their gifts to an admiring public. The people watching were of every possible kind: workmen, teachers, housewives, soldiers, schoolboys, students, babies, little girls, young motor-cyclists in leather jackets and their gum-chewing girls. But all watched the ceremony most carefully and appreciatively as a work of art. This instinctive appreciation of the native arts is something one finds in every Japanese. It is an extraordinary quality, one which sets the Japanese far above any other race I know.

There was a group of mutilated soldiers, casualties of World War II, dressed in white, kneeling in the sharp gravel on their bare stumps; one was singing a sad, wild song, another was holding a collecting bowl; yet another held a written notice in artificial hands of steel covered with white woollen gloves. How can I give them anything? But I am not, and never was, their enemy, so I donate a coin. The collector, head already bowed, bows. I am glad to see that his bowl contains a few hundred yen already. Some Japanese refuse to give alms to these unfortunates, claiming, quite correctly, that the Government should give them adequate compensation. In fact the Government does almost nothing for them, and if the maimed are Koreans they get no assistance at all. If one waited for governments to take pity on those it has mercilessly used for violent ends, and then cast aside when they are of no further utility, one would wait for ever. Why do people not remember these things when the papers tell them they must fight yet another useless war 'for freedom'?

The picnic parties under the trees were orderly and happy; there was a feeling of great good nature and sunny relaxation.

As I stood gazing up at a sprig of pure white blossom (faintly tinged with green) a young tout sidled up to me, chewing gum. He must have thought I was looking for girls, because he told me to take a turning on the right, then left, and I would come to a 'house very nice'. I offered him a Hilite, but he preferred his own American brand. We chatted about business, which he said was very poor. 'Too many schoolboys,' he said, grimacing. 'Not money.' I declined his invitations. As I bowed and walked away he called after me: 'See you tonight, Joe.'

A sudden chill; the sky was packed with massive black clouds. Suddenly large lumps of snow began pelting down from the apocalyptic heavens. I jumped on a bus that jounced me back into town, where I looked for a snack bar and eventually found a dark coffee bar called 'American Snack'. The afternoon had turned very cold and gloomy, and there were ceaseless squalls of snow and sleet. I was soaking wet when I sat down at a table in the snack bar. The waitresses tittered shyly, obviously afraid to come and take my order because I might say something to them in English. A boy from behind the bar shouted to me: 'What you want?' I was served a gruesome 'Hambarg Stick'.

The city of Mito was crowded with blossom viewers. It is a very dull, plain town, like any other in Japan. If the weather had been finer I would have taken a bus to Nishiyama, where there stands, in a grove of Japanese cedars, the thatched cottage to which Lord Mitsukuni retired, or to Zuiryu Hill, where the Chinese-style cemetery contains the tombs of the Lord of Mito, buried there with Confucianist rites. The designer of the Korakuen Garden in Tokyo, Shu Shun Sui, is also buried there.

Another place in the neighbourhood worth visiting, especially in autumn when the autumn tints are very remarkable, is the mineral hot spring at Fukuroda, about thirty miles from Mito by the Suigun line. Here the Fukuroda Waterfall, two hundred and fifty feet wide, falls in a series of four terraces from a height of about five hundred feet, a most impressive sight, especially seen through maple foliage in autumn.

Before going to the station to catch a train back to Tokyo I visited a shrine on a hill overlooking the small gay quarter. It was deserted in the drenching sleet that kept flopping down from the lowering sky. Later, as I stood on platform 6 (at position 8, where the restaurant car would draw up), the extraordinary weather suddenly changed again, and there emerged from the black clouds a low sun of that peculiarly intense orange seen in Hokusai's prints. A train on another line was standing at another platform, letting off billowing clouds of dark grey, thick and viscous-looking smoke. This was tinged by the orange of the setting sun, which transformed the ugly little wooden foot-bridge across the tracks into a floating, celestial palace of dove grey and rose. Softly the orange sun sent its radiance right along the needle-like rails. In the distance two bright red signals looked hard and shrill by contrast with the sun's muted effulgence. On the entrance platform there was a real plum tree growing, venerable and dark, and grotesquely calm, with two small blossoms—white stars touched with orange light like pollen. On all the platforms there were pink decorations showing formal plum blossom. Youths waiting for my express to Ueno were wearing quilted jackets of black, blue or scarlet nylon: the colours added liveliness to the scene.

As the train drew out of the station lime green vapour-lamps gleamed against a sunset pink and grey as a flamingo, the whole composition mirrored in flood water. Spring had arrived that very moment, in magical Mito.

3
SPRING DANCES

An elderly man, in spectacles and sober suiting, was crouching today on the cement steps of a strip show in Shinjuku, taking his own personal pictures of the enlarged nude pin-ups—'Springtime Specials'—displayed on the stairs. This was the first time I ever saw such a thing being done, but it's a novel idea, and saves entrance fee (rather high in this case) for viewing bodies which are usually much more delectable in the photograph than in the flesh.

One of the great features of spring time in Japan is the number of spring dance shows put on by nude and review theatres, and by geisha. In Tokyo the geisha take over the Shimbashi Embujo Theatre for a month or so and display their talents in a show called 'Azuma Odori'. As I had been much captivated by the displays put on in the Gion district of Kyoto by geisha in former years—the 'Miyako Odori' there is the counterpart of Shimbashi's 'Azuma Odori'—I felt I ought to see performances by the Tokyo geisha.

The theatre entrance was a perfect bower of plastic cherry blossom. Most of the seats for these performances are bought up by business men with geisha mistresses—a hobby rather like keeping some expensive pet—or by companies that patronize certain geisha houses when entertaining influential clients, so it is said to be sometimes difficult to get a seat. I managed to get one quite easily, and indeed the house was only half full. I sensed that the geisha admirers had become somewhat bored by their protégées. Outside the stage door of the theatre was a row of old-fashioned *jinrickshas*, high-wheeled, with narrow, closed hoods and long, thin wooden shafts. They are usually pulled by oldish, but still lissom, dark-costumed men wearing white *jikatabi*. There are few young rickshaw men still plying their trade in the celebrated geisha quarters of Tokyo. As I stood outside the stage door a geisha, her stage make-up glistening a deathly white, emerged from the stage door and was helped into one of the *jinrickshas*. The rickshaw boy pulled down the shafts and set off at a steady trot while the tall, black, spindly wheels twinkled behind his white heels and thin black legs in their tight trousers. Once the geisha had entered her little canvas cabin it was impossible to see anything of her but a glimpse of dangling hair ornaments through a slit in the side.

The performance was not very interesting. At times it was sweetly pretty, but a bad, sluggish production caused a perfect miasma of boredom to settle on the audience; the geisha were all expert dancers and musicians, but somehow an air of stale amateurishness hung over their performances, which were tired and dull. The tedium was such that I fell asleep during the second item, *Shikikashenko*, dances portraying the four seasons of the year. *Kotoko*, 'A Fantasy', choreographed to songs based on Isamu Yoshii's languidly sentimental poems about geisha, danced by three of the most famous geisha in Tokyo, all of them good dancers and renowned for their various skills, gave off the stuffiest atmosphere of all. The three geisha, Marichiyo, Kokuni and Somefuku, strutted and postured with their fans to absolutely no effect at all. But the greatest disappointment of all was the third item, *Kotobukyoku*, with a scenario by Japan's leading novelist, Yasunari Kawabata.[1] This was a sort of dismal historical pageant, simply submerged in 'business' and dialogue, about ancient Kyoto. Part of the trouble is that geisha, though they may be interesting dancers, simply cannot act. There was none of the glittering spectacle of the Miyako Odori with geisha shamisen players and singers ranged right down each side of the auditorium. At the Azuma Odori only small groups of dark-dressed players and singers appeared at the sides of the stage, in structures like little hen-coops.

In the interval, trying to make up my mind whether to stay and see the rest of this deplorably weak show, I saw two lady shamisen players carrying their guitar-like instruments through the foyer. The bent necks of the instruments looked from a distance like the elbowed attachment for a vacuum cleaner, and for a moment I thought the women in their plain, dark-toned costumes were theatre cleaners.

Yawning through the sumptuous programme, I noticed that one of the geisha had a very pretty and unusual name: Maritama. One was called Tonko, another Yoko and yet another Mikiko. One, inevitably, was named Sakurako. Enchanting names. I decided to stay, after all,

[1] This leading Japanese novelist, winner of the Nobel Prize, is also the translator of *Little Lord Fauntleroy*, which, like most Japanese translations of European works, is severely truncated.

and was rewarded by a charming little play in three scenes written by Ryuichiro Yagi, *Mukashi Mukashi Nyobo Banashi*, or 'Once upon a time there were three housewives'. The second scene, *Kagami Nyobo*, or 'Mrs Mirror', had the following explanatory note couched in typical Janglish:

> This is a story of an age when the mirror did not known in the world. One day, a fisherman hooks a small beautiful box that contains a mirror. When he looks into the mirror, he sees his father's face. (He is an image his late father.) However, his wife is jealous of a woman (actually herself) whom she sees in the mirror and curses. Then a senior fisherman arrives and explains the mirror to them. Now, the wife understands and tries to keep herself beautiful and is no longer jealous.

It was prettily done, though geisha as fisherman have to be seen to be believed. The Grand Finale, *Azuma Sugata Haru No Nigiwa!*, showed us all the geisha girls dancing together in the main hall of a big geisha house in the Shimbashi district, and wishing everyone a happy spring season. The programme contained a passport-sized photograph of every geisha in the performance. Only one, with a witty face and a sweet smile, was really my type. Her name: Umeyakko. The rest seemed to me to have conventional and characterless expressions, though each one was in fact different.

I missed the glamour of the Kyoto performance at the Gion Kaburenjo Theatre. Tokyo and Kyoto geisha are great rivals, but this year I felt that the Shimbashi geisha were not at their best. It costs a small fortune to put on these shows: this year the cost was estimated at about fifty thousand pounds, but there are many rich and influential sponsors in business and in the Cabinet who help to defray costs. Another less formal version of the Miyako Odori is the Kamogawa Odori of Pontocho, which takes place at the same time in Kyoto at the Pontocho Kaburenjo. Both are performed by geisha and *maiko*, or apprentice geisha. The geisha of Akasaka have their Akasaka Odori at the Kabukiza in Tokyo; and those of Yoshicho have their Yoshicho Odori at the Meijiza, Hamacho, Tokyo.

Another pleasant entertainment in Kyoto during spring time are the farces in masked pantomine, the players wearing ancient kimono, performed on a stage of the Mibudera Temple. This type of play is called Mibu Kyogen and dates back to the thirteenth century. It has strong affinities with the Kyogen farces of the Noh Theatre. In some cases, the costumes worn by the actors date from the Genroku era in the seventeenth century. There are also some very old masks preserved at the temple, but these are not used in performance, as they are too frail and precious. The farces are performed from 21st April for ten days, and are well worth seeing: the humour is broad and perfectly easy to follow, since the actors are accomplished dancers and mimes. Before the performance one should pay homage of some kind to the chief image of the temple, a statue of Jizô-Bosatsu attributed to Jôchôy, a renowned eleventh-century sculptor. It is listed as an Important Cultural Property.

One day, in honour of the spring, I wore a suit of plain mole-grey velvet, snug-fitting, and with it a *sakura*-pink shirt with a white silk tie. Also my rose-tinted monocle with the plain gold rim. My feet were shod in shoes the colour of cherrywood bark. Just for that one day I felt I was the spirit of *sakura*. . . .

I had lost my way in Sendagaya, and asked a small boy where I was. Petrified by my blond hair and blue eyes, the little boy replied, in Japanese: 'You are in Japan.' He must have thought I was a visitor from outer space. He had a five-sided face, flat-topped, close-cropped head, hair like fine plush pile, pointed chin, tiny ears on the pentagon's vertical sides. He looked like a peony.

I was fortunate to catch, on a public television set, a telecast of some spring dances which I had seen in northern Japan two years before. There were seven spring songs and dances native to Miyagi-ken, and they were transmitted from the lovely Funaoka Park in the pretty town of Shibata. The River Kajikawa here has one of the most beautiful avenues of cherry trees in Japan, stretching for over ten miles along its banks, and I well remembered, with patient nostalgia, the songs and dances I had enjoyed in the pink shade of the lantern-lit blossoms: *Yamako Uta*, *Ochaya-bushi*, *Ta Ue Odori*, *Tanarashi Uta*, *Honen Koi Koi Bushi*, *Sansa Shigure* and the quite remarkable and unique Deer Dance called *Shika no ko Mai*. In this, a team of nine masked men, each disguised as a deer, dances with wild leaps to the music of flutes and drums in a kind of fertility ritual. How I longed to go back there again and climb up to the shrines on Mount Niôji! I still have a piece of fine carved Murakami lacquer which I bought on a trip to this district.

Japanese men exercise their neck muscles by jerking their heads from side to side and backwards and forwards, with sometimes ominous clicking sounds.

A Japanese woman's broad feet, in white *tabi*, spread out like great puddings over frail little silver-decorated pink plastic *geta*. Someone has stood on her big toes, each of which bears the mark of a man's rubber heel.

An amusing notice outside a building in Sendagaya made me smile for a few moments: 'Tokyo High Speed Knitting and Cooking School'. It reminded me of Hokusai's 'Cooking at a Moment's Notice'.

At Kurugama, a small police box crammed with people asking where houses are in the locality. Submerged at his little table, a bewildered policeman. It is indeed terribly difficult to find addresses in a Japanese city. The streets are so confusingly named, the houses so illogically numbered. Sometimes several houses in one street will have the same number. The best people to ask for directions when one is looking for a certain house are postmen, wineshop keepers, newspaper boys or dustmen.

Japanese directness in English expressions: an advertisement saying 'Less Money Sale' on Hankyu department store windows in Sukiyabashi. I am delighted by a pen called 'King Jim' and a notebook called 'King Jim Memo'. I also noticed at Kuguhara station 'Ledis Wear', 'Shoes Shop' and 'Lovely Sack'. When I got on the train to Kamata I was surrounded by a crowd of young people carrying drawing books, sketch pads and instruction books entitled 'How to Drawing'.

So many Japanese on the train look perfectly neat and composed and almost inhumanly clean, as if none of them had ever had a bad thought or done a wrong thing. Sometimes an air of tranquil, bland self-satisfaction makes them look unutterably smug. But often I believe this self-satisfaction is the result of right living and thinking, and is justified. When they look so perfect, so balanced, so calm, correct and respectable, I feel untidy, lost, lonely, degenerate and unclean. And also very large. Many foreigners feel like this. The best solution, I have found, is always to wear good and spotlessly clean shoes. This is very difficult in Japan. After a day spent trudging round Mito's dusty, stony, pot-holed and then suddenly muddy roads, my shoes were filthy. But all the Japanese on the train from Mito looked neat and spotless. It was not until I got my shoes cleaned up by a shoe-shine woman at Ueno that I began to feel equal to the Japanese.

On the other hand some boys, particularly students, look as if they had not washed for weeks, and their shoes and clothes are often a disgrace of dirt and untidiness that cannot have poverty as an excuse. Occasionally one meets men and women who are terribly coarse in appearance and loud-mouthed in conversation; though this should make me feel better it does not. Often the coarsest-looking Japanese have beautiful souls.

I was taken to see the Spring Dance at the Kokusai Theatre in Asakusa, a huge popular all-girl revue theatre with long lines of pseudo-Tiller girls all kicking their legs up at the same time. It was quite devastatingly pretty but massively dull. All the male parts were taken by skilful male impersonators who had all the mannerisms of old stars like Fred Astaire, Jack Buchanan and Carl Brisson. Their affected male walk was very amusing. It is purely popular entertainment and is visited by thousands of country people every day. I did not like the long-bodied, short-thighed, bulgy-calved Japanese chorus line. From the sixth row, we could see all their pimples, chilblains, crater-like vaccination marks, armpits blue with depilatory creams, and big-boned, bruised ankles. Enormously brash production numbers, vulgar without being coarse.

But some of the English programme notes were amusing: Scene 2, *Shibaraku*—'During the Tokugawa Shogun Era, the common people were severely suppressed. Shibaraku was a Robin Hood-type hero who fought against the Tokugawa lords. This story was adapted from the famous play *Shibaraku*, which is among the top eighteen Kabuki plays. We present this story in the traditional Kabuki style, except the hero, Shibaraku, is portrayed as a woman'.

Scene 3, *Atomic Girls*—'Costumed in red, our line-dance beauties undulate their shapely legs to a quick-stepping swing beat'.

Scene 4, *Alluring Flowers*—'This is a modern dance which represents the enchanting and mysterious passion of the tropical insect-eating flower, refflesia'.

In Scenes 6 and 7, *The Legend of Sen Hime*—a wonderfully contrived fire scene, 'the most spectacular fire scene ever produced on any stage', had me almost rolling in the aisle at its crudity: hinged walls and segments of roof kept flapping down, choking smoke came pouring out, nearly asphyxiating the audience, and revolving slides projected very repetitive flames on the backdrop and the quaking wings, while all the characters ran about as if hell itself had been let loose. This was quite the funniest thing in the show, while the unfunniest were the Three Canaries singing trio and the Comic Kewpies giving their version of *Carmen*.

All the music and singing were pre-recorded, and the girls just mouthed through their parts. It was all very unreal and ordinary, and perhaps that was the reason why the packed house never once applauded. The stage show alternates with a Japanese film show, usually a *chanbara* sword-fighting film, which is often much more worth seeing than the revue.

A slicker and more sophisticated, occasionally witty Spring Dance, with near-nudes, was put on at the Nichigeki Theatre in Sukiyabashi. This is also decorated every spring with plastic pink cherry blossoms round the entrance, where the touts from as early as 8 a.m. ask politely if you would care for a 'private show, girls, boys or all together'.

This passage from Saikaku Ihara's *Tale of Seijuro from Himeji* (in the translation by Ivan Morris) illustrates well the feeling one gets at a Japanese strip show or the Nichigeki or Kokusai Revue theatres, and which perhaps explains the silence and unenthusiastic gaping of the male audience:

> Next, Seijuro's face turning to that 'Isle of Nakedness' which he had seen on maps of the world, he bade all the courtesans in the room disrobe. Among them was a courtesan named Yoshizaki, who for many years had contrived to conceal the white macula that she bore on her hip. Now this blemish was exposed to the whole company. . . . Thereupon the men's enthusiasm cooled, for as they looked about at the assembled women, they saw that there was not one but suffered from some imperfection. Gradually, a chill fell over the company and their revels seemed to lose their savour.

Everywhere this spring there is dust, confusion and head-splitting banging and hammering. Huge yellow girder-lifting, pile-driving and earth-moving machines block the roads and pavements of Yurakucho, Akasaka and Shibuya. At Sendagaya immense upheavals are taking place round the station, where new roads and underpasses and overpasses are being constructed to take Olympics visitors and traffic to and from the stadiums that are going up like gigantic cement gasometers in Meiji Shrine Outer Garden. Pylons, flyovers, tunnels, cables, drains. One has to watch carefully where one is going or one finds oneself sprawling on a pile of gravel in the middle of the pavement or dropping into a large, unprotected hole as one steps into the road. Planks or girders are falling from new heights of bamboo scaffolding everywhere, and there are frequent showers of sand, cement, gravel and mud as a chute or a bucket or a mixer overturns. It is all carried out by jolly lemon-yellow- and lime-green-helmeted workers who stagger along in pairs, laughing uproariously, carrying pipes and girders, their *jikatabi*'s blue cloth daubed with yellow clay.

Spring time and autumn are also the times for token strikes. I watched a very orderly procession of strikers rather listlessly carrying home-made banners in Aoyama one night. Police were directing the sections of this very long but very perfunctory demonstration calmly and efficiently and respectfully, blowing polite blasts on whistles and obsequiously waving yellow plastic lanterns. It was all just a formality that had to be gone through. There was no passion. It was just another weary gesture for more pay. The strikers were not even singing or chanting. They had hired a few loudspeaker vans which were playing records of martial music. No one bothered to keep in step with it. It was a sorry sight. It is degrading that workers should have to go through this ridiculous display twice a year in order to force minimal improvements in working conditions and small rises in pay from their employers. The Japanese trade union movement, *Sohyo*, is split by internal quarrels and seems inefficient and weak in its handling of industrial disputes. The average Japanese worker has no 'future' at all, and therefore no hope. No wonder his strikes are lethargic token gestures. More impressive and determined are the miners, who frequently come *en masse* to Tokyo and hold up the traffic round Hibiya Park. Their faces are grim, their heads swathed with the white towels that denote effort and sincerity. But sometimes they sing and dance along through the indifferent streets. Their strikes, protests and demonstrations are noble. Many of them at this season wear a sprig of flowering cherry stuck into the towels tied round their brows. Why must it be like this? The miners perhaps more than any other workers deserve a good wage and every additional benefit that progressive employers could give them. They need all their courage and their strength for their work; why should they have to squander them in this way? Why can't men treat fellow human beings decently, like human beings? There are constant mine disasters. In Hokkaido mines are being closed down. The case of the miners in Japan is an endless tragedy. The sight of their processions in Tokyo tore my heart with shame for the human race.

Hair bandeau called 'Show Off Band'. A device for wetting gummed labels is called 'Jewel Moistener'.

The fruit seller at a stall in Shimbashi where I buy exceptionally good fresh fruit lets me appreciate the soundness and juiciness of the Aomori apple I select for my supper by giving it a sharp flick with his forefinger, making it give an almost drumlike note. I also buy from him a packet of five big, luscious, dried persimmons, all strung on a length of clean twine. They are deliciously soft, fragrant, chill, bloomed with their own richness, the shining deep brown seeds, like abacus counters, dark with their own essences distilled by the sun. The neck of the plastic bag that holds them is fastened by a piece of plastic raffia in what this evening seems to be a peculiarly deep, vibrant, poignant green. An inch-square coloured picture of the fruit's amber globes on an autumn tree reminds me of the persimmons that used to hang over my fence at Sendai. I think of the mellow ripeness of the last few fruit hanging like dim lanterns in bare trees on Christmas day, on a road near the Hirose River where I walked alone, kicking icy pebbles. I remember the fruit being tenderly picked in a fisherman's cottage garden near Shiogama, and in Hokkaido being hung in hanks to dry, with the corn-cobs, under the steep straw- and reed-thatched eaves of Otaru's farmhouses. A fruit rich in memories for me. Even the seeds feel light now, as if their souls had flowed into the flesh they made and that made them. Each dried fruit has a bit of its own stalk and branch, agreeably authentic. A delicate, dusty, dusky, subtle, faded flavour they have, one that is like nothing else, and cannot be imagined. But when one tastes it again, one wonders how one had ever forgotten what it was like. In early spring, dried persimmons are dreams of past summers, dead autumns. A fruit of noble weight and sadness. It is said to be excellent for curing hangovers.

Spring time often brings unusually dry weather to Japan. The Meteorological Agency states that humidity is very low in the capital —as little as 16 per cent. This alarmed Metropolitan Fire Board officials, who said that because of the current dry spell the average wooden pillar in a Japanese house could be lighted with an ordinary match. People were recommended to keep their wooden bathtubs and buckets filled with water in case of emergencies. Nevertheless in one day eighty-two fires broke out in Tokyo alone. These fires spread swiftly among the predominantly wooden buildings of the Tokyo suburbs.

I took a visitor from the country to Tokyo Tower, that monstrosity that tries so unsuccessfully to outdo the Eiffel Tower. The sprawling, ungainly girders at its base make it look like a cherry-blossom drunkard on straddled legs. The ascent by lift, however, is thrilling. One is allowed to go up only to the central observation platform, where there are souvenir shops, cafés and telescopes that can only be used if one puts ten yen into a slot. They are big, heavy, double-barrelled telescopes which are almost too unwieldy to move: it is difficult to hold them still and to focus on the place one wants to observe. There is a splendid view of Tokyo Bay, with the vessels all pointing the same way, parallel to the shore. And all around us is the wonder of modern Tokyo, the packed streets, the endless traffic, the seething parks, shrines and temples. Far away, as if projected against the blue sky by some gigantic magic lantern, the snowy top half of Mount Fuji's ethereal trapezium is suspended on air.

Tokyo Tower, once the highest structure in Japan, is now dwarfed by a rival tourist attraction which is also an office block—Kasumigaseki building at Toranomon. It is 490 feet tall and has an observation lounge on the top floor. From this vantage point, on a clear day, it is quite easy to see the tip of the Izu Peninsula. It is the first skyscraper ever built in Japan, and is said to be proof against earthquakes and typhoons with gusts of over thirty miles an hour. Beside this oblong, vertical box—it cannot be said to have any architectural distinction—Tokyo Tower looks very trivial and insubstantial.

The sun is hot on the tower's orange girders, that vibrate ceaselessly, and from time to time the whole structure seems to lean slightly, or sway with passing earthquakes. In one of the suburbs a big fire has broken out. We train a telescope on it with difficulty. It is a big school. Farther to the west there is another blaze, and to the north smoke pours from a burning factory. Fires in the Plain. These fires are known to Tokyoites by a poetic name. They are called the Flowers of Edo. (Edo was the old name for Tokyo. Tokyo people still refer to themselves as *Edokko* or Children of Edo.) These Flowers of Edo are now the true symbols of a Tokyo spring, and not the *sakura.*

PART THREE

AT HOME IN TOKYO

I

SHINJUKU

February 25: I have been without a watch for nearly a year. Today I bought one at last, very reluctantly, at a shop in Shinjuku. It is a watch that needs no winding, Japanese make, Seikomatic. It is made here in Shinjuku. Diashock twenty jewels, whatever that means. The five hundred yen discount (the shopkeeper called it 'service') was also automatic, as I did not expect it and did not ask for it. I noticed that on the lid of the presentation box Shinjuku is spelt 'Sinjuku', which is a very appropriate name for this palpitating amusement area.

It took me half an hour to cash a fifty-dollar traveller's cheque at the bank. There were three different forms to complete, one of them in duplicate. The girl assistant indulged in what seemed to be a never-ending stamping of the forms with seals and date stamps. (How prettily the Japanese round their mouths to breathe on their *hanko*, or little personal seals, thus moistening the vermilion paste embedded in them before printing them carefully on bills and official forms!) Then she made lengthy inscriptions on the forms in Japanese characters. The forms were then shown to a supervisor, who also appended his seal on each one, after the girl had worked out the very simple sum three times on an adding machine and twice on an abacus, or *soroban*. Then her supervisor did the sum twice on an adding machine and once on an abacus and added another, larger, confirmatory seal. The girl ran to the head cashier who after prolonged scrutiny gave his *imprimatur*, after which she took all the paper-work round to various cashiers, one of whom actually consented to cash the cheque. She came back to me in triumph, bearing the notes and coins on a blue plastic dish; she took ages to tell me the exact amount, in English; but still the end was not in sight. A receipt had to be made out, stamped, sealed and signed, before I was able to get away with my ill-gotten gains. There were Japanese customers dozing on benches; they looked as if they had been there for hours and expected to stay all day.

But the tedious experience was worth it for the sight of the bank manager lording it at a vast desk, occasionally casting an eye over his minions, but otherwise doing nothing except glance at the newspaper, open invitations to geisha parties, perform a lengthy curettage of his nose, wait for lunch time and preserve an unalterable hauteur. Round him milled clerks and girl assistants and workmen trundling sacks of money about on small trolleys. All the time I was there not a soul spoke to him. Such is the lonely eminence of the great.

The best place to change traveller's cheques quickly is at Isetan department store, ground floor, just inside the door on the corner. If you must go to a bank the Nippon Kangyo Bank in Shinjuku, just next to the Hollywood Bowl and the Shochiku Cinema, is the best place: they have very pleasant and efficient and quick personnel, speaking good English, at the foreign exchange counter. Mitsui Bank is always unfailingly efficient and used to handling foreigners.

Service is deteriorating day by day in restaurants, which at this time of the year, though it is quite warm outside, are unendurably overheated. At one restaurant in Shinjuku I ordered a steak. It took twenty-five minutes to arrive. While I was waiting the manager persuaded his extremely incapable organist to start playing a sort of musical diarrhoea of semi-classical airs, all played in the same dead tempo. The steak, when it arrived, came on a huge, sizzling cast-iron platter that did not look very clean. These black iron plates are a fad in certain Tokyo restaurants and I hate them; one burns one's fingers on them, and they splash grease all over one's clothes. A simple china plate is so much nicer. When I asked her for rice, the waitress looked quite incredulous, as if I must be out of my mind, a Westerner eating rice. Many Japanese think that foreigners never eat rice, only bread; they think that rice is eaten only in Japan. The word for bread is *pan*, and a roll is *rollo-pan*: most Japanese restaurants however have trained their staff to ask all customers, whatever their nationality, if they would like *rice ka pan*—rice or bread—and many Japanese in Western-style restaurants choose bread, as being the correct thing to eat with Western food. They sometimes look with great surprise at a foreigner eating rice, especially with chopsticks, as if rice were something only Japanese people could eat, and chopsticks tools no Westerner could possibly master; they do not know that in my childhood I had rice every day and never tired of it. I was practically reared on rice.

In every coffee shop and restaurant, when the waiter or waitress brings a cup of coffee, it is always presented to the customer with the handle and the spoon on the left-hand side of the saucer. Japanese waiters and waitresses serve it as if they were serving themselves, and seem incapable of presenting the cup with the handle and spoon on the right-hand side of the saucer. However, this enables one to turn the cup round slowly, as one does in the tea ceremony.

At the 'Catleya' coffee bar, as in many popular restaurants, one buys tickets for drinks and food from the desk by the door. I went in one day and ordered a cup of coffee and a 'Clab Horse Sand' or Club House Sandwich. The waitress brought the coffee but forgot the sandwich. After waiting half an hour I decided I must leave and presented the ticket desk with a request for my money back. The flustered waitress, overcome by giggling shame, flew to the serving hatch and shouted to the kitchen boy, who immediately began cutting very thick slices of 'toast bread'. '*Chotto mate kudasai*,' or please wait a minute, the waitress pleaded, her face blanched with make-up more than fright, and her beehive hair-do falling in strands, making her look like some demented woman character in Kabuki. But I had no time to wait by then. I got my 130 yen back and smiled and bowed to the waitress as I left. I intended to be pleasant and to make her feel it didn't matter, but I had forgotten the sinister impact of my smile and as soon as I had given it I realized that this and my little bow were the last twists of the knife. She thought I was trying to insult her; but all the same she smiled bravely back and bowed in reply. A much lower bow than mine. Such peculiar and distressing encounters are very frequent in Japan, and are provoked by the smallest things. But the situations, apparently insignificant, hold a wealth of complication which is both fascinating and appalling.

There are three good little restaurants in a big building in Shinjuku not far behind the Red Cross Hospital in Nishiokubo. One is a *sushi* restaurant, owned by novelist Tamura Taijiro, which serves perfect raw fish slices but is expensive: as in all *sushi* shops now, the bill is added up in some mysterious fashion in the boys' heads, and prices vary according to the quality and scarcity or otherwise of certain types of sea food; prawns are nearly always the most expensive item. Next to it is a little rustic-style restaurant that specializes in grilled frogs and sparrows and thrushes and has very good bean-curd soup. The best restaurant of the three is the Maison Paul, which is more or less Western in style. In the basement of this building is a sumptuous night-club called, oddly, Tokyo Country Club. One night the Maison Paul was full of kimono-clad hostesses from the night-club. The girls had all been given free hair-do's and facials at the beauty parlour next door, and the empty cruelty and lacquered hardness of their pale, dissipated faces were even more repugnant to me than usual. It passes my comprehension why intelligent men should pay out thousands of yen for the dubious pleasure of an hour in their company, and spend more thousands on a bottle of beer. These expense-account Japanese are the nation's real degenerates, not the pimps, drunks, assassins, drug-pedlars, gay boys and prostitutes who batten on them.

A 'special' strip show: it was given, in dead silence, by only very old, crippled, wrinkled women, some of whom were so decrepit they could hardly unwind their *obi* and let their kimono drop.

One sees everywhere appalling human wrecks, lying dead beat on pavements, dead drunk in subway entrances, slouched asleep on the Yamate loop line, scavenging rubbish bins, all sunk in the deepest depths of degradation and misery. These are the real beatniks, though there's nothing 'beatific' about them. Most appear to have been ruined by drinking cheap Japanese spirits known as *shochu*, which can be obtained at wine shops and at some of the small shacks selling *o-den*, or stewed titbits.

The stars over the Hanazono shrine's sharp-horned gables seem to be ruffed with frost fur; they are almost immobile, and quiet as mirrors through the neon glow that rises like a great dome over Shinjuku. Amid all the noise and despair and terror of the streets this Inari, or Fox shrine, recently gaudily restored, is a haven of peace, with its little grove of orange *torii* or arches that I have to bend my head to walk under to the little altar. Here I clap my hands twice, loudly, to call the god's attention, cast a small coin into the box, pull the bell-rope and bow my head over folded hands for a minute or two. What good it does I have no idea, for the Shinto religion is beyond my understanding.

An American couple, Quakers, spoke to me in Isetan department store while I was looking for some razor-blades. They were people so extremely nice, so intelligent and interesting, I wished I could meet more Americans like that in the East. It was the Quaker lady who spoke to me first. She said: 'I like your peace badge.' They had left theirs at home. They were the first people in Japan to notice my C.N.D. badge.

I like riding up and down the escalators in the department stores of Shinjuku. There is always a neat and pretty girl bowing and speaking a quiet welcome at the bottom of the rising escalator on each floor. She is usually in a smart but unobtrusive uniform, with white lace nylon gloves, like a bus tour guide. As she bows she gives the Japanese welcome: 'Irrasshaimase.' No one answers, and very few of of the Japanese seem to take any notice of this purely formal greeting, but I always like to bow in return—a procedure that tends to unbalance me on the moving steps—and say: 'Doh itashi mashite', or something like that, which means roughly, 'Don't mention it.' The girls are always surprised when I speak to them. It must be a rather sad and lonely job, standing there all day, wiping the rubber handrail of the escalator with a white cloth and welcoming thousands of people who never answer your greeting.

I like Japanese department stores, their floor upon floor of every conceivable object, but they have one very great fault: it is very difficult for a foreigner to get service in these stores. The assistants laudably do not pester anyone to buy, but so great is their reluctance to insult us with the sordid matters of business and money that they will watch a customer standing with an object in his hands without moving to serve him. Only if he calls out or beckons will an assistant come shyly forward. Of course this is always the standard reaction to foreigners. The majority of assistants are terrified of perhaps being forced to use a few words of English in front of colleagues who will laugh at them for their brave effort to speak elementary phrases. Or perhaps they don't know *any* words.

There are notable exceptions to these rules, for example in the self-service food department of Isetan there was a bright young fellow, Kazuhiro Katase, who would always go to a foreigner's assistance without being asked, and used his nice English in an attempt to help and advise. In Mitsukoshi department store, just across the road, there is a very pleasant young man in the men's wear department who speaks good English and advises one about fittings for clothes. (Nearly all Japanese clothes, though delightfully designed, are too small for most Westerners—the sleeves usually are much too short, even in their 'Large-Large' sizes, and the collars too tight. Isetan, however, stocks some outsize garments, though these are not well designed. A Japanese tailor who stocks excellent ready-made men's wear in Western sizes is Nakaya, 1, 5-chome, Ginza, in the next block to the Matsuzakaya department store and on the same side of the street.)

I believe some Japanese harbour deep resentment against English-speaking foreigners simply because it has cost them so much effort and trouble to learn our language, often with very poor results. The resentment in most people is hidden or subconscious, but I think much frustration and this damned sense of inferiority in the Japanese come from their inability to master the language of the conqueror. The frustration and resentment are often sublimated into giggles on the part of girls and stammered apologies on the part of men. One gets so exasperated hearing them say, as soon as they meet one: 'I'm sorry, I speak bad English.' Or: 'Please excuse my broken English.' Especially when they speak, in fact, quite decently and colloquially.

Some of the Japanese frustration and resentment comes out in those television viewings of all-in wrestling, broadcast every Friday evening over the N.T.V. (Tokyo) network under the sponsorship of the Mitsubishi Electric Comapny. This is the nation's most popular showing, with ratings of 70 per cent and more. During these bloody fights between American and Japanese pro-wrestlers, spectators round the ring throw beer bottles and seat cushions (*zabuton*) when the American defeats the Japanese. When the Japanese wrestler wins they naturally enough go mad with enthusiasm. A recent article in *The Mainichi Daily News* by an outstanding Japanese journalist, Koji Mori, attacked the gratuitous violence of this programme and the irresponsibility of a great company like Mitsubishi Electric in sponsoring it. He also deplores the attitude of the Japanese towards these programmes:

> The many television fans who watch the programme are no better. Keeping their eyes glued to the bloody fight scenes appearing on the tube, they are cheering Japanese wrestlers to defeat 'bad Americans'. Rikidozan, a world pro-wrestling champ, said the show is designed to show the audience that man's physique can stand such a tough and rough battle if sufficiently trained. But to the audience it is undoubtedly a show to disperse their pent-up 'inferiority complex' against the whites.

(Rikidozan was soon afterwards assassinated in an Akasaka night-club by gangster rivals.)

Indeed some Japanese become so heated about these contests that they have heart attacks, and there have been many cases reported in the newspapers of men and women dying of apoplexy while watching some particularly gory bout.

Perhaps this bottled-up frustration and resentment lies behind many of the cases one reads of brutal, outrageous violence inflicted on innocent pedestrians by roaming gangs of youths. In the Shinjuku district one is particularly prone to this kind of attack, or to intimidation and extortion. Quite often, not wishing to get involved in the affair or to have anything to do with the police, passers-by merely stand and look on, or hurry past without doing a thing. In Japan it is in fact inadvisable to attack one's attackers in self-defence or in the defence of others, because then one is liable to a police charge of assault and battery!

One constantly sees people, sometimes drunk, breaking into queues at bus stops and railway stations without being reprimanded by anyone. This is due partly I think to a childish Japanese egotism that makes the offender imagine that no one else's business could be nearly as important as his own; one sees this in shops and post offices when people shove themselves forward to be served, and at once the assistant drops everything to serve the importunate client. Ant-like behaviour.

On this subject of violence in Japanese society there was a fascinating letter in the *Asahi Shimbun*, translated in the 'Japanese Viewpoints' column of the English-language *Asahi Evening News*. The writer is Saburo Satoya, a school manager:

> Passengers on trains and buses pretend not to notice when somebody acts up and makes a nuisance of himself. People here tend to think it best to 'keep clear of the devil'.
>
> Last fall, I restrained a drunkard who was acting wildly in an Osaka streetcar. It was about 9 o'clock at night and the streetcar was about 60 per cent full. The drunk wanted a fight and found a pretext. He shouted that he did not like the way the conductor was handling the passengers.
>
> The drunk hit the conductor, and made his eyes and nose bleed. The drunk then started smashing the streetcar windows, but still no one did anything but gape.
>
> The drunkard approached the motorman's platform and tried to take over the controls. A scuffle ensued.
>
> I had had enough by then. I told the drunk off. He then turned on me. As I had studied judo at school, I threw him down and dislocated a joint in his arm. He could no longer act wildly. Still none of the passengers offered to help me to quell the drunk.
>
> The man promised he would go quietly if I let him go. But when I loosened my hold on his arm, he suddenly hit me in the face. I subdued

him again and turned him over to the police. In the struggle, I broke two upper teeth.

I learned a lesson in that incident. Most people will not even try to help someone brave enough to resist violence. That is why we cannot eradicate violence. We should not act merely as spectators when we encounter trouble. We should have a strong sense of justice and help one another to wipe out violence. Only then will we have an orderly society.

The need to be skilled in the various Japanese arts of self-defence becomes very apparent when one walks about the amusement areas of Shinjuku, Shibuya and Ikebukuro. An interesting and somewhat amusing story was related recently:

A Tokyo cabaret hostess single-handedly overpowered a pickpocket and regained her purse at Ikebukuro station. Miss Tatsuko Otsuki, 26, employed as a hostess at the Shinseiki Cabaret in Ikebukuro, heard the jingle of a bell as she got off a Seibu Line train at the station. Realizing that she had a bell on her purse, she put her hand in her coat pocket and discovered the purse was missing.

She looked behind and saw a man putting his hand in his inside coat pocket, and she heard the jingling again. The young woman pulled open the man's coat and saw the bell. 'That's my purse,' she exclaimed, and pulled it out of the pocket. At the same time she seized the man's right thumb and twisted his arm behind his back. Miss Otsuki pushed the man to the stationmaster's office on the platform and turned him over to station employees. Miss Otsuki said she had studied *aikido* [an art of self-defence].

She indignantly criticized men who were near the scene of the theft and who did not offer to help her in catching the pickpocket.

Recently there have been several reports of bar madams and hostess girls putting sleeping pills or dope in drunken customers' drinks and robbing them while they were asleep:

The bar girls allegedly lured already intoxicated customers into either of the bars [on a main street in Shinjuku]. They themselves took drinks that the customer did not order and charged exorbitant prices. When they found their customers had more money on them they took them to the other bar and plied them with drinks containing sleeping pills. When the customers passed out the girls allegedly robbed them of all their money and threw them out into the street.

But there is much innocent amusement and entertainment to be had in Shinjuku, and foreigners are almost never molested. It is the poor Japanese who suffers at the hands of his compatriots, and occasionally at the hands of foreigners.

There are many small bars which one can visit for the length of a single drink; e.g. opposite Shinjuku station, that 'Western' bar with a cowboy in a stetson at the door expertly twirling a 'six-shooter' on his forefinger. The bar boys let off their guns in welcome when I enter, tripping slightly over the doorman's spurs. There is the Gakuya coffee bar (the name means 'backstage' and it is near the *yosei* or story-teller's hall, an old variety theatre that is a delightful experience, in one of the quieter areas of Shinjuku); at this coffee bar there is always a special display of flower arrangement, or at festivals there will be displays of armour or dolls or Tanabata decorations. There is the Fugetsudo coffee shop in Shinjuku, where one listens to classical music and views very original displays of modern Japanese painting. This is one of the few Bohemian centres in Japan, but perfectly respectable; one often sees writers and painters there, self-consciously scribbling or sketching, as well as the usual crop of phonies, dressed to suit the part, that one always finds in these circles. I personally do not care for the celebrated 'gay bars' of Japan, but there is one worth mentioning which I entered quite by accident when I was exploring the 'quiet quarter' of Shinjuku, behind the Art Film Theatre. It is not one of those places like the Bar Genet in Osaka where the boys dress up as women or put on kimono and lacquered wigs. It is a quiet, sober little bar, the Bar Ibsen, up a rather steep flight of stairs. (Usually I distrust bars where you have to go up or down stairs.) Here Japanese men, and occasionally foreigners, come for a drink and a quiet chat; there is nothing effeminate about it: it is simply a normal bar catering for men who prefer the company of their own sex. Now that Japanese women are invading the bars in such large numbers, they are beginning to drive out men who like to have a quiet place to sit and drink and talk. So many 'normal' men have now begun going to 'gay bars' with their 'normal' friends. The Bar Ibsen is a model of its kind: no hysteria, no rowdyism, no dancing, but a perfect place to have a drink or two some otiose eve before going on somewhere else. Another attractive small gay bar is the Benihana with a charming proprietor (he wears a sailor's earring) and amusingly designed phallic matchboxes. Not far away are two enchanting Lesbian bars always full of tired Japanese business men who can't face the strain of another geisha party or hostess cabaret: Sunnyside (Sannysaid) and What's New Pussycat.

A curious advertisement says: 'New boom in an instant!' What *can* it mean? Perhaps it is not intended to mean anything, but is simply used as a sequence of smart foreign words to give a certain fashionable *cachet* to an otherwise undistinguished shoe shop. Women's bags are now frequently printed with foreign words, all quite meaninglessly arranged. Nowadays in Japan, everything is 'boom'—the 'leisure boom' is a stock phrase which everyone understands only too well—and 'instant'. There is even 'instant sex', I noticed, in the advertisement for a cheap strip show. Girls' dress styles are given names like 'the jump look' (presumably because they are so seductive, they make men jump) and 'the switch look'. The excellent men's fashion magazines are now advertising 'the stun look' for 'Men with Yen'.

Marriage arranged by a go-between in Japan is called 'an interview marriage'. One sometimes sees at a restaurant or in a hotel lounge meetings of the two family parties, and of the demure bridal pair having their first good look at each other, subdued, at first hardly daring to look at one another. Such marriages are nearly always very successful. Another method is for the couple to be given tickets for adjoining seats at a symphony concert: if they don't like the look of one another they don't speak, and leave at the interval, unless they like music or find someone better.

Many modern Japanese terms are like the approximations, often so poetic, that one encounters in modern Mandarin. For example, refrigerator is 'electric icebox', and vacuum flask is 'magic bottle'. Candy-floss is 'electric candy'.

In the main street of Shinjuku there is a small shop with huge bottles in the window containing pickled snakes—one horrible dead-white, corpse-like, one unpleasantly wrinkled. Another, laid open by an expert vivisectionist, displays, against a dark blue glass slide, its pallid structure, its dark, navy blue liver and lights. Snake's liver is supposed to give great sexual power. Also in the shop window are dozens of tiny monkeys' heads, fur and everything, in neat cellophane packets. Another big jar contains snakes that have apparently been roasted, for their flesh displays long, charred cracks. A glaucous mandrake or *ginseng* root inhabits another flask. In a glass case, a collection of live vipers, all huddled together, absolutely motionless in one corner, seemingly inextricably knotted and coiled together.

At the Shinjuku Toruku (Turkish) bath—the cheap end (150 yen)—it is fascinating to watch (very discreetly) Japanese men undressing. At this time of the year (early spring) some of them still wear two sets of underclothes—vests and shorts surprisingly Hawaiian sometimes—and a sort of thick, heavy woollen tracksuit, brown or grey.

Some also wear an extra pair of long white drawers and even a ribbed woollen body-belt, often bright green or scarlet, but usually fawn. It takes them ages to dress and undress, and during these procedures they look touchingly like tired children slowly getting ready for school or for bed.

In the bath itself I have noticed a decline in manners; some men, instead of first washing all over before getting into the pool to soak, just dash a wooden pailful of hot water, scooped from the pool, over their private parts and then get into the water. Some even smoke in the hot pool, a thing unheard of two years ago. (At the smaller public baths, only nineteen yen, the woman in charge soon ticks them off if she sees them doing this.)

In the public bath-houses men and women now never bathe together, except in some country districts and certain tourist resorts in northern Honshu and southern Kyushu. (Mixed bathing is in fact against the law, but this is never enforced.) One sits on a six-inch-high stool with an oblong seat the size of a postcard, and washes oneself all over with the small towel provided, using a small plastic bowl of hot water. One squats in front of two taps, one scalding hot, the other cold; the taps are pressed downwards, not turned. At the cheap public baths, serving limited localities, one takes one's own soap, towel and plastic bowl, and any washing one wants to do; men and women can often be seen strolling towards the local bath-house carrying their plastic bowl, towel and soap; for some reason, men often carry the bowl behind their backs. It is a favourite meeting-place for a gossip. Some of the larger bath-houses, for example those in Asakusa and Kanda, actually put on shows ranging from Kabuki to folk-dances and singing.

Jean Genet, in *Notre Dame des Fleurs*, has two good expressions which are very accurate descriptions of the appearance and movement of Japanese eyes: '*ses yeux minces*' and '*coulisser les yeux*'. The most beautiful Japanese eyes are not those which are widest, but those that are longest, whose outer corners reach right up almost into the temples. Again and again one sees a lovely pair of eyes, like the upper wings of a black and gleaming butterfly, or like dark snowflakes.

I cannot stop looking at Japanese faces. Some foreigners in Japan complain that the Japanese are always staring at them; I really can't agree with that. In any case, I like people to look at me, and I like to look at people. If a Japanese stares at me, I stare right back. Their faces have a number of distinct types, yet they are all different: the lovely and the plain, the young and the old, the noble and the naughty have a gentle strength of feature, a vitality that seems to come from the mouth, usually perfect in repose, vital when smiling, sometimes with the odd glint of gold- or silver-work in the teeth—those often purest white, short, regular teeth that make one think of the wholesomeness of baked rice. I like that firm, bold, well-shaped and relaxed mouth. Yet it is not just the lips that give the face its beauty. Often there is no especially beautiful feature in the face. The loveliness comes from an inner calm, a happiness which masks every face at times with a look of hidden radiance. Sometimes the mask breaks; the joy of a moment's wild vitality, packed with the energies of rice, the flesh of fish, the juice of fruit and wine, bursts out suddenly, overwhelmingly, and transforms the beholder into a sharer of happiness.

I like the often kittenish look of the eyes, the pretty bulge of the epicanthic fold, the mysteriousness of the subtly sloping, sleepy looking lids with their sooty fringes, jutting down straight and black, like thatch, and the well-marked but delicate eyebrows, often shaved into crescent or moth-wing shapes. The hair a shining black helmet of lacquer, or fringed, or like a dry, thick, stiff brush. The fairy ears. The oval of the jaw and the often shallow but broad, well-proportioned brow; the short distance between upper eyelashes and brows, faun-like. The nose, delectably small and tilted, but sometimes with a bold, aristocratic line. This type of nose, called a 'high nose', is much admired, and much sought-after at cosmetic surgeries. The smile of the Japanese is without strain because it comes from the heart, because the eyes smile and dance too, because the smile is for the pleasure of smiling, not to show off perfect teeth or impress anyone. The fullness and generosity and whiteness of the smile, so frank and open, are in odd contrast with the veiled presence of laughter in the barely sparkling eyes, which always give, yet hold something back.

The faces of Japanese men can be grouped as follows: most common is the worried look. Then comes, in young men, the cheeky monkey look, the sulky look or the childlike look, with full, parted lips seeming fresh from the mother's breast. Then there is the excited, flushed look, a-glitter with glasses, the look of students eager to practise their English on foreigners. There is the composed look, denoting great inner strength, which one often sees in the faces of little boys. There is the intellectual look of many Japanese business men, and often, alas, the dead look of some cabinet ministers. Worst of all is the stupid look, the look of a business man on the crowded Nagoya–Kyoto train who placed a bag on the seat beside him so that I would think it occupied. Later, he gave up the seat to a Japanese. I don't think his action, however stupid, was meant unkindly. He probably felt he couldn't cope with a foreigner sitting beside him, a foreigner who might start asking questions in English to which he would be unable to reply.

Some of the young—especially uniformed high-school boys with cropped hair and muddy complexions—look curiously old, prematurely aged, with touchingly puzzled expressions. (A sudden smile transforms them.) While old people often have an engaging air of youth and high spirits: the lovely little-girl faces of some old ladies, the rosy-cheeked little-boy faces of old men.

The things that Shinjuku bar boys and bar girls do *under* the bar (out of politeness to the clients and also to obtain a little privacy): they eat all kinds of cake and fruit, noodles, soup, *sushi* brought to them by restaurant boys. They crouch down under the counter to pop a sweet or a vitamin pill into their mouths, to take a sip of a private drink, to arrange their hair, to pick their teeth with toothpicks (holding a refined hand in front of the mouth, even when no one is watching except me); they make out interminable bills and accounts, writing on big blank sheets the debts of patrons who get drinks on tick and pay up at the end of every month. (Bar madams have now taken to sending gay boys to the offices of defaulters, demanding they pay up. Now bills are nearly always paid on time.) Sometimes, in the lower type of bar—the kind I like best, and where the drinks are cheapest—the bold girls make amorous passes at the boys behind the bar, like good-natured, joking, playful little kittens. These erotic passes are sometimes meant to provoke customers, and do.

In the bar called Urashi (beauty) the madam is a graceful and refreshing picture by Utamaro; her neck is so straight and round and pure above the opening in her jade green kimono, with a little plump fold of fair flesh just under the pointed chin. Her hair is arranged in deliberate yet natural wisps and curls; her smile is pure sweetness. She points a slender, descriptive finger at her nose when talking about herself, a moving, childlike gesture used by all the Japanese.

The gay boys (I prefer to call them 'joy boys') are a regular feature of the Shinjuku streets, and arouse absolutely no comment, whether they are dressed in ladies' kimono or Paris-style dress, in Bohemian male or 'camp' or ordinary sober Western suitings. Their make-up attracts no attention, because now, according to recent surveys, about 30 per cent of Japanese males have embraced the art of cosmetics, and Japanese cosmetics manufacturers are now vying with American firms in producing full ranges of creams, salves, lotions, 'business men's suntans', hair sprays, eyebrow pencils and 'neutral-tinted' talc for men. *Rippu kurimu* (lip cream) or *rippu pomado* (lip pomade) and various kinds of tinted lip-salves are very popular with Japanese men. Electric curling-irons and combs are used openly in all barbers' shops on young men's hair. Perfumes and toilet waters for men are in great demand; at the make-up counters in any department store one can sample any number of scents, spraying them now here, now there, on this pulse-point and that, entirely free of charge. The Yanagiya company's advertising booklet for male cosmetics says boldly:

> Today is the beauty treatment age for men. They say stockings and women have become stronger since after the war. Japanese men should not stay defeated by women. Why don't we rise in order to restore men's lost pride by demonstrating men's original 'sekkusu apiru' [sex-appeal], that is our 'Masculin Odor' scent?

While the great number of plastic surgeons in Tokyo are now giving Japanese women new busts with silicon injections or foam rubber, new hymens and restored vaginas, the men are having their noses made bigger, their eyes enlarged by the removal of the epicanthic fold, and even their usually rather small codpieces made more prominent. Some males have hair transplanted from their heads to their chests and backs. Many Japanese women are without body hair, and they too have hair transplants and graftings, always recognizable by their unusually silken quality.

One gay boy who is frequently seen in the streets of Shinjuku has a long, pale, refined, degenerate face with soft mouth, flower nose, dark, perverse eyes, vaguely squinting; his face always bears a slightly stupid yet cunning and malicious or perhaps just mischievous expression. A long, thin, waxen neck, tiny ears half hidden under urchin-cut mop of bright orange hair, with which his dark eyebrows, like faintly blurred antennae, stand in quaint contrast. One or two bad teeth in a 'sultry' smile. He is reminiscent of the boys in Harunobu's and Suzuki Harushige's prints, who are indistinguishable from the *oiran*, the geisha and other women. His extreme slightness and emaciation in his bright terracotta shirt-blouse and skin-tight, dusky pink pants. His large-jointed ankles, his narrow, bare, bony feet with green-painted toe-nails are in silver, backless sandals ('scuffs' in American English), that he slurs over the pavement like musical instruments, each giving a different note. He carries his lilac *furoshiki* in a delicate, nervous hand with a skinny wrist, and he has a lightly dancing, almost prancing walk, like a young faun's; I imagine that Coleridge must have moved with those erratic, irregular little steps. I look at him with interest as he passes me, and he looks back with equal interest and politeness. No vulgarity, no pestering, no self-pity. He interests me only as a human phenomenon.

Then I saw another gay boy, a hideous one, in glaring red jumper and orange jeans, with vivid off-orange hair. He was big-boned, with raw-looking hands and bare, grimy feet (toe-nails red) and coarse make-up. Skin rough and greasy, with a few hairs sprouting round a mouth he had outlined in brown eyebrow pencil and blocked in with luscious pillar-box red. A strong, heavy jaw. An impression of great energy, vitality, native intelligence. His long string of bright yellow wooden beads was gaily swinging as he walked. He gave me a long, malicious, inviting, *goguenard*, summing-up look, discreet, from his heavily mascara'd eyes, and a kind of brutal smile, showing large, yellow, lipstick-stained fangs.

A few years ago there were many films made about the lives of homosexuals and gay boys, and these films had artistic merit apparently. They were ostensibly treating a 'social problem', which in fact they helped to aggravate, for with the publicity given to the lives of these boys came an interest in and a liking for the real thing. Sometimes the gay boys appear about three o'clock in the morning, when their bars have closed, at the many bowling centres in Shinjuku and other amusement areas. Many are skilled bowlers, but most of them go just to show off their ultra-feminine wiggles. Bowling is the perfect opportunity to display their best points.

In the Ginza and many other busy areas of Tokyo one can fairly frequently see people in women's fashionable clothes, or in the traditional kimono, who are obviously men. When they are wearing Western dress the bony ankles and large, long feet give them away; when they are wearing Japanese dress it is their walk, more womanly than any woman's, that betrays their masquerade. (Very often such 'women' are Kabuki actors or professional female impersonators.) All this is accepted as part of this 'floating world' of illusion, and all these creatures are embraced in the wise, all-comprehending arms of Buddha.

They sometimes add to the gaiety of nations. But of course the majority of Japanese people are as 'normal' as normal can be, which is sometimes not very much, for we are all strange mixtures of sexes. As in other lands, even the 'normal' ones have their little deviations, like molesting women in packed trains, where one often simply cannot avoid contact, or slitting women's clothes with pencil-sharpener blades or dropping lighted cigarette ends into the long sleeves of girls' best kimono, or haunting the magazine stalls in Shinjuku or Kanda where the most peculiar (and often wildly comic) aberrations of sex and behaviour are illustrated in glossy magazines that are sold quite openly. Despite occasional protests in newspapers and in the many unprincipled 'scandal rags' these things go on and are helplessly accepted. In a country so packed with diverse humanity as Japan, it is a question of 'live and let live'.

Nowhere is this truer than in the more concentrated areas like Shinjuku, where gangs of hoodlums will stage sit-ins at bars and cabarets where they imagine their leaders have been insulted; where the all-night coffee shops are patrolled by youths looking for young girls who have run away from home, and who, after being raped, will be sold to bath-houses at pleasure resorts, to geisha houses at hot springs or to girlie bars in all the big cities; where dope-fiends, deprived by concerted police action of their dope, come staggering out into the open streets, raving for a 'fix', their faces white, their limbs shaking with terrible palsies of yearning and frenzies of horror; where a popular singer like Yukio Hashi can be attacked on the stage of a huge auditorium by a jealous fan waving a naked *samurai* sword. (I sent Yukio Hashi a huge basket of roses when I heard he had been injured slightly.) Everywhere—in lavatories and public telephone boxes, stuck on lamp-posts, dropped in one's lap through the open window of a taxi waiting for the lights to change—one finds little printed slips of paper giving the phone number of some highly qualified 'Miss Orgasma', often described as 'high-school graduate' or 'speaking all languages'.

Yet the capricious Shinjuku scene, despite its never-ceasing traffic, its swarms of taxis waiting to pick up bar girls, its fevered neon and its jazz coffee shops and gay bars, is essentially a respectable, very ordinary place. There is nothing remarkable about its appearance, excepting at times its extreme vulgarity. Hundreds of thousands of ordinary and respectable people work and live there and throng its stations, that are the busiest in Tokyo. Here and there, among all the student riots, the frenzied jostling, the modern buildings and discount stores, there are gardens and temples, shrines and softly beaten gongs; coming out of a noisy strip-tease show, one's nostrils smell the perfume of incense from the temple next door; walking in Shinjuku Gyoen, a most beautiful public park, one sees a gang of hoodlums, their hair well lacquered, their smart suits well brushed, taking each other's pictures in conventional poses under the wistaria bower by the ornamental lake near the reproduction of a Taiwan mansion. It is all a mass of contradictions that do not contradict: like myself and the Japanese they simply exist side by side, in true oriental fashion, with cumulative inconsequentiality, safe in the hands of Buddha.

2

LIFE WITH A JAPANESE FAMILY

I HAVE had much experience lately of Japanese house and apartment agents, for I have been looking for somewhere to live. Their advertisements are in all the English-language newspapers, but the prices they ask are outrageous, and I simply cannot afford even the cheapest flats, which are about thirty pounds a month for two small rooms and bath. In addition, one has to give the agent a present equivalent to one month's rent; then the owner requires key-money and often demands as much as six months' rent in advance. The agents are mainly a slick and shifty lot of Japanese, chewing gum and speaking American slang; they have had a lot to do with Americans who are partly responsible for the exorbitant prices of property and the high rents in Tokyo. But not all these agents are rapacious rogues. Last summer one of them, a very pleasant and efficient young man, found for me a rather poor two-roomed apartment in Sendagaya, and would only accept half his commission for it. He also went out and bought cheaply for me a few household goods—sheets, a pan, a teapot and a cup and plate.

Some of the newspaper advertisements are inserted by Japanese who have one or two rooms to let in their houses, and these people always state that there is 'no agent' and 'no commission'. (The agent's 100 per cent commission is quite legal.) I replied to an advertisement which said there were two rooms available in a Japanese house, sharing kitchen and lavatory and bath. I went to Shinjuku to see them, and though they were very small and dingy I took them because they were unusually cheap—only eighteen pounds a month, not including 'utilities'. The house was of wood, in Japanese style, and the elderly owners, Mr and Mrs Sato, were most friendly and helpful. They could both speak a little English, and they were both mad about folk-dancing, Japanese-style of course, not the American square dance. I liked the place and the two old people, so I moved in immediately.

There was a rather ramshackle wooden fence round the house and its tiny garden. On the outer gate was a bell which tinkled every time I went in and out. In the garden were a few sooty azalea bushes and a stone tank containing a few goldfish. The house door was of sliding glass panels, leading on to a concrete space where one put one's umbrella and took one's shoes off. (One should take off hat and overcoat *before* entering a Japanese house.) The hall floor of shining boards was raised about one foot above this, and there were always house slippers lined up along the edge for guests. A wooden beam in the hall held a motto on wood (*gakku*); the Chinese words, written in lovely old Japanese characters, were *shi sei*, which meant, I was told, 'sheer sincerity'. After changing into house slippers in the hall, one had to remove the house slippers on entering the Satos' rooms, which were covered with *tatami*; but one kept on the house slippers to go to the kitchen. When one went to the lavatory one had to slip off the house slippers outside the lavatory door and step into a pair of wooden clogs inside the door. When one took a bath in the big wooden tub, heated by a cheery small fire underneath, one had to discard the house slippers and step into yet another pair of wooden clogs. For wandering in the garden or going to the rubbish bin, there was yet another pair of clogs, this time ordinary *geta*, or a pair of heelless sandals. All this chopping and changing of footwear was at first extremely tedious to me, and downright confusing. I would find myself going into the bathroom with my house slippers on, or coming out of the lavatory into the hall wearing wooden clogs.

Sometimes I come into this neat-as-a-pin Japanese house when no one else is in, and I don't take my shoes off in the hall. I walk over the shining bare boards in the shoes that have been soiled by the street; it gives me a tremendous feeling of guilt. No Japanese would ever do it, of course; he simply couldn't after being educated from childhood to change into slippers immediately he enters the front door. It is a very good way of keeping the house clean, and one which we might well adopt in the West.

The lamps are too low for me. I am always knocking with my head the rather heavy bronze Western-style hanging lamp in the hall and the cream porcelain bowl of the ugly hanging lamp in my sitting-room.

At the corner of the lane, reassuringly, stands a very tall, bright red post with a red light on top; a fire-alarm. Mr Sato shows me how to use it if the house should catch fire when he is out. He takes me all round the Nishiokubo district, showing me the best shops, the best bars, the best restaurants and the best barbers. He even takes me to the public bath at the corner of our little lane and introduces me to the presiding dame, a formidable lady who keeps a watchful eye on both the male and the female sides of the bath and has a long ear for all the gossip she hears. Mr Sato is really extraordinarily kind; we take a bath together and he massages my neck which is rather stiff; nearly all Japanese are expert masseurs, and one often has glimpses of Japanese interiors where small boys and girls are giving massage to mother or grandmother.

All over the house Mr Sato has put up demotic little notices in slightly worried, agitated style, like some Viennese refugee landlady's instructions in a Finchley Road or South Kensington boarding-house. In the crouch-down flush toilet, one enjoys a coloured picture of the Imperial Palace and a notice which reads: 'Attention! before useing [*sic*] please put a paper in the botton [*sic*].' In the adjoining, tiny lavatory, which contains a lily-shaped stand-urinal with a few inches of white tile set in the wooden floor beneath it, the notice runs: 'Attention: Please take care and keep clean. Please put your foot on the tile and watch!' Above the telephone in the hall: 'Attention! Please turn off a radio, play a record from 8 a.m. to 10 p.m. Owner.' I am not quite sure what this means, but as I have neither radio nor record-player it doesn't affect me.

Mrs Sato, who must be about sixty-five, is surprisingly youthful and slender, her figure straight and lissom. Every day she practises Japanese folk-dancing with Mr Sato and this is what has given her such a good figure and allowed her to keep it. She has a slightly Malay face, with big, dark, lucent eyes and a charming smile, for she still has all her teeth. She is up early every morning sweeping and polishing the hall and cleaning the cement entrance with buckets of water. Then she sprinkles the little stone path through the garden to the gate with a toy watering-can, painted with improbable golden roses and silver ferns, to lay the dust. She brings in the milk bottles from the little yellow-painted wooden box specially provided for them and fixed inside the main gate. The papers arrive at six o'clock, and I have already taken mine out of the glass-fronted post-box attached to the front fence. I am such a big and awkward foreigner in this delicate little house; I am always bumping into things and breaking them: today I broke the glass on the post-box and put my finger through a paper screen. Both clumsinesses were greeted with delighted laughter and radiantly forgiving smiles by both old people.

Mr and Mrs Sato have no children with them now. Later, when I was often taken into their own part of the house to sit with them and watch their television programmes of folk-dancing and sip beer and nibble rice-crackers with Mr Sato, I saw the little shrine they had set up in an inner room. It was very small and humble, but always adorned by a few fresh flowers and fruit, and sometimes, on anniversaries, there would be candles and a few joss-sticks burning in front of two faded photographs of good-looking sons killed in the Second World War. They never mentioned their loss, but I felt those two dead sons were always in their minds, and in their little house, even at their most light-hearted moments when they were singing and clapping hands encouraging each other in their dance practices. An enchanting couple.

I liked the way Mr and Mrs Sato chattered away together in their two rooms. After years of marriage, they still obviously have much to say to one another. He always seems to be talking about politics and general cultural matters in such an interesting and amusing way, while she breaks in frequently with her charming Japanese lady's laughter, like a wind-bell, and sweetly spoken phrases of her own. They are like two children playing at keeping house.

I do not listen deliberately to their conversations, but I can't help hearing what they say sometimes when I am in the kitchen, and in any case, though they know I am there, they make no attempt to lower their voices. Sometimes Mr or Mrs Sato would come and join me in the kitchen and often Mrs Sato gave me samples of her delectable cooking; her pickled egg-plant in particular was delicious, and she knew how to make all kinds of peppery, spiced sweetmeats and sugared vegetables and crystallized flowers and herbs. She would present one or two examples of each to me on a doll's dish of blue eggshell china, with a pair of chopsticks sheathed in hand-made paper, a gardenia in a saké cup and a paper napkin printed with an old woodcut by Sharaku, dug up from heavens knows where, for it must be at least fifty years old; they don't make things like that napkin nowadays.

Owing to an excessively dry winter and spring, the water is cut every night from ten until six next morning. Mr Sato always fills a bowl and a pail of fresh water for me, as I am usually out late in the evenings.

The happy chatter of the two old people is so vivacious and continuous, broken by little peals of laughter, that often I think there must be more than two people in their rooms, and have to look down at the smooth wood floor outside their paper sliding doors; but there are only two pairs of house slippers there. I like the pitter-patter of their feet in the hall. One morning I found them doing physical jerks to instructions from an announcer on a children's television programme; they were performing them with the utmost seriousness, as if they were part of a folk-dance.

They go off together to the bath-house at the corner every night about eleven o'clock, each carrying a plastic bowl with towel and soap, chattering and laughing away like two children going to school.

Sometimes Mr Sato seems a bit grumpy and silent, but that is only when Mrs Sato is out. When she comes back, the delightful 'newsing' and trills of soft laughter start again. When it is raining Mrs Sato puts out three umbrellas in the cement entrance for the use of the household. Her devotion to Mr Sato is quite wonderful, but it is the normal devotion of any Japanese wife to her 'interview marriage' husband. One morning it was snowing, and when I brought in Mr Sato's *Yomiuri Shimbun* from the broken post-box in the little garden the paper was sopping wet. Later I saw Mrs Sato lovingly spreading out the sheets and hanging them on the black-lacquered clothes-horse usually reserved for kimono, so that they would be dry when Husband-san woke up and grunted for his first cup of green tea.

Mr and Mrs Sato are so sweet, perhaps because their name means 'sugar'. Mr and Mrs Sugar. They gave me a little, very modest present of some paper handkerchief-towels, the sort that a Japanese carries everywhere with him and uses for every conceivable purpose. The name of the paper towel is 'Catleya', and on the cover is printed the delightful English phrase: 'All paper for your life: 100 sheets.'

Misprints in advertisements for houses to let: 'sinny living-room', 'bed-wetting room' (for 'bed-sitting room') and 'bedroom furnished with telephone'.

I opened the sliding doors one morning to the sudden shock of a deep snowfall: the little bushes and dwarfed trees in the garden were so weighed over by it that their branches hung together, interlocking, from either side of the path. I had to give a number of little shakes to make them spring back and make way for me. The goldfish were invisible at the bottom of their murky green tank. A snow of unexampled softness that clots the thousands of criss-crossing telegraph wires and clothes the television aerials—horizontal in Japan—with supernatural flesh.

The view of the sunny, snow-hung gardenette through a bamboo screen as I lie on the matted floor sipping my hot green tea is enchanting. Snow in Japan is unlike snow anywhere else, in the way it so elegantly and thickly drapes every leaf and bough with monumental stillness. But today's unseasonal spring snow is soon gone, melted into a mass of mud and slush.

Mr Sato is unusually tall and thin for a Japanese elderly gentleman. His long, sharp, witty face is something like a fox's, full of sympathetic cunning, the eyes lively as pebbles winking in a stream under the shaggy black eyebrows in which two or three extra-long hairs are cultivated with great care. His smile, a great boyish grin, showing long, yellowed teeth touched with gold. His great, chortling laughs as he converses on the telephone are like the crowings and barkings of Kitsune, the mischievous supernatural fox of Japanese legend.

When I wake up in the mornings through my thin wall I can hear movements in the house next door: the young wife is bustling about making Husband-san's breakfast; finally she calls to him by his family name: 'Yamada-san! Time to get up!' She has to call three times before there is any answer, and then Husband-san grunts: 'Oi!' He falls asleep again, and again she calls him, and again he grumbles 'Oi!' This is how most Japanese husbands address their wives: if Husband-san is entertaining his friends, males, at home, Wife-san does not participate; she runs about buying food and drink, getting out long-unused dishes and glasses, preparing curious seaweedy titbits, cooking rice and fish and telephoning for *sushi* (raw fish or rolls of vinegared rice). If Husband-san wants anything, he will interrupt his jovial conversation with the friends to shout, rather loudly and crossly: 'Oi! Okusan! Oi! Oi!' Whereupon *okusan* (literally, 'person remaining inside the house') comes running, casting herself down on her knees to excuse herself and taking orders with nods and frequently repeated 'Hai! hai! hai! hai! Wakarimashta! Wakarimashta!' (Yes, I understood first time.) The couple next door are still fairly young; sometimes at night, after Husband-san has come home stewed with saké or *shochu* (cheap sweet-potato spirit)—he was then working on the great Olympics Stadium—I hear him shouting for his bath, and after that there is the sound of amorous *ébats* on the matted floor, and pants and muffled screams of amorous brutality. (Japanese men, despite the 30 per cent who are said to use cosmetics, are the malest males in creation.)

But in the morning it is all different. There are groanings and grumblings, and horrible hawkings and spittings. The sliding doors slam backwards and forwards as Husband-san gets ready for work and Wife-san finally trots to the front door to see him off.

The fire-engine sirens are always going, and, as we live close to a maternity hospital, ambulance and blood-transfusion van sirens add their howlings to the demented uproar of Tokyo. Whenever a siren goes, the dog next door moans in frantic sympathy. But it is surprising how quiet our little lane is: occasionally a three-wheel van manages to get down its narrow ruts, and sometimes we hear people running and panting as if being pursued by ghosts, murderers or burglars, but on the whole the peace of this little backwater, only one block from the main road, is remarkable. Because we live near a maternity hospital, people sometimes think I am an erring G.I. father who comes to pay his respects to his Japanese wife at the lying-in hospital. One day, as I was coming back from shopping with an armful of fruit and flowers for my flower-arrangement practice I was stopped by a young working man outside the Red Cross Hospital who grinned at me and asked when we were expecting 'Baby-san'. 'Any time now,' I told him. He made a significant phallic gesture which I returned in full measure, and we parted well pleased with one another.

Mr and Mrs Sweet Sugar have one other great hobby besides folk-dancing: they are passionately concerned about local politics, and as there is a somewhat fevered local election this spring they are always dashing out with banners and placards, as soon as they hear a loud-speaker van bawling in the streets, to support their candidate. I was never very sure what their political views were, but I believe they were good members of the Liberal Democratic Party, which in Japan is not as Liberal nor as Democratic as one would expect from the name; in fact it is merely a dyed-in-the-wool Tory party under a fancy 'progressive' name. The Japanese, at least the older ones, seem to take a genuine interest in politics, but perhaps this is because of all the illegal entertaining that goes on during an election campaign. Year after year more and more candidates are prosecuted for entertaining voters to lavish dinners, for giving them gifts and even presenting them with money. The prosecutions seem to do no good at all, and in any case one never hears anything about the sentences which are supposed to follow. Many politicians sagely book private wards at hospitals and conveniently have a 'nervous breakdown' after an election to escape prosecution. Private wards before an election are unobtainable in Japan; they have all been booked up in advance by vote-buying politicians intent on staging a well-produced state of mental collapse.

Richard Storry in his admirable *History of Modern Japan* has this very perceptive comment to make about the Japanese and their idea of politics:

> In the past the Japanese undoubtedly lacked political maturity; and to this day purely social, personal, and, indeed, monetary considerations can dictate the voting habits of large masses of the population, especially in the countryside. At the same time the Japanese are becoming more sophisticated, politically, with each year that goes by. They have long been literate and have long been interested in matters of public moment; but until very recently they have tended to accept the views and interpretations presented to them by local officials and men of standing in the community. There are many signs, however, that younger people are beginning to think for themselves.

I must say here that I have seen very little evidence of political maturity among young Japanese. Among the workers, as I have already indicated, there are massive, regular but apathetic token strikes; among students, perhaps the most politically conscious body in the community though by no means mature, those revolutionary pacifists and socialists, communists and anarchists take up politics and political demonstrations because these activities form part of the conventional image of a manly young progressive student; a student interested in politics gets the reputation for being an 'intellectual', which is a very important status symbol in Japanese academic society, and his reputation as a student leader of political movements may influence the kind of degree he gets, irrespective of his true academic merits. Indeed when the time comes for these students to apply for jobs in sometimes ultra-conservative companies who yet have the welfare of their workers at heart, the interviewers are known to look favourably upon young men who have taken an active part in organizing movements, in assassinating political figures, in leading Zengakuren snake-dancing demonstrations; the interviewers also favour those who have contributed to anarchist and pacifist magazines (always of short duration) or who have staged sit-down strikes in their universities or outside embassies. (The new type of aggressive rioter is also popular.) The point would seem to be that, despite their extreme views, these students can be taken to be sincere Japanese who are concerned with the welfare of their own country and will have no truck with foreign domination. They might turn out to be important leaders in the business war that wages relentlessly between Japan and the West.

Once these students have entered a big prestige company like Matsushita or Yawata Steel—a plum position for any young man in

Japan, and the competition for such positions is ferocious—he tones down his views, wears baggy Western clothes, thinks, however unwillingly, of the inevitable interview marriage, children, washing-machine, television set, car, and gradually adopts the essentially a-political conformity of the Liberal Democratic majority. This is one of the saddest aspects of conformity in Japan: a rebel is usually active only for a year or two. Those who remain rebels, like the novelist Kenzaburo Ohye, a pacifist anarchist, youthful and ardent and utterly dedicated to what he conceives to be right and just, are very rare in Japan.

Meanwhile the local elections go on, with loudspeaker vans bawling out tape-recorded speeches from six o'clock in the morning. No one minds, not even the police, though it is illegal to use these loudspeaker vans. (But once an exasperated householder shot at a college girl campaigning too vigorously.) In the main streets at lunch time, when the workers are leaving shops and small factories for lunch, one can see vans drawn up by the pavement with a bland, baggy-suited candidate, his lapel adorned by a large artificial chrysanthemum, standing on the roof, surrounded by his fawning, chrysanthemum-adorned minions, rattling off some pedestrian speech. Once or twice I saw the Sato couple standing beside one of these vans, chatting with neighbours, giving their support but not listening at all to the rubbish being doled out to the public, or to the fine promises that are in fact never kept.

In the lane, the cry of the sweet potato man, and the bell of the man collecting empty bottles. There is the call of the ragpicker and of the old lady who collects bundles of newspapers and wrapping-paper. Late at night a man passes in the lane shouting a curious street-cry which sounds like *Yakiyo* or the name 'Iachimo' in *Cymbeline*. I wonder what it means. Later I find out he is shouting 'Yaki-iimo', or baked sweet potatoes. They are baked on a bed of hot pebbles, and are delicious. Another man, shaking bamboo clappers, comes round every month or so selling long green bamboo poles which are used as washing-lines: the poles are threaded through the armholes or legs of garments hung out to dry. Some of the poles are painted with lime green enamel. Another sweet potato seller bellows through a battery powered megaphone. Then there is the brass trumpeting of the noodle seller, the hoarse call of the fishmonger or the whistle of the vegetable man. People are constantly shoving the sliding doors apart and shouting across the hall: 'Gomen nasai! Sato-o-o-o san!' ('Please excuse me for bothering you, Mr Sugar!') The way the Japanese prolong certain words and names when they are calling to someone gives their voices at times a cat-like wail. Then, always after two or more cries, Mr or Mrs Sato will come trotting softly to the door, saying 'Kon-nichi-wa' or 'Hajime-mashite' or 'O-machi-doh-sama'. (The first two mean 'Hallo, I am glad to see you', the last 'Sorry to have kept you waiting'.) These formal politenesses, even with ragpickers and tramps, are exquisite. The postman and the men who come to read the electricity and gas meters are given especially formal and respectful greetings, because they are government employees; they are never insulted by the offer of a tip at Christmas therefore, though the laundry boy will receive one at New Year, and the dustmen get fifty yen every month. (Though this is supposed to be against the law.)

Laundry confusions: I am presented by the laundry boy with several articles of clothing that do not belong to me, including handkerchiefs, long woolly underpants and some rather gaudy socks. I declined these offers, and said I would rather have my own things, many of which were missing, probably farmed out to Japanese clients. But apparently the laundry boy is offering me these strange items as 'service'; so many articles of clothing go astray or are never claimed that many Japanese laundries make a practice of handing out garments to customers after a certain time has elapsed. These items are never very desirable, because the laundry workers, naturally, get the first pick.

Many Japanese boys, especially working-class boys with their wild brushes of black hair and tight blue ex-American Army surplus jeans, are perfect Li'l Abner types.

Question put to his parents by a little country boy (aged six) visiting the Satos and Tokyo for the first time and getting his first glimpse of a foreigner: 'Does he go to the *o-benjo* [honourable lavatory] like us?'

The bedside lamp, in this unseasonal cold, becomes a 'bed-inside' lamp for me; it warms the icy mattress and the sheets, and the big green shade keeps the hot bulb from contact with inflammable materials; the large top *futon*—a thick, red-bordered quilt—holds the heat in well.

I had a long hunt for the ribbed zinc hot-water bottles such as the Satos use to warm their beds. I went to all the department stores and ironmongers' shops in Shinjuku. 'Sorry, sir, season over now.' Outside deep snow and freezing winds! But indeed, spring has officially started, though snow thickens the white plum and pale pink cherry blossom. So no water bottles and no gas or electric heaters are available in any of the shops except in the second-hand stores, but even here the prices are too high: nine pounds for a tiny electric radiator? Absurd!

But my rooms are simply arctic. (They'll be boiling hot in summer, I know.) So I bought a small electric ring, for boiling kettles, and use this to keep my feet warm; I find that if my feet are warm I don't mind about the rest of me being cold. When I hear the hot sweet potato man's call in the lane, I hurry out and buy a large one, not to eat, but to wrap in a muffler and hold in my lap, to keep my hands warm.

In the kitchen, while Mrs Sato and I are cooking our suppers, the electric light keeps going out. Mr Sato is away, so I have to climb on a stool in the little pantry and switch on a special, dangerous-looking red switch, that at once brings all the lights on again. After a few minutes, *clonk*, and all the lights go out again. Mrs Sato is reduced to giggles and eventually we have to resort to candlelight. It is lovely to see my big fat prawns slowly turning many shades of delicious salmon pink in the pan of gently seething water. Then I cut open the diminutive cauliflower—so expensive!—after I had steamed it; oh, the tender flush of pure green down the central stalk! And a red lacquer bowl of rich *miso* soy (bean paste) soup.

In my bedroom there is a gas heater. I had lit it to take the chill off the room before going to bed. But I turned both taps off before going to sleep. I awoke about 3 a.m. with a splitting headache. I was only half conscious, but I managed to crawl out of bed, struggle to the lavatory and be sick. The cold, fresh air revived me. I had been half poisoned by carbon monoxide fumes. Fortunately I did not disturb the Satos, who would have been most upset. Even when the gas heater is off, it seems to give off noxious fumes, and Japanese gas is the most viscous and evil-smelling stuff in the world. There is heavy black carbonization round the new clay cylinders and on top, also on the kettle I used to boil on it. My chest is tight and when coughing I bring up big gouts of jet-black phlegm. Everything needs a good clean-out: I put in some new cylinders.

Mr Sato gave me some delicious Japanese nougat. Each little piece is wrapped in transparent rice-paper. The sweets are made by a Japanese firm called Poupée which has printed on its bags the following legend: 'Recommendable to all ranks of people for its best selected material with rich nourishing ingredients.'

I bought a very dull Japanese cake, imitation Parisian gâteau, called, amusingly, *Rumpelmeyer Izumiya*, a strange marriage; its cellophane cover was stamped with a picture of the Arc de Triomphe and the legend Paris-Tokio. 'Tokio' is the old-fashioned spelling of Tokyo; I notice that many correspondents from abroad (like Hessel Tiltman) and the *Guardian* still use the old-fashioned spelling.

Fugetsudo coffee shop, Shinjuku, the walls adorned by an exhibition of gigantic red abstracts. A boy with the air of a wildly pretty girl, his long, curly hair done in the 'chrysanthemum cut', has a sudden, surprising bass voice. Many Japanese men are girlish-looking, but are far from effeminate. In England they would be remarkable, but here no one wonders about them; they are 'normal', but gentle.

So often, in 'Help Wanted' advertisements in English-language newspapers, foreign firms demand 'aggressive' Japanese office staff or salesmen. The Japanese are aggressive enough in big business, but in their own quiet way that bewilders foreign dealers, who think they are having a walk-over and then find they've come away with nothing. Japanese firms, regrettably, will make any kind of promise and quite blandly not keep their word or fail to deliver the goods; it is not that they want to deceive, but they want the foreign buyer to feel that everything he says or wants is right, even if they cannot possibly carry out his desires. It is not really lying; it is the way Japanese have of being 'aggressive' in the cut-throat business world.

After knowing me a few months Mr and Mrs Sato expressed concern that I was not married. (The Japanese consider it a terrible disgrace for a man to refuse marriage, and indeed practically every Japanese male, unless he can escape abroad, is sooner or later pressured into marriage, often with some 'suitable' partner he doesn't care for particularly, but who usually makes him a good wife, though he may not make a very good husband.) My stock answer to the perpetual and boring and embarrassing Japanese question about why I am not married is: 'Divorced. Twice.' The shock of this shuts them up, because divorce is also a disgrace to the Japanese. This is what I told Mr and Mrs Sato, and they were shocked into stunned silence. (Like most people, the Japanese do not like being told unpleasant facts.) The subject was politely dropped. A few weeks later, however, I was invited to a little party in their big room, and I accepted. They often invited me to such intimate little gatherings of their friends, where Mrs Sato would twang the *shamisen* and sing her strangulated folk songs while Mr Sato did a sort of step dance with comical hand gestures and occasional 'noble' attitudes with his fan. We would sip green tea and beer and nibble peanuts and seaweed biscuits and *o-mochi*, or sweet bean cakes.

This time the gathering was rather small. There was an elderly lady and gentleman in their best kimono and *haori* (jacket), accompanied by their pretty daughter, about thirty, and their son, about twenty-five, who had a much-envied position in the Mitsui Bank. There was much talk and music and singing; the daughter had been to America, where she had 'majored' in something or other. She said her hobbies were listening to classical music, making dolls and the tea ceremony. I was invited to attend her tea-ceremony class.

It was a pleasant evening, but only later did I realize that I had been put on display by the Satos as a possible suitor for their friends' daughter. Apparently at this 'semi-interview', as Mr Sato called it, she had been quite taken with me and had expressed her interest in a further meeting. Mr and Mrs Sato deftly questioned me about what I thought of her. Trying to conceal a growing horror, I said every polite thing I could think of to them, to their growing satisfaction. They were deeply puzzled and, I suspect, offended when I did not attend the tea ceremony and refused to meet the young lady again, after giving some face-saving excuse. The girl sent me a curious present, a box of highly coloured *hanabiki* or crackers (it was the time of the Boys' Festival) which I immediately set off in the garden, hoping that their little scented detonations would drive away any further interest in me. They did. Perhaps Mr Sato had realized that as a go-between he had bitten off more than he could chew.

Copulation with a woman: so nice, but oh, so surgical!

In the *o-benjo*, or honourable lavatory, Mr Sato has placed an enormous, heavy magnifying glass. What is it for? Some kind of haruspication?

I am living at the heart of a gay quarter. All round the house are small hotels, and some new, large ones, which the Japanese call 'avec' hotels. They all advertise their usually rather moderate charges outside. The charge for a 'rest' of one hour is from three hundred to six hundred yen; 'rest' is a euphemism for you-know-what. And 'avec' is a term which the Japanese have taken to whole-heartedly: it means in general 'going together', whether steady or not, necking, petting and close dancing which is known as 'avec dance' or 'cheek dance'. All day and night the little lanes round my lodging-house are full of young and not-so-young couples looking for a good place to 'rest'. (Japanese girls are surely the world's most readily available partners for a little light sex in the afternoon.) Others drive up hastily in cars, for there are also some new 'avec' hotels which are 'avec' motels. Some of these establishments have pretty 'literary' names, like the palatial new 'avec motel Utajima', which means 'Poem Island'. Others are called 'Chikamatsu' (after the great Japanese dramatist, 'the Shakespeare of Japan'), 'Bamboo' (sign of maleness) and 'Cherry Heaven'. I have seen one with an English name: 'All Miracle'.

The cheaper 'avec' hotels are not really recommendable, unless one has a taste for slightly sordid squalor, used sheets and the excitement of using *futon* still warm from the previous pair of lovers. The interior of a good-class 'avec' hotel is as enchanting as its exterior; there will be an exquisite little rock-garden outside the dimly lit sliding front doors discreetly veiled from the street by a brushwood or some other kind of 'rustic' fence. The hotel's name will be painted in bold characters with black, simple elegance on the gate lantern. Inside there will be smooth, cool, shining wooden floors, sliding doors of thick paper called *fusuma*, often painted or printed with charming designs of clouds or waves or mountains; in the small room (with flush lavatory and shower adjoining) there may be circular windows with paper panelled screens, a flower arrangement of rocks, freesias and camellias in the *tokonoma* (alcove) under the hanging scroll of a leaping carp. There will probably be a television set, for many Japanese like to make love to a popular programme or under the very noses of respectable matrons giving the daily cookery demonstration.

There is a feeling of mystery and kindness; to put one at one's ease there is the proprietor or manageress, a discreet, distinguished-looking lady in dark kimono, followed by the gentle maid who lays out the *futon* and pillows and brings green tea and sweet bean cakes. One can order a meal to be brought in from a nearby restaurant, with beer or saké. The sense of guilt is completely removed from what in the West would be regarded (officially) as an improper assignation. The only time I ever encountered any embarrassment in such a place was when I went alone, simply to have a short 'rest'. This is something unheard of. The madame was very confused because I had not brought a girl with me, and one of the maids modestly offered her services. But my Japanese friends, after initial shyness on first entering such an hotel and removing their shoes (always the most fatal step for a Western woman, but one which has no significance for a Japanese girl), soon feel at home and happy in the perfect little rooms where everything is done to make things easy for us, to shield us from embarrassment or agitation in our love-making. If so wished, it can be arranged for the couple next door to peep through holes in the paper doors at one's love-making. Attached to the room is a small tiled hot bath in which we lie drowsily, afterwards, until the maid knocks and whispers that our time is up. We dress and—this is a Japanese formality—the girl lingers behind while I wander to the corner of the lane to wait for her after paying the bill. (Very often a Japanese man will allow the girl to pay the bill, or give her money to pay it with.)

Then we go to a dim-lit coffee shop and listen to modern jazz or *chansons* or the enormously popular records of *West Side Story*, according to my companion's taste. A perfect way to spend an afternoon.

3
DIVERTIMENTI

JAPANESE envelopes and notepaper are often small and delicately designed. There are some of hand-made paper, others of wood shavings or bamboo paper on which it is a pleasure to write with brush and Chinese ink. There are 'seasonal' envelopes also, plain white, with interior envelopes printed with blossom or maple or summer butterflies, whose clear colours glow faintly through the outer covering. (These are really designed for use by young ladies, but I often use them.) The other day I bought, for only forty yen, a packet of very restrained envelopes: narrow, off-white oblongs whose only pattern is made of thin pale grey stripes. When sending one of these letters by *sokutatsu*, or express post, one has to pay forty yen. (Now recently raised to sixty-five yen.) But the forty-yen stamp is a dull colour, so I ask for one ten-yen stamp, a vibrant cherry red, and a thirty-yen stamp, a pale lavender grey. The effect is entrancing, especially when I type the address with the vermilion half of the typewriter ribbon. But this use of the red part of the ribbon has caused consternation among my Japanese acquaintances: they say it gives them a nasty shock to receive a letter with the address typed in red, because red signifies anger or some disastrous event.

Today I did not shave as I wanted to test the electric razors on display at a department store. (The girl at the counter rubs your face with Blue Chrysanthemum after-shave lotion, entirely free of charge, and if you are very good she will give you a tiny sample flacon.) About 4 p.m. I wandered out, looking all bristly, and of course I *would* run into someone particularly nice whom I wished to enchant. I succeeded in doing so, despite my hirsute appearance. So many Japanese do not show they notice the physical appearances of others, or at least do not evince surprise when one appears dirty and unshaved, in rags, one's shoes and gloves a disgrace. They themselves, despite their well-founded reputation as the world's cleanest people, are quite often negligent and slovenly in their personal appearance, though on the whole the standard of elegance, neatness and cleanness is very high. From babies to elderly sages, from school children to great-grandmothers, they are nearly always a joy to behold.

Some American cigarettes are now on sale clearly marked 'Tennyson'. *On aura tout vu!* Crushproof box, dual filter, and, like all foreign tobaccos, bearing a little blue label saying: 'Imported by the Japan Monopoly Corporation.' Poor, dear Lord Alfred, what an insult!

In my almost rustic lane only a block from a turbulent main street I enjoyed one morning the sight of dog-rose-pink camellias on a bush hanging over the bamboo and brushwood fence of an 'avec' hotel, outside which a *sushi* boy was collecting the empty noodle bowls, used chopsticks and saké bottles left by the night's innumerable clients.

A pretty letter from Yoshie Nakajima, envelope and paper very fine; on them is painted in faint greys and bloomy blacks a 'floating' picture of the Nigatsudo Temple in Nara, with Mount Wakakusa's range drifting in distant mist, the mountain tops like dark icebergs: below them the outlines of two long, horned roofs seeming also to be adrift in mist. She writes, in her enchanting English: 'Shozo Tokunaga wrote to me that you've returned. How nice of you to be back again here. It is the latest happiest news for me. How is everything with you? I'm all right, ever unchange. . . .'

I was arrested by the sight of young-man dolls from the U.S.A. in the American Pharmacy at Yurakucho. They are in various types and stages of dress and undress, and only one foot high. Universal crew cuts, noses snub, almost simous, Caucasian features, genuine all-American boys. One or two of my Japanese friends have a display of these male dolls in the *tokonoma* (alcove).

At last, a bilingual subway map in the subway trains. Larger subway maps in English appear only at the larger stations. One can obtain on request at the ticket offices a small pocket map of the subway system in Tokyo, that each year gets more and more complicated, and more expensive as well as extensive.

Most foreigners visiting Japan belong to well-hosted delegations, and so find no need to ride in subways and on trams, buses and 'street-cars' or on the overhead trains. The transport ministry is very worried about the frantic overcrowding of these trains at rush-hours (and nearly every hour of the day in Tokyo seems to be a rush-hour). The brawny students who were recently hired to push passengers into the already tightly packed coaches have now been instructed to pull people out instead of pushing them in. All this pushing and shoving and manhandling goes on with the greatest good humour; one's feet get bruised, ankles kicked, shoes ruined by being trodden on by heavy wooden clogs or stiletto heels, and buttons get ripped off one's attire. The subway trains and streetcars are driven by men who stop and start their motors with disconcerting suddenness, so that quite often everyone is thrown on the floor in a milling heap. Nevertheless from time to time it is an exhilarating experience to travel in the rush-hours; there is no more direct method of getting one's finger on the pulse of the public and, for a foreigner, of gaining contact with the people. But one mustn't forget those poor victims, the patient and long-suffering Japanese, who have to travel under such conditions every day of their lives.

Most department stores now have floor guides and maps in English; a good way to pick up a few words of Japanese is to listen to the musical chanting of the lift girl as the lift rises from floor to floor. Most stores follow the same pattern, with food and drink in the basements (fantastic displays of every imaginable kind of stuff at Seibu department store in Ikebukuro), shoes, jewellery, shirts, cosmetics and pharmaceutical goods on the ground floor (called in Japan the first floor); kimono and women's wear on the 'second' floor, men's wear on the third floor. furniture and soft furnishings on the fourth floor, electrical equipment, stationery, toys on the fifth floor, cameras, watches, jewellery, art on the sixth floor, cafés on the seventh floor, playground, carousels and observation platform on the roof.

Today I saw a little girl dressed in a vivid red tartan kimono, bought perhaps at the 'Black Watch Shop' at Isetan department store in Shinjuku.

Tourists who live in hotels in the centre of Tokyo do not really get the feeling of the true city. In order to appreciate the peculiar quality of the real Tokyo, one should live in one of the many small districts in the city zone—Sendagaya, Mejiro, Shibuya, Nishiokubo, Bunkyo-ku or Meguro. Each of these districts is like a small town or village on its own, with its main shopping street, its own shrine, temple and amusement area, its station, park and public bath-house. One soon becomes known in these areas at shops and bars and hairdressers' saloons, and one gets the feeling of living in a village community right in the heart of Tokyo, a city ever on the move, ever changing, ever expanding. (One must never forget that Tokyo has been practically rebuilt twice during the last forty years.)

At the Maison Paul I am now an *habitué*, and go there almost every day for lunch or dinner. The young waiters and cooks—some no more than fifteen—shout a glad greeting when I enter, bowing and smiling. One young waiter, who has obviously not attended the 'Shinjuku Bartenders' Academy and Waiters' College and Finishing School', comes up to the table, all seriousness, and hands me the menu for lunch. There is a 'special today' notice clipped on to it, giving the names of two dishes in both Japanese and English. One is the excellent Japanese shish-kebab; the other is something called 'Dorada Veal and Rice'. I point to this, whereupon, to my utter astonishment, the waiter, who can't speak a word of English, suddenly contorts himself, bends double with the speed of a jack-knife and, convulsed with fits of laughter, beckons to another, more experienced waiter, who can say a few words of English. While I am wondering what it is all about this waiter thumbs through his 'Waiter's and Bartender's Guide to Conversational English' (which contains, like many Japanese conversation books cashing in on the English conversation boom, all our four-letter words) and comes out with: 'I am extremely sorry, sir, the veal is off, —— it.'

If one ever gets into difficulties in a Japanese restaurant, try asking simply for Curry Rice (*Kare raisu*) which is always understood.

The passing show: a gay boy with a beehive hairdo and heavily made-up face running across to the post office in Shinjuku, his upper eyelids painted with pale green fluorescent eye shadow, mouth soft, dusky red, large as a pussy-moth. He wore sky blue jeans and a bright red sweater. He ran very clumsily—so unexpected with that sylph-like figure, that moth-like face—in great clumping boots, making a lot of noise.

I have been reading Jouhandeau's exquisitely devout and funny and touching *Saint Philippe Neri* (Séries 'Hommes de Dieu', Librairie Plon, 1957). This queer saint, I find, was very much like myself, and a perfect Firbank character. It contains some of the purest French prose, limpid and exact, that I have read for a long time. One of the saint's disciples, too, is like me: the nephew of St Charles, Frederico Borromeo, who founded the famous Ambrosian Library and 'reduced to the minimum his relationships with everyone' (except Philippe). Page 37 of the book begins with my favourite words, *un caprice*.

In the food basement of department stores jams are sold by weight in polythene bags: there is something curiously revolting about this sticky sight. I long for nice glass jars. It is simply horrid to watch the assistant ladling plum jam into the gooey bag with a flat wooden spatula and weighing it carefully on the scales, occasionally adding a gule or two or subtracting one. Eggs also are sold by weight in polythene bags, usually in fives, never in half-dozens as in the West. Incredibly varied counters of sweets, cookies, rice-crackers, seaweed biscuits, bread of every colour and description (usually very poor, like cotton wool). On a polythene bag of *croissants*—terribly tough, I discovered—there are the lines of an old French rhyme:

On prend le café au lait au lit
Avec des gâteaux et des croissants chauds.
Ah! que c'est bon ! Nom de nom !

The Japanese make mistakes in printed French or German words much less often than in English. When I am buying what for the Japanese are 'strange' or 'exotic' foods like cheese or bread or steak, a small group of housewives gather round to watch. When I have been served they buy exactly what I have been buying, presumably thinking that I must be an 'expert' in foreign foods.

A girl serving me at the fish counter dropped a ten-yen coin out of my change on the floor. She picked it up, but gave me another, 'clean' one, from the till. After counting up the price of my purchases twice on an automatic adding machine another shop girl checked her result on her *soroban* or abacus, clicking away prettily at the glossy beads with neat thumb and forefinger. She got a different result each time and finally added it up on a bit of paper.

In Japanese restaurants they take the menu away from you as soon as you have ordered. Waitresses never seem to think you might want to order something else. In most restaurants there are only two or three menus to serve all the tables. The waitresses in Tokyo today are often extremely inattentive and undisciplined. But if one leaves a newspaper behind on the seat, they will run out into the street after one with it. It is touching.

In the self-service department of Isetan everything is on sale, including motor-cars. Just get in and drive away; it's one way of getting one's paper 'sack' of groceries home.

A pet shop in Shinjuku: poor little white Spitz puppies shuddering at every horn, bell and squealing brake from the horrifyingly close and merciless traffic.

In the lane near the police box and the children's playground in the grounds of the fox-deity's Hanazono shrine, there is a strange trio: a big brown and white collie, with long, noble head and proud-plumed tail; a small Siamese cat with pale blue eyes and chocolate brown paws, tail, nose and ears; and a tiny, silent, appalled-looking monkey in a cage. The dog and cat are chained, as is the monkey in his cage. A tin dish of scraps of fish and rice has not been touched by them; I can hardly bear it when animals don't eat. The dog and cat play affectionately and fearlessly with one another, gently nipping and pawing, patting and wrestling. The small, forlorn monkey from time to time puts out a withered, doll-sized human hand and grasps the collie's coat or the cat's tail, but neither of them takes any notice of him. None of the animals, except occasionally the monkey, blinking powder blue lids on puzzled round eyes, looks at the passers-by, and no one stops to look and speak and touch except myself. They are truly Japanese animals—self-reliant and expecting nothing, absolutely nothing, of anyone. It is extraordinary to me that animals can thus take on the characteristics of the humans inhabiting the land they live in.

The unreliable Japanese are nearly always those who chew gum, drink Cokes, ape Western fashions. And Christianity often seems to attract a dull type of Japanese, or 'rice Christians', or at any rate Japanese who are dulled and inhibited by Christian religious guilts and superstitions.

Sometimes, after sex, a Japanese will say to me: 'May I love you?' I find that heart-breaking.

Whenever I see a shirt I like in a shop window, I nearly always find it is in the boy's wear range.

I lost a glove at Ginza Mitsukoshi department store. I reported the loss to the lovely girl at the information desk and left my telephone number with her. The next day Mr Sato excitedly told me that she had telephoned to say the glove had been found. When I went to collect it I found she had herself neatly mended slits in the thumb and fore-finger. I made a date with her for lunch on her off day, and we rounded off the afternoon with an hour's 'rest' at Poem Island. I didn't want to lose my nice Austin Reed winter gloves when it is so hard to find big sizes here. The best chance one has of finding sizes to fit broad hands is to rake about among the 'left-overs' at seasonal bargain sales.

Men at work: on top of the enormous scaffolding of a new building they are hoisting a huge, red-painted metal cistern into place. Near by, a dozen men in *jikatabi* are scrambling like nimble spiders about a sparkling metal structure that is the framework for a neon sign of giant proportions. All wear crash helmets of a beautiful lime green. Over them waves the symbol of industrial safety, Japan's Green Cross flag.

A woman smiles at me in Asakusa. She is a brawny country wife with ruddy cheeks and shining, jet black hair, wearing a padded jacket and those sad-sack trousers called *monpe*. I smile back at her. She does not cover her teeth with her hand as most Japanese women do, perhaps because she is proud of them: they are almost entirely covered with silver, and the effect is startling. The habit of plating the teeth with gold or silver or lesser metal alloys is fortunately on the decrease in Japan, excepting in remote country districts, where plentiful gold teeth are an advantage in the arranging of a marriage. In former times women were very modest about showing their teeth, for this was thought to be unseemly. Today one still sees modern, 'emancipated' girls and women modestly covering their smiles with hand or fan or scarf or kimono sleeve or whatever they happen to be holding, be it brush or box or bunch of flowers. Custom dies hard in Japan. In the feudal era, which lasted well into the eighteenth century and was not nearly as 'backward' as the word feudal suggests, married women had to dye their teeth black with *o-haguro*, which is a thick liquid made from stewed tea or vinegar in which iron filings and dried gall-nuts have been steeped. The things women will do to be fashionable!

Black is the colour of invisibility in Japan: the scene-shifters who appear on-stage at the Kabuki theatre wear black clothes and black veils, and all but the star operators in Bunraku wear black clothes. During the Tokugawa Shogunate the art of making oneself invisible was developed to a high degree. *Ninjutsu* men dressed in black from top to toe and were experts at scaling walls with secret folding ladders or grappling irons; they were said to be able to enter and leave houses and courtyards without being seen. Several films and charmingly absurd television serials have been made about their escapades, but the art has long since died out, and there are now only a few practitioners of this family skill. Nathaniel Hawthorne's story, *The Minister's Black Veil*, a most extraordinary tale, always reminds me of the black-veiled faces of Japan.

Bonsai or dwarfed trees: there is a great nursery of these curious objects of unnatural art at Nishiokubo. Firbank's description of a tree on the horizon and a figure moving towards it in 'an agony of dumb regret' always recalls to my mind the 'typical' attitudes of these tiny trees. One can watch the whole process of shrinking and stunting and grafting at the nurseries in Nishiokubo while sipping a cup of green tea thoughtfully provided by one of the apprentices to a delicate craft that takes a lifetime to master.

In Asakusa I saw some lace handkerchiefs hanging outside a stall; they were printed with large black-and-white photographs of Japanese film stars and pop singers. I bought a whole bunch of them; now I always carry one with me everywhere I go, in my breast pocket, with most of the face (and none of the lace) showing. Japanese young men nearly always show only a regulation half-inch of white handkerchief in their breast pockets. When they see me sporting gaily coloured silk handkerchiefs with all the corners flopping about wildly in the breeze, they look at me as if I am demented.

A young taxi-driver who would not take me and a Japanese companion from Tokyo to Kanda gave as an excuse that he was from Yokohama. We had been waiting in a queue outside the Yaesuguchi exit of Tokyo station, where there are men controlling the taxis. These men did nothing about the taxi-driver's refusal to take us. The two Japanese behind us, however, were immediately accepted for a destination in Tsukiji. This proves my growing suspicion that there is among a small number of Japanese taxi-drivers a reluctance to accept foreign passengers. However, most Japanese taxi-drivers are perfectly ready to stop, provided one hails them at the right place—that is, not on an intersection and not at a part of a street where 'No Parking, No Stopping' signs are displayed. (Though even if one does this in ignorance, as I have often done, many taxi-drivers will stop.) When I consider the sordidness of taxi-haggling in other parts of Asia, the ill temper of many London taxi-drivers, with their mania for big trips, and the perfectly awful taxi conditions of Vienna and Paris, the cheapness and courtesy one meets with in Japan are things to be marvelled at. It is true that many Tokyo taxi-drivers do not know their way around, but these drivers are usually fresh imports from country regions who are 'earning and learning', as there is no system of teaching drivers the geography of the city.

3rd March: Hina Matsuri, of the Doll Festival Day. For weeks all the department stores have been giving displays of beautiful sets of dolls representing ancient court characters. All kinds of ingenious miniature accessories go with these very gorgeous dolls—lanterns, fans, musical instruments, palanquins, thrones, tables, utensils and miniature potted flowering shrubs and food made of tinted rice and bean paste. A full set of dolls with all their accessories will cost as much as five hundred pounds, but this would be a luxury set indeed. Most sets begin at about ten pounds. Many Japanese people buy a few dolls and accessories every year until they have made up a complete set,

New Year decorations outside a restaurant

Lanterns at Toshogu shrine

Doll Festival

New Year toast

New Year writing ceremony

New Year acrobatics
performed by firemen

(*Right*) Geisha parade

(*Below right*) Firemen in *happi* coats

(*Left*) New Year visit to the Imperial Palace

(*Below*) Cheering students at a baseball game

秀太郎
千津子

Stall at the Asakusa New Year Festival

and these are carefully wrapped and put away after the period of the festival is over. The festival derives from the *hito-gama*, or 'human form', dolls made of paper in ancient times; it was believed their making and casting into streams, lakes or the sea prevented sickness and misfortune.

My favourite Japanese magazines are the fashion magazines, both male and female, the latter covering both Western-style dress and kimono. They have riotously mad 'camp' and gay poses and wonderfully kooky clothes, all preposterously silly, but consciously so, and utterly enchanting. The mad-looking girls in modern hair-do's and make-up, modelling traditional kimono, are hilariously funny.

Bar hostesses dining at the Maison Paul. 'Good-class girls', I am told. Some of them are pretty. There are always one or two wearing glittering 'harlequin' glasses; these are known as *interi-jo-san*, or 'intellectual girls': apparently tired Japanese business men often make passes at girls with glasses. Some hostesses were wearing white Western suits: one of them had a sort of Elizabethan ruff, not round her neck but round her hips, and when she walked it seemed to have the centrifugal gyrations of a hula-hoop. Those in kimono have pretty *geta* studded with paste jewels; their upswept hair is sprayed with rainbow glitter frost. The girls in Western clothes all wear sharply pointed, sharp-heeled, vicious-looking red shoes. These remind me of the time when I was stricken by the 'dancing madness' in central France after eating rye bread contaminated with ergot. During that awful mania, the sight of sharp-pointed shoes, especially red ones, used to drive the poor sufferers into exhausting eccentric dance routines and me into fits of frenzied high kicking which lasted for hours. (In the Middle Ages, when these dancing manias were very prevalent, owing to the presence of ergot in rye bread, pointed red shoes were regarded as signs of demonic possession.) Today I am always reminded of those madcap days of demented dancing whenever I see people doing the twist, which is very popular in Japan. (They do it much better than jiving, the frug, the swim and so on, at which their efforts are very poor.)

Little tins of the excellent Meiji fruit juices bought at stations (where all kinds of alcohol except gin are freely on sale) have a plastic cap to keep the top of the can free from dust and dirt; a small metal tin-opener is inside the cap, together with about four inches of plastic tubing. One punches a couple of holes and drinks the good juice through this plastic 'straw'. It is very hygienic, convenient and an extremely good idea, I think.

Even in 1959, just after it was announced that the Olympic Games would take place in Tokyo in 1964, one could see youths in brightly coloured tracksuits or shorts padding round the leafy alleyways of Meiji Park. Now they are trotting all over the place, training for the Games in Munich in 1972. There is a craze for weight-lifting among Japanese youth, though on the whole I would say the typical Japanese physique is not really suited to this kind of strenuous exercise. Barbells often stand rusting in the rain outside the sliding doors of shops where the willowy and delicate male personnel are trying to develop tremendous muscles. There are many home-made dumb-bells—a concrete block at either end of a bamboo pole. They stand in the gutter, waiting for the boys' lunch-time practice after a meal of rice omelette or noodle soup. Japanese body-builders, like their brothers all over the world, are indescribably comic.

At a shop selling model aircraft construction sets, a pair of Japanese youths are openly sniffing up glue in hopes of getting high. This is now a favourite sport among high school pupils.

The visual effect of lambdacism—and rhotacism—in a restaurant menu boldly printed with the phrase *a ra calte*. Everywhere one sees enormous, expensive but misspelt neon signs; one of the most common mistakes is 'cabalet'.

The Japanese, when they are alone, are like the sea when no one is looking at it. It is more than ever sea, sea pure and simple, as the Japanese are when foreigners are not present. I am sad because I shall never know the Japanese like that—in their pure state, like the ocean when no one is looking at it.

Restaurant boys bursting out of their second-hand jeans—seams giving way, pockets tearing, flies popping, zips slipping. The latest fad is to rip off the two back pockets—or, more stylishly, one only—to reveal one or two square patches of dark blue, unfaded cloth neatly outlined on each buttock against the *délavé* denim of the rest of the garment; this gives plump-bottomed Japanese boys somewhat the air of blue-bottomed baboons. But nearly always the elegance and natural vitality of the bodies underneath them transform the most extraordinary garments and the cheapest clothes into magic modes that express and reveal most beautifully and attractively the vigour and perfection of the natural Japanese physique. It is a pleasure to walk the streets, anywhere in this land of youth, merely to feast one's eyes upon so much native elegance, feminine delicacy and male glamour.

In entertainment districts there are placard men at almost every corner directing prospective clients to restaurants, bars and clubs. These men often are dressed in fancy costume; there is one in Ueno who struts about on six-foot-high stilts.

At the Bar New Salary Man in Shibuya there are nice bar girls, but as usual the one who served me just stood and stood right in front of me, watching every sip I took. I really didn't know where to look, so whiled away the time by gazing through the Japanese kaleidoscope I carry everywhere with me.

In the little cardboard barrel of the toy, with its twistable tip that makes the patterns alter, I was tranced by the sight of coloured ink-blot arrangements, an unfolding sea anemone, the swarming shapes of colours behind pressed eyeballs, the spreading damps of blue, green and mustard yellow lichens, the opening and shutting of crisp coloured fans, the hanging and lighting of paper lanterns, the casting and spreading of tiny, bright, flower-printed playing-cards on a dusty white cloth. Brief affirmations of an endlessly changing vivid variety, leaves shifting on leaves in a wet, glistening wind, water flowing and turning over scented and tinted pebbles in the sun-shot shadow of swaying willows, the endless expressions of a single mask, all the smiles of a single face, repeated to infinity—like Japan itself, like the whole of the East. This dome of many-coloured glass, a child's toy, stains the white radiance of eternity as much as 'life' does, and in fact rather more. And these stains, fortunately, are less ineradicable and ineluctable than the stains the world tries to lay upon our souls; they are like the superimposition of shades in the printing of a wood-block picture, like the mingling of pale wines, the overlapping of wistaria and lilac blossoms. This little cardboard tunnel leads into illumination. With Mr Sato's approval I have hung one in the *o-benjo*, next to his enormous magnifying glass, for speculations far from idle.

At the Bullpen Bar one of the customers sitting beside me at the counter is a boy with a nice male baby face, coping with a large, new, black pipe. He cannot get it to draw. His infant face is almost weighed over by it, like the tail wagging the dog. In all Japanese bars there is always at least one bar girl who is in top form, gossiping animatedly with a group of two or three men clients. Then they leave, and at once, if she has no new customers, she collapses like a tired rag doll, leaning her brow on the counter, beating her head with the edge of her folded hands to give herself the light relief of automassage. Then one feels the desperate boredom of a bar girl's life.

The Rikki Sports Palace with its glittering crown of neon jewels in Shibuya: the only sport I could find there was bowling, though there is also an extensive (and expensive) turkish bath (1,200 yen and up, according to the nature of the attentions you require from the pretty masseuses). In the steep little street outside, one of the commonest sights at night in Tokyo, a group of giggling hostesses pushing drunken business men into a large car with lace curtains over the rear window. At the door of another club, hostesses in kimono are bowing and giggling, seeing off helplessly drunk clients. As they stagger away one of the hostesses stands in the bright doorway for a while waving, or rather fluttering, a tiny white hand so rapidly that it is like a star twinkling. She turns away, switching off the smile to give a busy burp, and hurries inside to her next customers. A sweet, empty face, all convention and tradition, and below it all just a longing for a settled life, a home, consumer goods and babies. Sometimes the way I see into people's hearts and minds and live within their bodies quite frightens me.

At a bar curiously named 'Black Tennis' there is a bar girl with extremely long, thin, narrow eyes whose pupils sharply slide from one end of the leaf-shaped flat ovals to the other like well-oiled abacus counters. She never turns her head, but only slides her eyes from side to side in their black-fringed slots that only very occasionally blink in her thin, pale, intense, irregular face. Then it is suddenly upset by a smile, and I realize why she has been keeping her features so immobile: she has just come from the beauty parlour called 'Maliryn'. A *jolie laide*.

At the Eye Bar near Mr Sato's house, the sign is painted with a large *hitomi*, or eye. The eye is Caucasian. The bar is no bigger than a large cupboard. It match-boxes are covered with purple velvet, on which the name *Hitomi* is stamped in gold Gothic and Japanese lettering. The match-heads are white, the sticks black. The effect of this free match-box is charming in its slight depravity. The barman told me he had slept on the floor all night. He lists, for some reason, all the foreign words he knows in Japanese that are preceded by the honorific *O*: *o-toiletto*, *o-sauce*, *o-juice*, *o-cheesu*, *o-cup*, *o-matchi*, *o-tobacco*, *o-charm* (the name given to the little dishes of dried peas or beans or peanuts served with drinks).

One of the latest developments in Japanese bars and restaurants is the serving of hygienic hot or cold towels in plastic or polythene bags; these rolled and often scented towels are now mainly supplied by three big *o-shibori* companies. Formerly bars used to prepare their own, and the best bars would train their girls to hand a fresh one to a customer as soon as he came in and always after he had visited the *o-toiletto.* These polythene bags are sometimes difficult to open; one should always have a small pair of nail-scissors with one. But most Japanese now bunch up the towel in the polythene cover until a bubble is formed, and pop it with a sometimes disconcertingly loud bang. Even girls do this now, yet another sign of their regrettable 'emancipation'. Only as little as a couple of years ago no Japanese girl would do anything as immodest as making a loud noise like that.

After giving me a haircut and massage the young backstreet barber came to the door to see me off, smiling and waving to me in the rain. I was the first foreign customer he had ever had. These little backstreet barbers, however scruffy their establishments may look, are the best in Japan, and the cheapest. You will *not* get a typical Japanese haircut, with all the thrills of Japanese head and shoulder massage, at barbers' in Western-style hotels, where you are always given a regulation military clip. And a tip is expected. A real Japanese barber is never tipped.

Many elderly country people come to Tokyo for the day, visiting Tokyo Tower, the shrine of the Forty-seven Ronin at Sengakuji Temple, Ueno Park and the Kabukiza, Meigaza or Kokusai theatres. The old women carry one or two artificial flowers, red carnations, the edges of the petals dipped in glitter frost.

Skiers returning from resorts are tanned an almost blackish brown by the snow-reflected sun, eyes ringed with pale patches where their goggles have been. They always seem slightly ashamed of their blackened faces: the Japanese admire pale skins, not suntans, which are 'countrified'.

Touching, the two hooks and eyes fastening the fronts of student's stand-up collars in their black uniforms; inside, a strip of white celluloid, just peeping over the black cloth collar, gives a neat and clean appearance.

A promising newspaper small-ad says: 'Tea ceremony: learn it with an easy heart in a room facing Sumida River. But I can't speak English. Miss Harune Hayashi, 44 Ryogoku, Nihonbashi, Chuo-ku.'

The Japanese hiss (indrawn breath) before answering a question is traditional. It gives time to think, like the English 'er'. (The Japanese also use this cunctative interjection, protracting the sound into that of a creaking door in a horror film.) The Japanese 'ho!' (very short) is given on meeting someone unexpectedly, followed at once by a quick bow, sometimes performed with the additional tribute of hands placed on knees. Their long, serious 'Oh-h-h-h-h?' like a Noh-player's rising note during a chanted speech, expressing interest while listening to desultory conversation, is also very common. (It is the very sound of Japanese male gossip.) Another expression one often hears is 'Eh-to!' which means 'Let's see, now let me think a minute', and is used constantly by the Japanese, rather self-importantly, I always feel, because it usually means they know quite well the answer to the question they have been asked. The delaying tactic gives them the prestige of 'intellect' or 'considered thought'.

Outside my window, persistently staring in at me on a frankly very roughly cobbled web is a great, tigerish spider, his pop-eyes like clenched fists on thin wrists. He waves one tortoise-shell leg at me. There is something awfully familiar about him. Can I have been a spider in a previous reincarnation? It begins to look like it, and perhaps that would explain why I feel such warm sympathy for the creatures. I throw him a dead fly, but after examining it closely as if it were some inscrutable message, he deliberately disengages it from his web and casts it away. Whatever next?

When I move from my sitting-room to my bedroom, the spider moves from the sitting-room window to the bedroom window, and hangs there on a satellite web, staring in at me as I lie on the matted floor doing nothing. Then, as if to urge me to further effort, he begins scrambling round and round his very slack web, seeming, against the whitewashed wall, to swim in clumsy circles on the air. He never catches anything in his web, and indeed has made friends with a truly gigantesque daddy-long-legs that now lies spreadeagled on the ground where it suddenly flopped after doing an agitated eccentric dance round the web of the spider, who gazed at it with a mixture of admiration and consternation. It is at least six inches across. I believe it is the reincarnation of a friend, and I have named him Jumping Jack. Then one day I see the daddy-long-legs has been trampled on by some careless passer-by, and am reminded of Jules Renard's remark: 'Un ami de moins, quel soulagement!'

4

SPRING TIME IN ASAKUSA

AT A 'special show' in the Sanya area of Asakusa, a tattooed sailor was on view. The only English word he could say was 'please', and he repeated this several times as he did a kind of male strip-tease. Last of all he wriggled out of his brownish woolly belly-band as if it were a corset, and cast it professionally aside with another 'please'. I had the feeling that he was, in fact, an exhibitionist, and that he should really be paying for the privilege of showing himself off. He was certainly very eager to display his remarkable tattooing, though like many Japanese he was half ashamed of it.

But there was no need to be in his case: his designs had obviously been done by an artist. They covered his entire back, chest and thighs, except for a narrow strip of flesh running right down the centre of his chest and stomach. This type of all-over tattoo is still fairly common in Japan, and at public baths one often encounters young men who are in the process of being fitted for such an adornment, having one shoulder and upper arm completely covered, and the design for the other shoulder and arm already mapped out in blue lines of tattoo that will later be filled in with colour and shapes of flowers, carp, birds and so on. A complete tattoo is known as a 'suit of ink', and can be very expensive: many young men spend all their pocket money on these elaborate designs.

The colour on this sailor's body were a fine sugar-bag blue (a little *délavé*), black and a muted, rather orange-tinted red. It gave a lacy effect, this design, because of the scalloped edging, an intricate border of flowers, small butterflies, birds and beasts including fox cubs, spiders, lizards, carp and snakes. The whole design was beautifully interwoven with black characters. The back was completely covered by a large, splendidly composed, graceful figure of Kwannon, Goddess of Mercy in Buddhist hagiology; she wore a tiara and swirling robes and stood with lissom feet upon a sevenfold lotus flower. The buttocks were all frondescence—ferns, leaves and grasses, with a mouse appearing to peep out from between the cheeks. By flexing his back muscles, the sailor made the whole thing come to greater life, and the drapery of the Kwannon seemed to be stirring gently in a breeze from Nirvana. 'Please!' he said to us again, smiling. The thighs were covered with flowers and carp in a design which took the shape of a pair of old-fashioned culottes. There was no tattooing on the lower legs, nor on the feet, though there were small bracelets of flowers round the ankles, and on the soles of the feet crosses were tattooed, symbolizing a 'trampling' upon the sacred symbol of Christianity.

'Please!' said the sailor, lifting each foot to display his melasmic soles, that were long and narrow, shaped like slender gourds or egg-plants or like the leather tread of a ballet slipper.

The whole design was carried out in profuse detail that included many finely calligraphed Japanese and Chinese characters, one of which, I was told, stood for 'illusion'. It was all of extraordinary delicacy and, within its conventional limitations, of great originality, as satisfying to look at as a painting or a wood-block print. It must have taken years of work, and endless sittings, awful discomfort. The tattooist's signature was done on the instep of the sailor's right foot. The tone of the blue in particular was ravishing, set on the pale amber skin. There was none of the rather folksy clumsiness and jolly vulgarity of a British tar's illuminations. It was a work of calm refinement, without a trace of sentimentality, displayed to perfection on the body of a common sailor. Despite his shy good nature, I felt he was a haunted person, always seeking someone to display his gorgeous and usually veiled work of art to. (Many tattooed boys go to the public baths to display themselves as well as to wash; and they say that hot water and steam intensify the colours.) The sailor was obviously deeply conscious of the design's great aesthetic quality. He might almost have been designated by the government as an 'Intangible Cultural Treasure', except that he was all too tangible: he kept inviting us to stroke the designs. 'Please,' he kept saying: 'Please.'

But the most extraordinary thing was still to come. 'Please,' he said, and, in a final unveiling, drew back his foreskin, revealing, tattooed in two colours, a fickle butterfly on his *glans penis*. 'Symbol of Japanese male caprice,' declared our guide, smiling proudly.

I discovered a small toy shop in Asakusa which sells only Japanese toys: miniature, bright-coloured notebooks of fine rice-paper, only two inches by one inch, boxes (hinge on the right) printed with Kabuki and Noh masks, sets of 'Chinese' boxes made of gaily designed stiff paper, one inside the other, the largest as big as an apple, the smallest the size of a thimble. There were little white-tailed kites, about the size of a postage stamp, printed with a single character or with the face of a monster, a devil, a dragon. (These were miniatures of the gigantic kites flown at the great kite-flying and kite-fighting festival at Hamamatsu every May.) Tiny dolls in paper kimono, *crêpe* paper wigs, only half an inch high. Paper lanterns of all shapes and sizes from Gifu, made of finely painted rice paper on delicate bamboo hoops; the faint crackling sound they make as one unfolds them, drawing the lacquered top and bottom rings away from each other like a concertina, is a summer sound. There are fans of every kind, some no bigger than a match-box, fragrant and cool. Some large-paged notebooks, the paper scattered lightly with gold dust over designs of a few willow branches. Envelopes lithographed with misty Chinese black-and-white brush paintings. Other envelopes have a rustic texture, like dark porridge, and are made from chopped rice-straw. There are even some small garments, jackets called *haori*, made from decorated paper. Wood-shaving envelopes and writing-paper, paper pressed with real butterflies, dragonflies, moths, flowerlets and ferns. Other sheets of paper were woven from grasses and split reeds; these were to be used for decorating small wall-spaces. I bought a dwarf chest of drawers made entirely of cardboard covered neatly with several different patterns of printed paper. It has one big drawer and two small ones, and is three inches high, two inches wide. What shall I keep in them? Some tiny balls covered with fine silk thread; they are smaller than moth-balls—gleaming vermilions, greens, yellows and golds, the very colours of enchanted Tokyo this spring.

18th March: the first day of *Higan*, or spring equinoctial week, was very warm, afternoon temperature 14·4° C. But the sun went in at the end of the afternoon. This year is called 'the Year of the Rabbit' (some Japanese call it, in English at least, 'the Year of the Hare', and no one really seems to know which is correct). I went with a friend of mine who is a country boy born in the Year of the Rabbit to see the Dance of the Golden Dragon of Asakusa at the Sensôji Temple, more popularly known as the Asakusa Kwannon Temple after the Goddess of Mercy to whom the temple is dedicated. My rustic friend's first comment when we got to Asakusa, a famed amusement district, was: 'Such crowds of people! On a Monday! And playing *pachinko*! [1] In the morning!'

[1] *Pachinko*: a very popular Japanese pin-ball game.

The pink plastic cherry blossom was out all the way along Naka-mise, a long street of picturesque small shops selling every conceivable kind of souvenir as well as clothes, kimono, goldfish, shoes, sweets and food. We entered by the Nitem-mon or East Gate, an impressive structure which, together with the Asakusa shrine, was spared during the fierce fires that raged in this area during the war. Another fine wooden gate is at the other end of Naka-mise; it is hung with a huge lantern about twenty feet high, red and black, and is the subject of many a coloured wood-block picture.

There are swarms of pigeons. Sometimes in the compound of the temple it is difficult to walk without treading on one, for people throw them boiled beans that can be purchased at some of the small stalls near Bentenyama, the site of the pagoda. Near here is the belfry of Asakusa, often referred to in Japanese lyrics, and as celebrated as the one in Ueno Park. Right next to Rokku, or the amusement quarter, is the landscape lake-garden of the Dembôin Temple, created in the seventeenth century by Kobori Enshû, one of Japan's landscape gardener geniuses and also a master of the tea ceremony. Unfortunately the garden is not open to the public, but one can obtain glimpses of it from the precincts of Asakusa Park. In it we saw some *higan-zakura* (spring equinox cherry); the blossoms had just fallen on the ground under the naked tree.

We strolled with the dense crowds along Naka-mise and then back again towards the temple. The large crowds were composed mainly of country people in their best kimono. Sometimes an old lady, looking towards the shrine as she advanced, would be muttering prayers and rubbing her Buddhist rosary of well-worn brown beads. The married matrons from the country, fuzzy coiffed, have sometimes an awfully stuffy, frowsty look. One senses a limited life of kitchen and *kotatsu* gossip in some narrow-minded village, where the constant preoccupations are food and marriage arrangements. The rosy-cheeked countrymen, on the other hand, whether young or old, have a gaiety and swagger that can only be seen in Asakusa, which to them is Tokyo and their home ground for holidays of a day or two. Near the gate a blind beggar man in white clothes was praying, chanting in a singularly beautiful voice. My country friend remarked on the loveliness of the blind man's Japanese, and assumed that he must originally have come from Kyushu.

On our way back along Naka-mise we came to an open space to the left of the street, between a big stone inscribed in minuscule characters and a large metal statue of Kwannon. Here there was a crowd of men in *happi* coats, blue *tenugui* or cotton towels knotted round their heads. They were standing round their great gilded dragon which was at rest on ten six-foot-high poles. It was about thirty feet long, its serpentine back all glittering golden scales, its underbelly striped pink and white; it had a white beard and tufts of white hair round the mouth and the huge horns; the mouth was wide and red, with sharp fangs. It was a beautiful piece of folk art, a splendid beast reminiscent of the best Chinese dragons I had seen in Singapore or Hong Kong or Macao.

Near by stood a small canopied cart which I was to see again later, during the procession. About twenty small boys, also in *happi* coats, and carrying sprigs of pine, were lined up for the procession.

There was a long wait, as always at these affairs, but the little boys were very well behaved and stood patiently in the sunlight waiting for the show to begin. One of the men, a dragon carrier, saw my camera and came over to my friend and me and started to make conversation with us. He said he was one of the dragon dancers and that this dragon dance was the only one of its kind in Japan. (This is not strictly correct, as there are dragon dances at the Minato Matsuri, or Port Festival, in Nagasaki, at Juzaimachi and in Iwate Prefecture in northern Tohoku, though with different kinds of dragon.) He asked me the meaning of my C.N.D. badge and where I hailed from, hearing of England with the utmost delight. He introduced me to another young man, 'my greatest friend', who was indeed very large and broad and who was the 'head man', carrying the heavy, gilded dragon head in the procession and in the first part of the dance. They insisted on having their photo taken with me. They were absolutely natural, delightful people; and indeed among all the Tokyo people the only ones I really like are the residents of Asakusa. The people of Asakusa still retain much of the ancient traditional attitudes of old Japan, and speak its language. They are direct and friendly in a way that the somewhat effete students and residents of areas like Shinjuku and Shibuya can never be. Even Sanya, a flophouse district in Asakusa, though often horrifying in its spectacles of drunks and poverty-stricken, diseased workers, is an area where I often encountered strangers, who, though wild and sometimes alarming, never did me any harm and rather showed me the utmost affection, dragging me off to their own little bars and cinemas and into the dismal flophouses themselves, where they would show me the sad relics of their youth and of a degenerate past. One should really go accompanied, I suppose, but I never did, for often I simply found myself there by accident. And when I go to Asakusa, I never carry more than a few hundred yen on my person, and wear my most ordinary and unobtrusive clothes. Two of the most interesting places in much-abused Sanya are 'Dumpling Alley', where one can buy a bowl of hot dumplings in a sort of soup for only thirty yen, and 'The Ten-Yen Market', which is open every day, including Sundays, in Tamahine Park. Here one can buy old boots and shoes; broken electric fittings; second-hand underwear; wonderful old baggy workmen's breeches, *jikatabi*; bits of furniture made from old packing cases; and a host of other fascinating items, for only a few yen. For a few packets of American cigarettes one can buy an entire working man's outfit, from *fundoshi* (breech-clout) to broad, worn leather belt with big brass buckle.

There are street performers everywhere, both amateur and professional, and wandering girls who give their services for as little as twenty yen. A familiar busker in Sanya is a ragged pantalooned figure nicknamed Sanya-no-Kantara, who for a few yen will do a very unsteady folk-dance and strum an unrecognizable tune on his toy ukelele. One of the workmen I met in Sanya had been unemployed for months and had managed to live by gambling in the streets; he took me to a decrepit, noisy doss-house—a scene reminiscent of Gogol's *Lower Depths*—where we rented, not a bed or a bunk, but a space cleared on the floor between scores of other sleepers, for a hundred yen. (I was overcharged.) Another interesting spot is an 'avec' hotel, for males only.

Our friends of the dragon told us that the procession would not be starting for another half-hour, so after shaking hands (with *all* the men and *all* the little boys, a ceremony that took some time) we bowed and went to the shrine where, at the enormous, fuming bronze brazier in front of the temple steps, we took handfuls of incense smoke and 'bathed' our heads, necks and shoulders with it. The incense is supposed to preserve one from sickness during the coming year. A mother was rubbing handfuls of the smoke on the head of her delightedly smiling little boy, who wasn't big enough to reach the bowl. Women were wafting incense discreetly into their cleavages and down the backs of their necks, where the kimono collar dips so gracefully.

Inside the temple the altar was gorgeously decorated and illuminated with great masses of small, thin candles, which were constantly being renewed by priests and worshippers. In front of the gilded figure of the

Goddess of Mercy stood piles and pyramids of pastel-tinted rice-cakes, and oranges and apples.

Gagaku, an ancient kind of Japanese music with Chinese origins, and mostly played on gong, drums large and small and a sort of plaintive hoarse flute (*fue*), was being performed by a group of priests. Two shrine maidens in yellow robes and wearing brilliantly conceived costumes, representing the formalized wings and tails of birds, were doing a slow, very undemanding dance—that is how it appeared—clashing from time to time the small cymbals held in either hand. It was all deliciously mysterious and abstruse. People in the crowd were throwing coins through the railings at them.

We went down into the compound again and saw the arrival of the abbot, walking at the head of the procession to the temple and followed by many retainers in medieval dress and a number of 'company men', looking rather embarrassed in *happi* coats worn over baggy office suitings.

The canopied cart was also in the procession, drawn by young men in white *fundoshi* and blue *happi* coats and blue-and-white cotton towels knotted round their heads. In the cart sat six lovely young ladies in kimono and lacquered wigs, three of them playing the *shamisen* and the other three playing what looked like and sounded like piccolos. Then came the little boys, solemn and charming, taking slow paces which they tried to make as long and manly as possible.

Then came a band of two dozen very old ladies in kimono, chanting faintly, giggling a little and striking small brass images with tiny hammers.

Finally, the dragon, curvetting and caprioling, twisting, prancing, rearing and diving, snapping and biting high on the black six-foot poles. Sometimed it writhed shudderingly downwards, seeming to snake along the ground, then as it rose, snarling and worrying at imaginary fleas in its flanks of gold, the heavy padded gold-brocaded tail would slap at the air. The end man had to work very hard to control it.

The pleasant man who had asked to have his picture taken with me was walking in front carrying a gilded lotus flower at the end of a six-foot black-lacquered pole. The dragon, later in the dance, endeavoured unsuccessfully to snap at this.

In the courtyard in front of the steps the procession forms a big ring, and the mild, bespectacled abbot gives his yearly explanation of how Kwannon came down from heaven, accompanied by her guardian dragon, and founded her temple. (It is said that a tiny golden image of Kwannon was found in their nets by three fishermen who founded the temple to enshrine it in the seventh century. Another legend has it that the golden dragon once lived on a hill behind the Sensôji Temple.)

Then, after proceeding round the temple, the men performed the writhing and twisting dragon dance to the shrill, strangulated music of *shamisen* (a stringed instrument), flute and voice. The tail flapped and scales rattled most realistically. The same festival is also celebrated here on 18th October.

A little sideshow: a *bonze* doing tricks, balancing rocks, apparently defying all laws of equilibrium, on 'cider' (lemonade) bottle necks, on the ends of bamboo sticks which actually leaned under the weight but did not fall. He put some sort of spell on one of the rocks so that, though he could lift it easily in one hand, no one else could. He gave a long speech about the Year of the Rabbit, and said that March of that year was a month most favoured by good fortune, and proved this by saying that the managing director of the Fuji Bank (success symbol) had been born in March in the Year of the Rabbit.

Then the sun suddenly went in as the dragon departed; a chill wind sprang up and flapped the temple's purple-and-white ceremonial draperies; it grew dark. We ran to the nearest coffee shop through a shower of hail, passing, I noticed for a fraction of a second, an advertisement for a brand of milk called 'Homo'. Later we went to the big public bath in Asakusa, where after getting warm in the hot water we sat in *yukata*, or cotton bath-robes, on the *tatami* floor of a small theatre, drank hot rice wine and listened to the performance of Japanese folk-songs and dances in which everyone joined.

I went to a famous Tokyo plastic surgeon, and asked whether he could give my eyes the slanting Japanese look. (Daily he converts scores of Japanese men's and women's eyes into wide Caucasian features.) He advised me not to try, though he said it was possible by the insertion of tiny foam-rubber pads under the upper lids. He told me it would be almost impossible to re-convert my Nipponized eyes back to Caucasian ones. I was disappointed. I have to make do with a pair of dark brown contact lenses which I sometimes wear with a black nylon 'shoe-brush' wig. Then, when I have stained my eyebrows with boot polish, I tell myself I am almost Japanese. I usually adopt this disguise when visiting 'avec' hotels, or restaurants which are 'for Japanese only'.

I undertook these changes in my appearance because of a nasty shock I received one day. After a late breakfast of Kirin beer and nougat, I was proceeding in an agreeably intoxicated state of numbed euphoria into Nihonbashi underground station. Every piece of mosaic on Taro Okamoto's coloured walls seemed to stand out with a new and startling clarity, and the thirty-yen ticket machine, blue as a sailor's collar, delivered my cool ticket with an almost musical note. I suddenly found myself in a twisty maze of people all walking in the wrong directions: I was floating past a wall covered entirely by vast, undulating mirrors like the distorting mirrors at a fun fair. I glimpsed the reflection of a strange Westerner in a dark blue slimline suit plunging and swimming, with gestures of infinite apology, under a mane of wild golden hair and with a lopsided smile on his upset face, towards the tender guardians of the ticket barrier. I turned, trying to get a better look at this shimmering eccentric, and to my consternation discovered that it was myself. The ticket clipper clipped my ticket with a sound like a snap of shark's teeth, clipping a T-shape also out of the long nail of my little finger, which I had been cultivating for months as a sign of leisured distinction.

On my ticket I engraved the poem:

In public mirrors
One is never oneself.

It was one of those mornings when the blue serge thighs of ticket clippers are snowed with spring ticket clippings, as with fallen plum blossom.

PART FOUR

SUMMER

I

KŌYASAN: LIFE IN A MOUNTAIN MONASTERY

I AM writing the notes on my trip to Kōyasan in a *kyo-hon*, or Buddha-book, the sort of notebook one buys at every Buddhist temple; it consists of two hard covers about four inches by seven, and in between these covers is a single length of paper, about a yard long, folded to make the leaves. Pilgrims use this kind of notebook for collecting the stamps and great vermilion seals of the temples they visit, often with finely written messages from the priests, who also use them for writing down the sutras. They are plain, pretty and useful, and I often use them for my writing. The paper is thick, soft and slightly rough, suitable for brush and black ink rather than pencils or ball-points. Fortunately I have with me my Japanese fountain-pen with a plump little brush instead of a nib.

The journey from Wakayama to the remote mountains of Kōyasan was long, tedious and uncomfortable in the packed, slow, local train. (I had made a mistake and got on the wrong train; I should have ridden on one of the daily expresses, but I didn't know, and no one at Wakayama station thought to tell me, that my ticket was for an express train. In a way, I was happier to be going by this endlessly slow and stoppy train: it made it more like a real pilgrimage.)

The journey became more interesting after Hashimoto, where I had to change trains. (I changed to the wrong train, and just discovered my mistake in time, or I would have been on the way to Osaka.) There was a long wait at the little country station of Hashimoto. But there was iced beer in the station kiosk's cooler. I had one can and a packet of salted peanuts and chewed some peppery rice-crackers wrapped in seaweed paper. Already I was beginning to feel quite ascetic and monkish. I had bought a Buddhist rosary of dark brown beads with a purple tassel, and spent a quarter of an hour or so practising rubbing it between my palms, as Buddhist priests do. Next to the sensation of grinding a cake of Chinese ink on a wet inkstone, that of rubbing a Buddhist rosary between the palms is one of the most soothing experiences one can have, and it does drive out devils and calls the good spirits around one.

My blissful abandonment to self-purification was rudely interrupted, on the stroke of noon, by the wheezy notes of an electric organ grinding out, very leisurely, a full peal of Westminster chimes from the roof of some public building in the little town. It seemed slightly odd, in this remote place, to hear the notes of Big Ben played as if by a broken-bellowed, rusty concertina. Then several sirens went off at rapid intervals, alarm bells rang and somewhere in the distance the sound of a gong came vibrating through the mist. For at least five minutes there was perfect bedlam; then, just as suddenly as it had started, the racket stopped, and Hashimoto relapsed into its customary country stillness.

The journey from Hashimoto to Kōyasan is one which takes the traveller into the very heart of the mountains, and into the heart of Japan. The mountains grow higher and higher as the little train winds its way slowly upwards for over an hour. The mists thicken, then clear to give thrilling views of long, deep, narrow valleys, in which the mountains seemed, as in a Chinese ink-painting, to be ranged flatly behind one another, in gradually lightening shades of grey, until they soared into the distant whiteness of infinity. By the railway line grew wild flowers including a sort of white Canterbury bell, borage, gentian and starry rafts of cow parsley.

The outlines of the steep slopes were furred with dense timber, and sometimes a far-off white waterfall would shine forth, splitting the misted greyness of its cloud-topped cliff like a thin, still crack of supernatural daylight between precipices. One waterfall was spread like a bridal veil of loose lace over black downpours of rock. The wild flowers grey among lush grasses in which from time to time I saw small birds like yellow-hammers. During a long halt I observed a golden-white butterfly alight on the rose pink flower of a feathery, grey-green, very spiky thistle. It fanned the air gently with its wings, as if enjoying the flower's sweetness, and calling to two other butterflies fluttering near by to come and share its pleasure. They did, and it was lovely to see the three butterflies on one flower: they added twelve white petals to it and six new stamens. How happy I was! In Japan, butterflies symbolize love.

From time to time small crowds of school children would swarm chattering on to the train, and it was amusing the way the chatter would always stop for a moment when they became aware of a foreigner watching them. There would be some hesitant smiles and whispers of *aoi* (blue) when they talked about my eyes. They all had big yellow plastic school satchels on their backs, from which a railway pass dangled on a length of black or white tape. The girls were all in summer frocks, neatly pleated and prettily designed. They looked cool and elegant. Even the smallest boys wore long trousers. The boys were in black school uniforms, very dusty and torn and patched in places, like the clothes of young boys all over the world. They wore battered, black-peaked caps pulled low down over their dark, rough fringes of hair and black, almond eyes; on their feet were white canvas track shoes which had not been cleaned for a very long time. Most of the boys and girls seemed recently to have visited the barber, because they all had clipped fringes and pudding-basin crops to prepare them for the heat of summer. Those ten-year-olds were so full of life, so happy, they could not keep still a minute, but kept trotting up and down the carriage with its long, green-upholstered seats facing each other on either side.

Sitting opposite me was a young man with liquid black eyes like *go*, or Japanese chequers counters of shining ebony, under his feathery eyebrows; he had beautiful naked feet, strong and square-toed in plain wooden pattens with black velvet thongs, the commonest type of *geta*. His feet were so clean and brown and healthy, with their little square pink toe-nails, I could have knelt down and kissed them, but refrained, because this might have embarrassed him. Instead we exchanged occasional glances; whenever our eyes met he would part his full, pale, peony-like mouth, as if about to speak, but he never did. We were like two butterflies. It was a communion of spirits.

There was also on that train a Buddhist nun with shaven head. She wore black and white and purple robes, and was obviously on a holy pilgrimage. She had two bundles wrapped in a plain pink *furoshiki*. She had a sweet, rosy face, almost like a boy's. Indeed at first I thought she was a boy, but then something indefinable in her bearing and movements told me she was a woman.

At Hashimoto she had bought a box of *o-bento*—cold boiled rice with bits of vegetable, fish and pickles. (These are sold to train passengers by station vendors at all but the smallest stations.) With such a box one receives, entirely free, a pair of plain wooden chopsticks in a pretty paper sheath; the chopsticks are joined for about half an inch at the bottom, to prove they are new, and it is a simple matter to break them apart and elegantly rub off any loose splinters. I too had bought such a box of food, and enjoyed it very much, eating it all with hungry relish, down to the last grain of rice. I did not want my lover to have any more moles. (The Japanese have a saying that if one leaves a few grains of rice in one's bowl, one's lover will be afflicted with an equal number of moles.)

I admired the delicacy with which the nun ate her lunch, plying her chopsticks with grace in her rough, work-reddened hands. She made the act of eating into a sacrament, though not an obtrusive one. And when she had finished she wrapped the empty box and the chopsticks in the sheet of coloured paper they had been sold in, tied the lot with the paper cord and laid it neatly on the floor beside her seat. I wondered at her care and tidiness; most Japanese would just have thrown their rubbish haphazardly on the floor. I admired her calm, that seemed to glow and be irradiated by an inward happiness. Her face, rosy as a well-scrubbed boy's, shone with quiet intelligence, and I knew she was carefully taking note, in her heart and mind, of everything she saw.

She provided a telling contrast to the crowd of middle-aged, gossiping housewives who were also on the train, making a sociable pilgrimage to Mount Kōyasan. Up to quite recent times, women were not allowed on the holy mountain, but now of course in Japan women are emancipated and one sees them simply everywhere. (Not that I have anything against them: some of my best friends are women.) And there is a particularly obnoxious type of Japanese housewife who, like the Wife of Bath, loves to go on pilgrimages. Hordes of these women, trailing all the stuffy staleness of their kitchen life, infest the sacred places of Japan, once reserved for men—gaping, giggling and gossiping. I don't mind the thousands of school children on school excursions so much; but these bands of frowsty females destroy the serenity and gravity of the essentially male domain of Buddhist temples.

I arrived at Gokurakubashi and there took the cable-car to the top of the mountain. It is best, I think, to stand right at the bottom of the steep-stepped cable-car, to watch the wooded mountain slopes dropping away into mist below. A bus took me on the long winding road, through groves of immense *sugi* or Japanese cedar (cryptomeria) to the temple where I was to stay, and where I was the only guest.

It was a relief to be greeted, not by some foolish, giggling maids, all agog and full of delighted apprehension at the sight of a foreigner, but by two quiet, practical men, priests in ordinary men's working clothes, who took me along smooth, shining planks of temple corridors, past many rooms whose sliding paper screens were open on cool, reed-matted interiors where *kakemono*, or hanging scrolls of Buddhas and Bhodisattvas, hung in plain wooden alcoves, each of which contained a flower arrangement or a dwarfed tree and some antique metal pot or incense jar. Above the hanging scroll, fixed to the beam across the alcove, were oblongs of white paper with designs cut out in them: they were delicately and precisely done, something I had never seen before. When later I asked my temple guide what their meaning was, he did not know, but simply said their name was 'Accessory'. (I later discovered dyed skeleton leaves called 'Accessory' used in flower arrangements. Why will Japanese firms persist in using English words as names for their goods, often inappropriate and ill chosen?)

My room was a large one of twelve mats divided by sliding paper doors (*fusuma*) of a muted grey into two rooms of four and eight mats. The whole of the rear wall was a shallow alcove divided into two parts, the smaller part, about six feet wide, containing an old scroll of a Buddha enthroned under a blue, white and crimson baldaquin and surrounded by saints, disciples, priests, Bhodisattvas, kings, princes and demons. Upon a rustic slab of lacquered wood that stood on the raised ledge, about two feet deep, of the matted alcove, there was a simple *seiji* vase, of the utmost preciousness, with a crackled, blue-green glaze, in which were arranged, in ascending order, one vermilion carnation, one golden chrysanthemum and one onion-seed head, all displayed in some sprays of fern and a brand of dwarf maple with feathery green leaves. It was placed with careful precision to the left of the *kakemono*, and on the right a curious little red-lacquered metal table bearing two small bronze objects that I was told were incense burners. I immediately fished out of my bundle some *neri-ko* incense balls (more commonly known as *ume-gako*) of that peculiarly lovely scent known as *Chiyo-noume* (Shadow of Plum Blossom) which I had bought at the shop of all divine incenses and perfumes, the

Kyukudo at Teramachi-Anekoji in Kyoto (it has a branch in Tokyo's Ginza near the Komatsu department store). These I placed in an incense container and laid on the glowing charcoal embers of the *hibachi* or stone brazier—for here, at an altitude of nearly three thousand feet, it was briskly cool after the sweltering heat of Wakayama. The grateful odour soon filled the room and charmed my roughened sensibilities into delicious languor and content.

The other, slightly smaller part of the *tokonoma* contained two tiny cupboards with sliding doors, in which *kakemono* scrolls were kept—providing a pleasant evening's viewing later—and two shelves, on one of which was a small bronze Amida Buddha. Both this and the Buddha in the hanging scroll were distinctly Indian in style. On the floor level of this section of the *tokonoma* was a small sliding window of opaque glass with a pretty bamboo-decorated framework. The whole effect was spacious, cool, clean and light, with plain wood ceiling and beams, and walls covered with a sort of silver-grey sand. No furniture apart from the *hibachi* (brazier), a tall lacquered clothes-horse, a big, low table and four dark, square cushoins.

I knew I should be happy here, in this room looking on a small garden, pleasantly overgrown, of tiny bushes and clumps of grass and a few trees.

I was looked after by two very attentive and pleasant students from the monastery's own university; their names were Mikio and Norio, and they were studying to become priests. Norio had a pale, ascetic face, but Mikio had round, ruddy youth's cheeks, a healthy mouth and brilliantly white teeth. Except when they performed the morning service at six o'clock, they were dressed in the dark uniform worn by all Japanese students. On the day I left Mikio came with me as far as Hashimoto, wearing smart Western clothes.

I expected only vegetarian food, but what the boys served me were Japanese meals with baked fish (*yaki-sakana*), pickled vegetables and that peculiar kind of soup (*o-misu-shiro*) that smells of old leather and has a base of seaweed stock or dried bonito flakes. It was hot, more than one can say about the meals in most Japanese inns. Moreover at Kōyasan I had the most delicious boiled rice in all Japan.

The Japanese word for love is *ai*, like a cry of pain. The Shingon sect at Kōyasan, like all other Buddhist sects, considers love to be the root of fear and envy. Buddhism in Japan has two great rival centres: the Shingon headquarters at the monastery on Mount Kōya, where its esoteric philosophy and complex symbolism are taught, and the centre of the Tendai sect on Mount Hiei, near Kyoto, a sect whose beliefs are based on pantheistic realism. The Shingon sect was founded by a remarkable saint, Kôbô-Daishi (774–835), in A.D. 816. The monastery with its many temples and gardens covers twenty-four square miles, surrounded by magnificent cedars and a tree called *Koya-maki* which is peculiar to this region. Though the monastery, like all other Japanese wooden complexes of buildings, has often been ravaged by fire, about 120 temples still remain. More than a million pilgrims visit the place every year, chiefly in July and August when they make the trip to obtain a brief respite from the summer heat of the plains. At this period the poor university students are run off their feet serving as guides and seeing to the needs of all the visitors.

At least two days should be devoted to Kōyasan, in order to see all the treasures of the monastery, to appreciate its quiet, relaxed atmosphere and to attend some of the services.

I find I have not listed all the furniture in my rooms: in the smaller part of my temple suite, a doll's house full-length mirror, only about a foot high, is modestly veiled by a special silk cloth. (One often sees this covering over mirrors—and television sets—in Japanese inns and houses.)

The master of the temple, when I asked if he had any soap, at first did not understand, then cried: 'Ah! Shabon!' (The Japanese version of the French word *savon*.)

Two workmen digging the road: one wears a lime green sweat-shirt, a brilliant violet ribbed wool belly-band and tangerine corduroy breeches with dark blue *jikatabi*. The other, in olive green trousers, is wearing a white sweat-shirt with a scarlet belly-band. They are both brown and handsome.

One of the serving-boys, Mikio, brings me a wooden-beaded rosary as a 'temple present'. The temple master comes in, kneels on the other side of the table, and asks if I would like a guide for the afternoon. I say yes. After half an hour of telephone calls in his office, my guide arrives, rather flushed and breathless, a nice-looking young student called Hideki; he had rushed away at the end of his class in Ancient Tibetan. After coming into my room and introducing himself, he kneels on the floor; then I invite him to kneel on a flat cushion or *zobuton*; when a person does this in Japan, it is then the host's duty to tell him to sit in a more relaxed position. The Japanese always say to a foreigner, 'Please make yourself comfortable', a rather ambiguous phrase. I was so taken up with chattering to my new friend about his life, his home and relatives, his girl friend—a Buddhist priest with a girl friend!—that I forgot to tell him to 'make himself comfortable', and in the end he apologized and asked me if he might do so. He took up the position, with legs crossed and feet tucked in, known as *agura*. Another favoured position when sitting on the floor in Japan is the 'Chinese' position with the left shin flat on the ground, the right shin vertical. It is a very comfortable position. When sitting back on one's feet in the conventional kneeling position adopted at a tea ceremony or some formal occasion, a good tip is to keep 'twiddling' the big toes, just as we in England twiddle our thumbs during a sermon. The action of twiddling the big toes cannot be noticed, and keeps the blood circulating in the feet. Even so, the feet sometimes go to sleep, and this produces an ethereal sensation when one stands up; if the feet have gone to sleep, touch something, a wall or a door or something solid, and this helps one to retain one's balance on torpid toes. One just doesn't fall over—it is simply not done.

When invited out to a Japanese meal, I recommend a day-long fast beforehand. It is only when one is very hungry that one discovers the true delights of Japanese cuisine. Also, hunger enables one to face with some enthusiasm certain concoctions which, to a Western palate, may be repulsive to begin with. (Such as raw sea-urchin.)

One of the students calls my little notebook a *shu-in chō*. He brings me a present of a sprig of *sankono matsu*, or three-leaved pine, a peculiar variety also found only in Kōyasan.

In the temple, well-chilled beer or hot saké are served, and one may bring in whatever other drink one wants; I often shared some cups of Suntory whisky with Mikio, Hideki and the temple master. There is absolutely no censoriousness. It is all enchantment. One evening I was astonished, in this sanctuary of Buddhism and presumed vegetarianism, to be presented with a dish of *sukiyaki*—slices of beef cooked in a flat pan with vegetables and flavoured with soy sauce and *mirin* (a rather sweet spirit distilled from rice, and often used in Japanese savoury dishes that consequently, to a Western palate, taste too sweet).

How shall I ever describe Kōyasan—its great beauty, both spiritual and physical? There is the early morning service in my temple at six o'clock, a ceremony performed and chanted by apple-cheeked Mikio and stern-visaged Norio, both looking unusually solemn in their robes, like little boys playing some grown-up game. I am the only congregation, kneeling for half an hour, twiddling my big toes, on a piece of red cloth in front of my incense stick and pinch of sandalwood chips burning before the Buddha of Miracles, a dark gold statue in a golden niche; the offerings laid before him include a well-scrubbed carrot and a giant radish or *daikon*. It is dark; the only light comes from the two candles I have lighted for myself and one other person, and from two tall, dim bronze lanterns. I cannot see the Buddha's face, but I know he is watching me, and this gives me comfort. I love him because he accepts my imperfection. Though he watches me, it is never unkindly, but rather he watches me with amused concern; there is nothing 'knowing' in that all-knowing look, nothing *goguenard*, none of the tedious *air entendu* that I meet in 'knowing' humans.

The student priests chant together, at first with a strong rhythm, then in a more relaxed and *legato* way. One of them, Norio, from time to time picks up a pair of cymbals; he takes one in his left hand first, and wipes its inner surface with the right sleeve of his robe. Then he lifts the other cymbal in his right hand, lays the pair gently together and, at exactly the right moment, begins clashing them to the rhythm of the sutras, making the rims tingle and vibrate against one another with a very thrilling effect. When he has finished he brings them quietly together again, until they are stilled, then lays one down on either side of his knees as his chanting continues. He also sometimes strikes a charming little gong with a slim brass hammer. The note is plangent and very sweetly penetrating.

Then came the moment I had been waiting for, when the two young priests took up their rosaries from under their aprons and rubbed them vigorously between their palms for a few seconds. The rattling noise they make is a true refreshment and a cleansing of the spirit. I rubbed and rattled mine too.

The ceremony is at an end, but first sticks of incense must be borne to the garden and to the great kitchen, where the master's wife is making breakfast. (I am always astonished at the easy way Japanese priests treat their vow of celibacy. It would shock a Burmese or Thai or Vietnamese Buddhist.)

Breakfast in my room, where the *futon* have been cleared away into the built-in cupboards by fairy hands and the sliding windows opened on the garden, that seems to enter the room with its shifting green light. Fresh charcoal is in the *hibachi*, whose sand has been neatly raked to represent waves, like a rock-garden. The first dish is soup, in a black-lacquered bowl with a lid on it; there is rice in a black lacquer box with an orange lacquer ladle. Bits of saturated pickle and egg-plant in a tiny white and brown dish, a little saucer of *sho-yu* or soy sauce, a succulent kind of extra sweet pudding in a savoury dressing, some stems of pickled ginger, dyed red, a plate of raw fish slices decorated with a little yellow vinegar-steeped button chrysanthemum (edible). A thimbleful of pistachio-coloured horseradish paste and some shredded *daikon* to mix with the soy sauce that the raw fish slices have to be dipped in, held elegantly in the chopsticks. A dish with a raw egg broken into it; I didn't quite know what to do with this—I think it was for some other course which somehow never materialized—so I slipped it into the soup. An unpeeled banana cut in half, on the slant, each cut surface dipped in strong salt solution. Some segments of peeled apple which also taste as if they had been dipped in salted water. Pale green tea in a little blue-and-white cup without a handle. An exquisite little terrine whose lid, when lifted, reveals the innocent wonder of a baked egg. Two hard-boiled plover's eggs, small and speckled. All served on a big black lacquer tray from which everything is unloaded one thing at a time on to my low table.

The meal is enchanting, both to the eye and to the curious palate, that palate for rare and delicate flavours that is one of Japan's most precious gifts to me. While Mikio is making a new flower arrangement, I drink cup after cup of instant coffee with instant milk as I watch his broad country boy's hands at work on the flowers. There is nothing instant about flower arrangement, however simple and empty the result may look. Indeed the 'emptier' it looks the better. Again he makes a variation with three flowers—it must always be an odd number—a bronze button chrysanthemun, a white carnation and a frail pink, late camellia, all leaning back in a handful of coarse grass that Mikio suddenly picks after jumping out of the window. He is in again in a moment, wrapping the grass with a bit of old raffia, and affirming it on the rosette of spikes in the shallow black bowl he has chosen for today's arrangement.

He bows and goes, taking away my breakfast things on the tray. The next I hear of him, he is out in the corridor with Norio, sweeping the broad, shining planks with a wide, wet mop they push in front of them with much gaiety.

My happiness is complete as I wander on the wooded heights above the temples, watching their tilting roofs and the pagoda roof of the Kompon Daito appearing to float in troughs of white mist between ranks of dark cryptomeria stacked one behind the other, in Chinese perspective, like wings of a great natural theatre opening across the valley to reveal the dark bulk of soaring mountains, also floating on mist.

On my return to the temple, I sit on the reed-matted floor by the open window, doing nothing, and from time to time exchanging a smile, a few words or a cigarette with the elderly workman who is repairing, with the precision and skill only the old Japanese carpenters know now, a screen in a building across the garden. Gentle mist rests on rocks, trees, flowers, grasses; then a brief, heavy shower that dances like swarms of white sparks on the roof tiles. On the glowing charcoal of the brazier my iron kettle is softly singing, and there is a peace so utterly complete that I am able to forget myself. I realize only now that during the morning service my mind had been elsewhere. I don't know how I managed to notice so much, for my spirit was out of my body; or perhaps it was my body that had gone away, leaving only the eye of the spirit.

I took a walk on high, tottery *geta*—I was wearing the temple's guest-kimono and *haori*, much too short for me, I did look a clip—round the pond in the little garden. At this altitude of three thousand feet the trees are later blossoming, and now the salmon-pink azaleas are only just beginning to come into bloom. The grassy slopes round the pond are planted with carefully placed rocks and stones that are supposed to represent gothic 'crags' in a wild landscape. Across the level bits of lawn, a few flat stepping-stones. Another garden with beautifully placed stones is that of the Sainan-in on Mount Kōya. Here the stones stand round a pool, and their reflections in it are most releasing to the imagination: they look like hanging scrolls of submerged mountains. A number of stones are also set in the lake, giving an effect of natural island formations or rocky archipelagos. Each rock is a different shape and height, and each rock has its own character, but they all blend to create a perfect feeling of simplicity, an unstrained emptiness. In the Heian period, garden architects submitted to long and severe training in the correct placing of stones. In the Kamakura period, and even later, Zen priests had the art of arranging rocks in appropriate places included in their strict Zen discipline. The stone arrangements in the Saihoji Garden (or Moss Garden) in Kyoto is an example of the Heian period training, while those of the Ryoanji and Daisen-in gardens represent Zen efforts to illustrate perfection or the absolute. (The Ryoanji Garden has a replica now in the Brooklyn Botanical Gardens, New York, constructed from stones sent from Japan; but Japanese people who know

Ryoanji are puzzled by the garden: it is not quite right. The stones have been set the wrong way round.)

A lunch of baked salmon, with a rustic salad of mushrooms, carrots, parsley and green peppers. Followed by two sweet, ripe loquats in a delectable sour green syrup and some candied ginger.

In the afternoon I loll about, sleep or walk round the temples. At night, after clearing away the evening meal, the boys lay my *futon* —they put down two end to end because my legs are so long—and one small, hard pillow, apparently stuffed with rice husks, on the sedge-matted floor. The only bad thing in this room is an ugly fluorescent lamp overhead. It is good not to be able to notice such things, but why have them at all, when there are perfectly lovely Japanese lamps? Neon in the streets at night is pretty, but strip lighting is the curse of Japanese houses, bars and restaurants. I will never enter a place that has such lighting. I prefer something quieter and less cold, less insanely efficient.

There are even sodium-vapour lamps lending an unearthly glow to the enormous forest cemetery of 300,000 graves surrounding the tomb of Kôbô-Daishi. Most of the graves are marked by a *tonosama*, a kind of obelisk composed of a cube, a sphere, a truncated pyramid, a flat cylinder and topped with a stone almost fig shaped or pear shaped. These shapes represent the five elements: earth, water, fire, wind and sky. Other tombs are marked by stones cut to represent the spires of pagodas, while the seventeenth-century poet Bashō's monument (he is not buried here) is a fine smooth rock carved with choice characters. There are many *jizu* deities in stone, both big and small, with red or pink or white bibs. Some of them have a few flowers placed before them.

Many famous historical persons are buried or commemorated here, the foremost being Kôbô-Daishi himself, the founder of the Shingon Sect and the builder of Kōyasan. Hideyoshi Toyotomi is also resting here, with members of his family; and here too we can see the *tonosama* of his great enemy, Mitsuhide Akechi, defeated and slain by Hideyoshi after murdering Oda Nobunaga, his lord, at the Honnôji Temple in Kyoto.

Many film stars, writers and actors, the latter including the first Ichikawa Danjuro, the founder of the great Kabuki acting family, lie here. There is also, inexplicably, the grave of the National Electric Company (N.E.C.) whose neon signs and advertisements dazzle one everywhere in Japan. Perhaps the tomb is just another business prestige touch.

One man has had built for himself a grave whose two stones are shaped like saké bottles. My guide, Hideki, remarks: 'That man very much loved saké, it is said.' 'Oh, yes?' 'It is said,' he repeats, gravely conscious of his worth as the conveyor of new but unverified information. The Japanese love this English phrase, which is a direct translation of a Japanese construction.

There are a number of cripples in white garments begging along the first section of the path through the graveyard, but there is no pestering. Poor Hideki seems rather embarrassed by them and we do not mention them. We also pass an occasional pilgrim monk in white summer robes and bowl-shaped sedge hat, a small bundle containing his few belongings on his back, a tall bamboo staff in his hand. Their faces and hands and straw-sandalled feet are tanned a dark brown with their wanderings round the holy places of Shikoku and the Kii Peninsula.

The dusky beauty, at twilight, of the candle-lit shrine where continuous prayers are said for the souls of the dead. People are also pouring water over a row of *mizukaki jizo*, or water-deities, whose statues are clad in bright pinafores and have handfuls of wild flowers before them. At a bridge over the Tamagawa River prayers inscribed on wood or wood shavings have been hung across the water from bank to bank, just dipping in the water. These prayers are considered to be spoken to Buddha every time they are stirred by the swiftly flowing stream. They are prayers for dead infants.

The mausoleum of Kôbô-Daishi is almost invisible: only the mossy roof can be seen, and some gilded lotuses within the stone fence. All around the mausoleum are some of the mightiest cedars in the land—immensely tall and broad-based, and straight as factory stacks. Some are charred from a recent outbreak of fire. A gnome-like little priest in white comes up to us and talks about them. There is in them something infinitely reassuring; they make one feel, as few things do nowadays, that the earth is good, to have borne such splendid giants. For a long time we stood there, as night fell, watching the waters of the river under the shade of those great trees.

The town of Kōyasan possesses, with Buddha-like all-inclusiveness, a coffee shop, a cinema and a *pachinko* (pin-ball) parlour. But still, thank goodness, no golf-course, no bowling alley, no night-clubs, though there is the *terebi* (television) in some of the houses. I notice no television aerials on the roofs of the temples, whose ridged roofs are provided instead with huge vats of water for fire-fighting emergencies should the thatch catch fire. But all temples are on the telephone. The quaint horse-drawn buses, called *basha*, reminded me of the one I rode in at Hiraizumi over two years before. They are an agreeable mode of transport from temple to temple.

The temples themselves, and the great complex of large buildings round the vermilion pagoda called the Kompon Daito, with its gorgeous orange interior and brilliantly painted walls and pillars, are marvels of construction. Wood has everywhere been used with a degree of understanding and artistry that has taken over a thousand years to form. The thick-thatched roofs are made of cedar-wood bark, compressed and beautifully trimmed at the eaves. There is also much paper and bamboo, as well as acres of sedge matting or *tatami*, and naturally it is all highly inflammable. Many of the buildings have been on fire time and again. There is also a certain amount of fire-fighting equipment, including white hoses with wicker baskets attached to the intake end, so that no weeds or precious carp are sucked up from the ponds when water is being drawn off to fight a fire.

The fine museum, or *reihokan*, with its priceless national treasures—ancient scrolls, paintings, letters and sculptures—is almost impossible to depict in words. There is a considerable Indian influence on much of the work, especially the paintings and the Amida Buddha statues. Indeed one of the most ancient paintings, on sheepskin, is called, with typical Japanese rhotacism, *Nepal Mandra* (mandala). The mandala motif, which Jung found so significant in art and dreams, and that is a feature of much of the art of primitives, children and the mentally ill, is seen again and again in the scrolls and paintings, some of which are extremely large and alive with thousands of tiny details.

The students are so eager to help and explain, though their poor command of English must make guide-work very fatiguing for them. They take great pains, even writing out certain explanations for me in both Japanese and English. Unfortunately one student with a foreigner slowly gathers a large crowd of the student's friends, none of whom speak a word of English, and one finds one is doing the town in a crowd of students, so that eventually when we have to go somewhere by taxi, three taxis have to be hired to accommodate all my guide's 'dearest friends'. I had arranged to go for a scenic drive along the splendid new motor highway that encircles the mountain, but when the time came I found that my guide had brought along four of his 'greatest friends', and I went back to my room with the excuse that I had to do some work. I am afraid I caused the poor boy to lose face with his expectant friends whom he had invited, without asking me, for a pleasure jaunt.

I was curious to learn the students' views on the celibacy of the Buddhist priesthood, for all these gay, strapping youths are studying to be priests at Kōya University (400 students, including only three girls). But all the students have girl friends or fiancées; one of them wears his girl friend's wrist-watch, which she exchanged for his as a token of fidelity. Others sport one finger-nail covered with the girl friend's nail varnish, a common method used by impecunious Japanese young people to plight their troth. None of them will be able to marry very young, because they have no money. Perhaps the Shingon sect is one that permits marriage: it is all very improper.

The Buddhist rosary they have given me has thirty beads, of which two are glass, and there is one wooden bead, larger than the rest, to which a brown silken cord loop is attached by a pale brown bone or plastic little bell shape. The beads are threaded on thick white cotton cord. At first the rosary was so new, it was just like a stiff circlet of beads, but with my constant rubbing of it between my palms it has stretched a little and relaxed. A stiff rosary is the sign of a not very devout person: a slack rosary, well polished by the sweat of the palms, indicates a good Buddhist who says the sutras every day. But it seems to me all Buddhists are good: the priests and student priests I met at Kōyasan were so obviously pure in heart.

The Japanese are the world's most terrible mockers. Once they find in you what they consider to be a subject of derision, their scorn is heart-rending. Many Japanese commit suicide because of ill-natured criticism or scornful gossip. It is something one has to suffer in silence. And usually even the worst Japanese mockers, when they see they are going too far, temper their scorn and show almost affection for the despised victim. It is a cat and mouse game.

In the deep silence of nights on Mount Kōya a thunderstorm suddenly breaks out. It lights whole windows of sliding paper with blue and white flashes. The rain dropping from the thatched eaves sounds like the expected footsteps of a longed-for friend who never arrives. I look at scrolls and picture postcards of Kōyasan. The latter describe the mountain as the 'Holy Ground' or 'Holy Land' of Kōyasan. Mikio came in to ask if I was frightened. I said yes, I couldn't sleep. He gave me a massage of such length and vigour that even before it was over I had fallen into a sound, health-giving sleep.

One of my last sights of Mikio and Norio: on their hands and knees, cheerfully pushing large damp cloths before them along the shining wooden boards of the corridors.

Then the master of the temple came to my room and respectfully presented his bill for beer, wine, one extra lunch and service: just under two thousand yen, in addition to the three thousand five hundred which is the value of my J.T.B. hotel coupon. I put the money in an envelope and handed it to him with a small bottle of Suntory whisky. Later he came again and gave me, in exchange for my present, another rosary, of lighter brown wooden beads, and a pair of chopsticks, both male size, of orange and black lacquer. I could hardly contain my tears, and indeed did not when he had bowed and gone.

Before I leave, the master, using his self-timer on a tripod camera takes a picture of Mikio, Norio, himself and me. It was very strange: three times the self-timing mechanism failed to work. Mikio puts his arm firmly round my waist. I lay tentatively my left hand on his right shoulder, then shift it to his left, in a gesture of friendship. The master said he would send me a copy of the photograph, but he never did, so it must not have come out.

Mikio's final words, with his frank handshake and jolly, rosy-cheeked smile, were, 'Be sure to come back.' Then he added: 'Without fail.' The latter phrase was perhaps one he had just swotted up from his dictionary, and he was proud to have remembered it and used it correctly. I was deeply touched.

2

A TRIP AROUND LAKE BIWA

THE LARGEST fresh-water lake in Japan is Lake Biwa, which can be reached from Kyoto in about one hour by train or by car along the National Highway Number One. Kyoto itself is now only about three hours' ride by the super-express train Hikari from Tokyo.

Lake Biwa has the famous 'Eight Views' which, in accordance with ancient Chinese landscape-viewing conventions, were selected as being the most beautiful. These classical eight views are: Evening Snow on Mount Hira, Flight of Wild Geese at Katada, Night Rain at Karasaki, Evening Bell at the Miidera Temple, Sunshine with a Breeze at Awazu, Evening Glow at Seta, Autumn Moon at Ishiyama and Sails Returning to Yabase. These are the eight 'ideal' views and, as you may well imagine, it is difficult to enjoy them all at the right time and under the right climatic conditions all in one day! Also many other places round Lake Biwa claim to be part of the Eight Views.

A good way to visit these Eight Views, or some of them, is to take the free daily bus from the Kyoto Hotel to the Mount Hiei Hotel for an excellent lunch with a splendid view. This trip takes only about thirty minutes, and after lunch another thirty minutes' ride brings you down to Hama-Ohtsu, the pretty little port at the head of the lake.

There are three interesting places near or in Hama-Ohtsu: if you want to visit them you had better take a morning train from Kyoto and, after viewing the three sites, lunch at the fine new Aquarium right on the shore of the lake at Hama-Ohtsu before embarking on your boat trip round Lake Biwa. The three places you should see before that are the vast, beautiful compound of the Miidera Temple; the grave of the *haiku* poet Basho in the small temple called Gichuji, east of the station; and the grave of the great American oriental scholar Ernest Fenollosa at Homyo-in Temple, a few minutes' drive beyond Miidera.[1] It is best to hire a taxi to visit these three places; some climbing of

[1] See my *Paper Windows* (Dent).

steep paths and long flights of stone steps is required, so you should reckon on at least two hours to view these three celebrated spots at Hama-chtsu.

The Miidera Temple's evening bell, with its plangent, mellow note, is famous in Japanese literature: you may strike it yourself, not just at evening but at any time of the day, on payment of the small sum of twenty yen.

After lunch you can choose one of the several trips round Lake Biwa on one of the pleasant steamers of the Biwako Kisen line. The longest excursions, taking in all or most of the beauty-spots, last from five to seven hours, but you may take trips as short as one hour which include certain of the attractions at the southern end of the lake. The Eight Views are all situated at this end. However, the northern end of the lake is the more beautiful, wilder and stranger, with its tiny, fantastic islands, rocky cliffs and the charming castle town of Hikone.

My own trip, which lasted all day, took me by train from Kyoto on a ride lasting just over one hour to this ancient town of Hikone. The main attraction here is the white-walled donjon, surrounded by four watch-towers and built 360 years ago, which is all that remains of the ancient castle. It stands on a wooded hill, and from the third floor of the donjon you can enjoy splendid views of Lake Biwa, the little islands and the mountain skyline on the opposite shore. The castle was the stronghold of the Ii family, feudal lords of the Hikone district. The most famous member of this family was Naosuke Ii, a progressive man who was largely instrumental in opening Japan to Western influences, to foreign trade and friendship. You take off your shoes at the door and walk about the spotless floors of the castle in your stockinged feet. Do not forget to look at the remarkable open beams of the ceilings, made of twisted, natural pine trunks and branches. Most of the woodwork is original, and floors and the hand-rails of the extremely steep, almost vertical, stairs are highly polished by the shuffling feet of millions of visitors. There are some low beams on the stairs: be careful not to bump your head!

Notice the triangular or rectangular funnel-shaped apertures in the thick walls, through which rifles could be fired against attacking forces. From the top-floor windows you can see and hear many birds, including large brown hawks gliding among the crests of the tall pines; and beyond, the waters of the lake shimmer with the tiny islands of Okinoshima (good for trout fishing), Chikubujima and Takeshima.

All these islands may be visited on a short round trip from Hikone, or on one of the longer excursions from Hama-Ohtsu.

In summer at Hikone there is a cool breeze from the lake, which stirs the wind-bells, and everywhere the song of cicadas pulses through the air.

If you arrive in Hikone in the morning, visit the interesting art museum in one of the towers that contains many beautiful scrolls, screens, ornamental natural rocks and fine examples of tray-landscapes. Then you may lunch at a delightful Japanese restaurant in an old house that was once the residence of the Ii family. It is situated in one of Japan's most famous seventeenth-century landscape gardens, the peaceful Gengkyu-en, with its dreamy lake crossed by arched bridges and islanded with artfully arranged mossy stones. The style of this garden is known as *Kai-yushiki*, which means 'rambling at leisure'. I should advise you to do just that.

I would also recommend a visit to the little-known Ryotanji Temple, about five minutes by taxi from the castle moat. (Ask the driver to wait or to come back in half an hour.) The Ryotanji Temple has a rock garden like that at Ryoanji in Kyoto, only smaller, more intimate, less austere and mercifully free from tourists. At Ryotanji the stones are arranged with patches of moss in subtle groups on raked white gravel. There is a teahouse where one may enjoy the refreshing taste of the frothy green tea of the tea ceremony while gazing out at the carp-rippled pond and terraced tea bushes and rocks of the other side of the garden. The place is dedicated to the art of gardening, and in the teahouse there is a small shrine in honour of Kobori Enshu, the famous Japanese landscape gardener who created the lovely formal classical gardens of the Katsura Detached Palace in Kyoto. The gardens of Ryotanji are superbly kept and of the utmost refinement, with many examples of espaliered pine trees and other horticultural oddities that would fascinate even those who are not gardeners. But there is also great natural beauty, tranquillity and sweet country air.

It is a place for relaxation and meditation where one can be at peace for half an hour or so listening to the cool sounds of water trickling from a bamboo pipe into a leaf-shaped stone tank.

A place which you must visit is the Ishiyama Temple, situated on holy Mount Garan near the town of Otsu. One of the curious features of this impressive group of temple buildings is a large outcrop of rugged grey rocks flecked with white veins and markings that resemble scattered salt or snow. Geologists will recognize this strange formation as Wollastonite, the only example in Japan and one of the very few in all the world. In the main building, which looks out on a deep gorge planted with towering pines, is the room in which Lady Murasaki wrote, or is supposed to have written, *The Tale of Genji*. Many articles said to have belonged to the novelist are displayed in this room, and Lady Murasaki herself—a life-sized doll—presides here, brush in hand, wearing the gorgeous and complicated robes of medieval Japan. The pagoda at Ishiyama has been featured on some of Japan's postage stamps. Overlooking Lake Biwa is an open platform called 'The Moon-Viewing Pavilion', a romantic name for a romantic pastime.

Finally, I would recommend a visit to the Floating Temple, known as the Ukimido Temple. It does not actually float, but stands on piles at the edge of Lake Biwa. Excursion boats do not stop here, so if you wish to examine the structure in detail you must go by car or by the quaint little two-coach train from Hama-Ohtsu to Katada, from which station the temple lies only a few minutes by taxi. The gate of the temple is very fine, in Chinese style, with a broad stone base surmounted by an airy wooden gallery and sweeping tiled roofs overhung by ancient, leaning pines. There is a friendly priest who sells postcards and talismans, candles and incense. In the small building housing an altar, just beside the priest's lodge, is a fine statue, a Shokannon or goddess of mercy from the Heian period, an important cultural treasure. The proper name of this temple is rather formidable —Kaimonzan Mangetsuji—and it is a small, modest Zen temple belonging to the great Daitoku Temple in Kyoto. It was built for the safety of boatmen and fishermen on the lake, for whom it serves as a beacon at night, when the shrine building over the water is brilliantly floodlit. The building containing the shrine is small, but contains one thousand gilded figures associated with the main image, which is of Amida-butsu. Look at this exquisite little shrine's coffered ceiling, which is constructed of hundreds of small plain wooden compartments about one inch square. The prayer-bell here is a bronze bowl standing on the offertory-box: the bowl, struck by a leather-covered stick, produces a deep, vibrant, musical note that mingles with the lapping waters of the lake, the sound of boatmen's oars and, more prosaically, with the whisper of reeds bowing in the wake of water-skiers' motor boats.

The Floating Temple is reached by a small, narrow wooden bridge, a striking contrast to the long, sleek, modern lines of the great new Biwako Bridge that can be seen a short distance away, linking the two shores of Lake Biwa at its narrowest point: it is the largest span in Japan. However you make your trip round Lake Biwa—by car or train or bus or boat, or preferably by a combination of all four means of transport—you will find everywhere a multitude of interesting literary and historical sites. Everywhere too, despite the growing industrialization of the shores, there are views of great beauty. See the eight famous views by all means, but do not forget that there are many, many more than the traditional eight. Keep your eyes open, and you will find beautiful views at every turn.

3
SEASON OF THE DEAD

August in Japan is called *O-Bon*, the Season of the Dead. It is a time when nearly everyone, particularly those people living away from home and working in one of Japan's gigantic cities, tries to spend a few days at his birthplace, or with his parents, to burn incense and pay tribute to the spirits of his dead ancestors at the small wooden family altar found in every house, or at his local shrine or temple.

It is ironical that the Americans, probably unwittingly, chose the Season of the Dead in which to drop their atom bombs on Hiroshima and Nagasaki. On those two days of black inhumanity many Hiroshima and Nagasaki people were absent from their cities, staying with their country relatives. But there were also many strangers in the cities, not including Japanese troops and foreign prisoners. One cannot help thinking of the many freaks of destiny that were evidenced in that season of ghosts.

During this season it is very difficult to get a seat on the crowded trains of Japan's already overworked National Railways. Plane tickets are at a premium, and it is almost impossible to find hotel accommodation. Hotel rooms were particularly scarce for the casual, single visitor like myself to Hiroshima during the Peace Festival, for all hotel rooms had been booked up one full year ahead by the three main (and warring) peace organizations.

I manage to get a seat on a train to Hiroshima after queueing all night, like thousands of others, at Osaka station. We just slept on the station floor, or in the station plaza, where the Japan National Railways thoughtfully puts up open marquees in summer for the convenience of those who have to sleep out all night or wait long hours in the sweltering heat of summer. On arrival in Hiroshima I was lucky to obtain, quite by accident, a room at an expensive but, as usual, highly uncomfortable Japanese inn.

The peace movement in Japan is tragically divided. What was once a genuine peace organization started in all sincerity by altruistic

Japanese women, housewives and mothers, has degenerated into a political platform. Let me make it quite clear that I believe all political parties should have the right to express their opinions and to demonstrate their beliefs. But I think it is wrong to bring a universal peace movement into the field of political wrangling. Peace is above politics. Politics has certainly debased the peace movement in Japan. Each of the three main groups wishes to be *the* peace organization, and there is a lot of petty bickering and scrambling for prestige and publicity (completely un-pacific) which to my mind is worse than any political slant the movement may be given.

The various organizations also vie with one another in inviting to Japan the largest number of professional conference-attenders from abroad, who are taken on strictly conducted tours, say their pieces and applaud in the right places at the interminable conferences, and then are seen sitting weary and bored in the lobbies of modern hotels.

It seems to me that these conferences and those attending them (though they may rightly denounce war in Vietnam, the American bombing attacks launched from Okinawa and the visits of American nuclear-powered submarines to Japanese ports) are often out of touch with reality, out of touch with humanity and, certainly, out of touch with the spirit of peace. It is my earnest hope that one day a truly independent, non-political and international peace movement may be born in Japan.

Among the conferences called that year at Hiroshima and Nagasaki were those sponsored by the Japan Council against Atomic and Hydrogen Bombs, called *Gensuikyo*, many of whose members are convinced Communists, usually with Chinese sympathies; the Democratic Socialist National Congress against Nuclear Arms and for World Peace, called *Kakkim*; and the Japan Congress against Atomic and Hydrogen Bombs, called *Gensuikin*, affiliated with the Japan Socialist Party and General Council of Japan Trade Unions, called *Sohyo*. *Gensuikyo*, the most powerful of the rival groups, is always referred to in the English-language press as being 'Communist-dominated'. Though this may be true, I think it is an unfair description. I am not a Communist myself, but obviously Communists have a perfect right to be pacifists also, and *Gensuikyo* has many non-political pacifist supporters.

These groups were all holding conferences while I was visiting Hiroshima and Nagasaki to offer prayers, in my own peculiar way, for the repose of the spirits of the dead killed by those two atom bombs twenty years before. The common people of Hiroshima on the night of 5th August, as I strolled in the Peace Park, seemed to have no relationship at all with these conferences, whose orators' voices, in many languages followed by Japanese translations, could be heard from loudspeakers booming over the Peace Memorial in hectoring, aggressive and abusive tones, regularly interrupted by bursts of applause.

What were the ordinary people of Hiroshima doing on this eve of the twentieth anniversary of the dropping of the first atom bomb? Young couples were strolling round the Peace Park, sitting whispering under the trees, never kissing, never even holding hands, but seeming to be happy to live in a world of their own, far removed from the world of peace conferences. Children with mother and father had faces buried in beards of candy-floss; others were playing with sparkling little fireworks; many were dressed prettily and sensibly in light, brightly coloured summer cotton kimono, their bare feet in wooden pattens.

Men and women fanned themselves in the intense, humid heat with small scented paper fans. There were crowds round the Peace Memorial and the Children's Memorial. They brought bunches of wild flowers and bundles of smouldering incense to offer to the spirits of the dead, bowing formally to their memory before joining hands and lowering their heads to pray: some crouched on their haunches to pray before the mounds of simple flowers and the flaring bundles of incense, whose clouds of smoke drifted over the whole park.

A solemn Buddhist memorial service was being held in another part of the park, attended by thousands of people, young and old. Here were being sold the coloured paper lanterns—red, yellow or green—which would be lighted with candles and floated down the river in the Lantern Festival on the evening of the next day. Near by, under a concrete dome, passers-by were striking with a big, swinging, horizontal beam a huge bronze bell whose deep, reverberating notes throbbed at irregular intervals through the chanting of the priests.

The skeleton of the ruined dome of the *Genbaku*, or 'Atomic Dome', of the former Industry Promotion Hall was flooded with light against the dark summer sky where the half-moon of August swam in torn clouds, casting its reflection on the slow river. Here couples were rowing small boats under the weeping willows on the banks. A few rockets kept bursting over the Atomic Dome. In front of the museum at the other end of the park large crowds were admiring the changing shapes and colours of a magnificent ornamental fountain, called poetically Fountain of Night.

As I left the park, already a few lighted paper lanterns were drifting dreamily down the dark river. Outside, in the city hectic with neon, green again with trees, people were drinking beer in the large, lantern-hung beer gardens on the roofs of tall buildings. Up there one had a faint breeze. At a dance hall opposite the baseball stadium teenagers were doing a rather tame shake. Young Japanese people, perhaps obeying unconsciously and instinctively ancestral promptings from centuries of highly formalized culture, are too self-conscious when doing Western dances: however much they try, they just cannot let themselves go in the shake, the frug and the monkey.

The bar girls were out round the station, squatting dispiritedly outside their little shacks. There did not seem to be much more trade than usual. The *pachinko* saloons were crowded: I spent a hundred yen on a handful of balls and as usual did not win anything. The restaurants and cafés were full. I went into the Oasis Café, which appears briefly in that very overrated and false film, *Hiroshima Mon Amour*, and found it full of *Gensuikyo* members wearing the wide-brimmed straw hats—very sensible in hot weather—which the younger ones affect. One or two looked suspiciously at my C.N.D. badge, which not a soul in Hiroshima recognized, though elsewhere the Bertrand Russell Peace Movement is world famous.

There were a number of *Gensuikyo* 'bodyguards' patrolling the streets and the park near the Shin-Hiroshima Hotel. One of them stopped me and spoke a few cordial words in English, probably thinking that I was one of the foreign delegates staying at the hotel. Then he saw my C.N.D. badge, bowed and went away, explaining that he was a 'bodyguard'. I was given very searching looks by *Gensuikyo* attendants at the door when I entered the hotel and strolled about the lobby for a while among all the dejected-looking foreign delegates. As I was not wearing the oblong *Gensuikyo* badge two pleasant young bodyguards, apparently students, did not let me out of sight until I had left the hotel.

I returned to my uncomfortable *ryokan*. My room overlooked the river. I saw a touching sight on the other shore, among a cluster of small wooden houses where the red light of a police box shone on a modest and beautifully calligraphed stone memorial. The local people there were holding their own little private lantern service, away from the fuss and splendour of the one promoted in the interests of tourism as well as of peace.

I crossed the bridge to the other side of the river and joined the worshippers. The cube-shaped paper lanterns were home-made, not mass-manufactured like some of those sold in the Peace Park. Each person had written carefully, with brush and Chinese ink, a name or two and a personal message or a little prayer on a red, green or yellow lantern.

A rowing boat was tethered at the bottom of the stone steps leading down to the water. In the boat two men were lighting the small candles in the lanterns and carefully placing the wooden floats on the still water. The lanterns clustered like jewels round the humble boat: only two or three had so far begun to drift out into the slow-moving current. In the prow of the boat sat a Buddhist priest, praying and chanting. On the bank three old women squatted on their haunches, chanting and striking small metal gongs which they drew from embroidered bags, using thin, silvery hammers. A few children and their elders and a policeman looked gravely on, staring at the gathering fleet of lighted lanterns. They took no notice of me, which for a foreigner in Japan is the greatest compliment. I was simply accepted, and in my own way tried to join silently in the prayers for the repose of the souls of the dead belonging to that little community.

The next morning, in a dawn of dark pearl with gusts of white rain, a few lanterns were still clinging to the shore, symbols of the dead who still clung to earth and would return repeatedly as ghosts until their restless, outraged spirits could finally discover peace through the prayers, flowers, candles and incense offered by the living.

I was out at 7 a.m. trying to get a taxi. When I finally succeeded I got quite a shock. Unbelievable as it may seem, the young driver did not know the way to the Peace Park, nor did he know the Shin-Hiroshima Hotel. I had to guide him there myself. He was puzzled by all the crowds of people converging on the park for the memorial ceremony. When I told him about it a faint light dawned on his smiling face, and after parking his taxi he accompanied me into the park, still smiling incredulously, as if he were attending some forgotten rite.

After the wonders of the night before, the memorial ceremony was an anticlimax. With its haphazardly scattered buildings, memorials of dubious artistic quality, tents and booths selling postcards, souvenirs, beer, flowers, incense; with all the apparatus of television, films and radio and numbers of helicopters buzzing low overhead, the Peace Park was an untidy and rather pathetic sight, its dignity redeemed by the hundreds of thousands of people coming to worship and pray and unostentatiously weep at bitter memories, among dense clouds of doves and incense and the flimmer of thousands of paper fans.

The last humble tributes of incense and bunches of country flowers were made, then khaki-clad police and boy scouts of all ages cleared the worshippers away from the Peace Memorial. The guards formed a cordon round the area; sometimes a late arrival would hand a bundle of smouldering incense or a little wilting bunch of garden flowers to one of the boy scouts who would obligingly run to place it on the steps of the Peace Memorial.

The ceremony froze into dullness, with many official Japanese gentlemen, in morning dress, making speeches that no one listened to and laying big, expensive, complicated floral wreaths.

The dullness seemed to settle over the enormous crowd. When the moment of the bomb-blast came, at 8.16 a.m., everyone stood up, a siren wailed, a young man and a young woman struck a bell several times.

We stood with lowered heads, trying to remember a crime beyond ordinary human comprehension, or hoping to recall a face, the voice of a dead person, and to speak silently, to pray. But we found that even prayer was impossible, and thought unthinkable. There was nothing we could do or say. We could only stand with lowered heads, as if in shame, and wonder why our eyes were capable of tears.

I left Hiroshima on the morning after the great Peace Festival. Almost as soon as the Memorial Ceremony in the Peace Park was over a spectacular typhoon unleashed itself upon the millions of visitors to the city. Soon we were all drenched, and all the flags and banners wet through. But the weather cleared up in the evening for the very moving Lantern Floating Ceremony, during which thousands of frail red, green and yellow paper lanterns, illuminated with candles, were floated down the river by mourners. It was a most beautiful and authentic happening. None of the foreign delegates witnessed it as far as I could see: another example of how out of touch with reality, and with peace, are the people holding and attending these political rallies in the name of peace.

So I left Hiroshima with a heavy heart. I have never liked the place, but I hate to see it and its A-bomb sufferers, whose genuine desire is simply for peace and health, being exploited and troubled in this insincere and useless way.

I was lucky to get a cancelled reservation on a small plane to Fukuoka: a lovely flight over the islands of the Inland Sea and right across the tremendous new industrial complex of Kitakyushu, a giant city formed by the amalgamation of five already existing cities in the north of Kyushu. From Fukuoka I caught a jam-packed train—more people standing than sitting, as is usually the case in Japanese trains—to Nagasaki.

Nagasaki is utterly different in atmosphere from Hiroshima. In my opinion Nagasaki is the real 'Peace City' of Japan, and of the world. For one thing it is really international, with strong Christian and particularly Roman Catholic leanings. Foreigners—priests, business men, tourists, sailors, teachers—are a common sight, and always have been during the last hundred years or so. Add to this the languorous, Italianate temperament of the Kyushu people, and you get a peculiarly sympathetic and kindly environment, on a wonderful harbour, surrounded by gentle green hills covered with bamboos and pines that in summer throb with the bell-like notes of the native cicada, *Homoeogryllus japonicus*.

Compared with Nagasaki, Hiroshima is provincial and narrow. Hiroshima merely has the distinction, dubious indeed, of being the first city in the world on which an atom bomb was dropped. In a way this act of senseless destruction was the making of Hiroshima. But Nagasaki did not need to have the second atom bomb dropped on it, three days later, to be known as an important international city, immortalized by the much-neglected, much-derided works of a great literary artist, Pierre Loti, who seems to have been disowned by Nagasaki. (The only memorial to him is a modest inscribed column in the gardens of the Suwa shrine.)

The attitude of Nagasaki people towards their bomb is one of forgiveness: though they cannot forget it, and no one wants them to, there is in their memories none of the resentment and possessiveness Hiroshima people display, and are still encouraged to go on displaying by certain groups. The Peace Statue in Nagasaki, grotesque and misshapen, almost completely lacking in artistic value, is intended by the people 'as the best expression of forgiveness for the past and hope for the future'. It is all of thirty feet in height, Germanic, thick-necked, with closed eyes that give it a boozy look. Its right forefinger, uplifted to heaven, seems deliberately to be provoking the gods to send down their wrath upon the city. The tucked-in chin makes it look as if it is burping. There is a vague loop of shapeless drapery over where the genitals should be: this completes the impression of impersonality and shallowness: it lacks character, virility and artistic merit.

(Incidentally I cannot remember one building, memorial or statue commemorating the atomic disasters in Hiroshima or Nagasaki that has any artistic merit: they are all too horribly slick and grandiose. An exception is the splendid ink painting by Iri Maruki in the International Cultural Hall in Nagasaki.)

I know Nagasaki well, and like to stay there. So I was surprised and shocked, but then amused, by the first thing I saw during the Peace Festival. This was a small American forces drum and bugle band from the barracks at Sasebo—scene of the recent violently disputed visits by American nuclear submarines—playing in the crowded shopping arcades of Higashi Hama-machi. It was a grim-faced, militaristic little outfit in puce khaki, with an 'unprejudiced' percentage of 'coloured' men. They marched and counter-marched, with a baton-swinging leader, playing incomprehensible military tunes, while a plump young American in tight sky-blue pants dodged about snapping them, a fatuous grin on his perspiring face. Apparently by pre-arrangement with the Hamaya department store, clouds of coloured paper petals were dropped by giggling shop girls on the men, who kept rigid faces and never missed a step. From the windows of another store the shop girls, not to be outdone by their neighbours, were showering down torn-up lavatory rolls.

This was surely a singularly tactless demonstration of Yankee good-guyism? I was sorry for the soldiers: they were deeply embarrassed by this awful chore, and the only way they could get it over was to do it all with a military precision that in the circumstances was pitiful as well as ludicrous.

There was a large and jovial Australian-New Zealand delegation to *Gensuikyo*'s Peace Rally staying at my hotel. At other hotels there were Indonesians, Chinese, Indian and African delegates; nearly all the European nations had also sent their representatives.

On Sunday, 8th August, after a hearty breakfast eaten in the hotel dining-room in their shirt-sleeves and braces, the Australasian delegation, or part of it, went off by special bus to inspect A-bomb sufferers at the hospital. Why increase these poor people's misery by making them part of organized tours? The victims—whose welfare has been largely ignored in the most cynical way by the Japanese Government—hate these visits by delegations and tourists, but in their helplessness cannot avoid these invasions of their privacy. On its return the delegation ate a hearty lunch.

Gensuikyo's other arrangements for its foreign delegates—who seemed to mix with one another, swapping reminiscences of previous conferences, rather than with their Japanese guests—included a memorial meeting for someone called Claudia Jones, a massive, chanting lantern procession for peace (lanterns were scarce and few foreign delegates took part) and the memorial service before the Statue of Peace on the morning of 9th August when, twenty years before, the bomb fell. I was interested to note that *Gensuikyo*'s notices in English in the hotel lobby stated that participation in the memorial service was 'voluntary'. What did that mean? What else could it be but 'voluntary'? Had the other events, perhaps, not been voluntary? (Then why had so many of the delegates stayed away from them?) And why should the most important event of all, indeed the only event, be labelled in this way? I noticed that a large number of the Australasian delegation did not attend the ceremony.

I arrived in front of the Peace Statue at 9.15 a.m. A huge marquee had been erected in front of the monstrosity. In a nearby park a Japanese Roman Catholic nun was rehearsing, with admirable verve, a choir of schoolgirls in the singing of a sweet but insipid peace anthem. Behind the Peace Statue there were swarms of young men and boys who had brought their homing pigeons to be released, from gaily decorated wicker cages, at 11 a.m., the hour of the bomb. This was quite the best part of the ceremony for me—watching those eager youngsters, so proud of their pets, stroking and fondling them as they transferred them from carrying baskets to the decorated wicker cages.

A police band arrived. The marquee was already packed with people, and others were standing several rows deep round the open sides. Dignitaries began arriving, wearing hired morning dress. Priests of the Shinto and Buddhist religions and one Japanese representative of the Roman Catholic faith took their seats. The contingent of foreign delegates made an entrance and went to their special seats. One *Gensuikyo* member tried to start a round of applause, but no one joined in. He beamed at the delegates, but when he saw me, alone, wearing my C.N.D. badge, he frowned, afraid, like so many Japanese, of the unexpected, the exception to the rule.

There were numerous speeches in Japanese and a long and elaborate ceremony in which all religious representatives took part, but which to my eye was largely Shinto. It all went on right in front of the Peace Statue, which, now that its base was smothered in scores of ostentatious wreaths, increasingly made me think of Baal.

A reporter from the Nagasaki studios of N.H.K.'s Foreign News Division, Masami Nagasaki, handed me his card, printed in both English and Japanese, and asked me if I thought this peace ceremony was 'impressive' and 'meaningful'. He obviously thought I was a foreign delegate and expected me to say yes. He seemed shocked when I told him frankly that the ceremony was a travesty. He said something about it being 'quite non-political'. I told him that it was both non-political and political, and went on to say that no ceremony performed in front of an idol of such inferior artistic quality could be sincere: only the feeling in the hearts of the mourners was sincere. He bowed, alarmed but smiling, and backed away. I feel pretty sure that my opinions were not broadcast in his report.

Then I began to wonder why the ceremony was not being held at the epicentre of the atom bomb, marked by a plain stone stele in a small park. That, surely, was the appropriate place to pray on this twentieth anniversary?

It was ten minutes to eleven, just time for me to run downhill and along the main street to the park. I reached there shortly before 11 a.m. There were very few people, and most of them were snapping each other in picturesque poses round the severely simple monument, at the foot of which a handful of bunches of country flowers lay among a few sticks of burning incense. There were no television cameras here, no film units, no recording electricians, no circling planes and helicopters, no reporters.

It was here, in company with a dozen or so Japanese, that I bowed my head as the rocket, bursting at 11 a.m. while somewhere a clock chimed the hour, told us the anniversary of the fatal second had arrived.

Again I wept, without knowing why, for I was thinking of nothing. My memories were beyond thoughts, and beyond words, and I forgot to pray.

4
HORRORS OF HEAT

In the wet, hot depths of a Japanese summer even the slightly built, lightly clad Japanese suffer. It is a period that has to be endured. Summer is the most demoralizing season in Japan. The best thing to do, if one can, is simply to sit still in a matted room, clay-walled, with the *shoji* (paper windows) slid open on the shady side of a small, water-rilled stone garden sprited with green bamboos, and to do nothing. One should wear a crisp cotton *yukata*, go barefoot, carry in one's left hand an *uchiwa*, that broad, flat paper fan printed with cool summer subjects, and sit quietly listening to the refreshing tinkle of a wind-bell of glass, porcelain or rough bronze with a 'cool' poem attached to the clapper, a poem on gold or silver paper. Such a summer poem might be one of my favourites, by the Dostoevskian, anarchist, early twentieth-century Japanese poet, hero of so many students, Takuboku:

Kakure-sumu
Waga ya no niwa no
Shira-yuri no,
Mazu honomekite,
Natsu no yo akenu.

It is perfectly possible for a foreigner to read this poem in Japanese, even if he does not understand it, and appreciate the sounds of the vowels and the subtle, hesitant, yearning rhythms; one simply has to remember that all vowels are open, all vowels are pronounced: in *honomekite*, for example, there are five syllables. Also, the Japanese 'g' is usually pronounced like our 'ng' as in 'sewing'. A translation of the above poem, from Dr Hiroshi Takamine's critical biography of Takuboku, *A Sad Toy* (Tokyo News Service Ltd, Tokyo, 1962), reads as follows:

In the yard of my humble retreat
Faintly loom white lily-flowers
At an early dawn of summer.

The deep summer in Japan is a time when unaccountable, extraordinary and grisly things happen. In the newspapers we read of an inebriated young man who fell from a railway bridge but landed on the roof of a locomotive that happened to be passing below and was deposited in a hospital four stations away. The man apparently slept through the whole incident and rubbed his eyes when he woke up and found himself swathed in bandages in a hospital in Shinjuku.

At the densely packed beaches of the Shonan Coast thousands of bathers—youths in their brief 'Bôsô Peninsula' trunks, girls wearing costumes featuring what one summer was called the 'switch look'—were badly stung by jellyfish, while hundreds of bathers drowned or were injured by hordes of motor boats and water-skiers who simply sliced people in two if they did not get out of the way.

There are many accounts of high-school students committing suicide by jumping off the roofs of high buildings because they have no 'summer friends' or have failed in their examinations for admission to a university; the competition here is ferocious. There is the account of an Ibaraki boy who, only eight years old, committed suicide by poison because he had lost a fight with a playmate and could not endure the shame.

An Osaka carpenter, intoxicated, pours gasoline over himself and sets fire to his clothes, burning himself to death in a fit of pique while his family looked on. There are many cases of babies or young children being suffocated inside refrigerators or overlaid in overcrowded rooms or being crushed to death by pulling the television set over.

Many reports of accidental death or suicide in the Japanese newspapers have an unfortunately facetious tone. One, headlined 'Farmer Meets Classic End', runs:

> Farmer Togo Kikuchi, 50, died in superb style today—drinking *shochu* on the summit of Mount Fuji. Doctors attributed his death to a combination of the powerful liquor and exhaustion after climbing the 3,776-metre mountain. A veteran Mt Fuji climber, Kikuchi died after his thirty-fourth ascent of the sacred mountain.

The official climbing season for Mount Fuji opens on 1st July and lasts about seven weeks; during this period it is considered 'safe' to climb the sacred rubbish-dump, and hundreds of thousands of Japanese walk rather than climb up the winding paths on the mountain's flanks. It can hardly be called 'climbing', though many young Japanese set out for the top equipped like seasoned alpinists. All one needs, if one really *must* go, are a pair of stout shoes, a pilgrim's staff (bought at the bottom) and a warm sweater for the top. And during the climbing season you will probably have to queue up to get to the top of this ugly, rubbish-littered pile of cinders, which is much better seen from a distance.

Another odd report said that a dead female foetus had been found in a bag 'to his surprise' by a national railway employee when he snatched it off a closed door of an electric train at Ueno station.

> But shortly afterwards, a postgraduate student, 25, reported to the Ueno station police saying that he had obtained the foetus for dissection at his medical university. In changing a train at the Shinagawa station, he had the bag caught by the electric train's door, he explained. But the railway authority maintained that his act had violated the Railway Enterprises Law as it prohibits bringing explosives and human bodies into coaches.

Even more horrifying was the case of the severed foot that suddenly flew through the window of a train and killed a passenger:

> A severed human foot crashed through the glass pane of a Yokosuka line train and fatally 'kicked' a passenger. The truncated human limb belonged to a young man who leaped from a dining coach of the express Daiichi Setsu coming from the opposite direction on the main Tokaido line. Several passengers fainted at the sight of the gruesome object. Confusion broke out in the crowded coach for several minutes. Railway officials said that the suicide must have been smashed and dismembered between the two trains since they could not find any signs that he had been run over. They added that he had lunged through a door of the dining coach of the express headed to Tokyo from Osaka and leaped outside. He left his sandals in the train—in the Japanese fashion when committing suicide.

One Sunday evening as I came out of Shinjuku railway station I was startled to see that the pavements and road outside the Odakyu department store were deep in foam. It was detergent foam pouring from three manholes. The breeze wafted great soft sponges of foam and blew bubbles all over the place, creating a fantastic effect in the traffic-jammed streets. (It reminded me of the time when I used to while away my boredom by blowing bubbles out of the window of my top-floor office near Fleet Street. They stopped the traffic, as people thought they were flying saucers.) There was a frantic group of store employees trying to beat back the foam down the manholes with rubber doormats, a scene worthy of a Marx Brothers' film. Next day in the papers I read that the store had held a 'Treasure Hunt in

Foam', at which thousands of Japanese women had been given spoons with which to fish for eighty-eight rings hidden in vast tanks of detergent foam:

> Finders of the rings were permitted to keep them. At the conclusion of the 'treasure hunt' employees of the department store poured the detergent down the drain and forgot about it. They later told police they were surprised to see it come back up again.

As the heat and the humidity grow more and more intense, people take to walking about in their underclothes, and sometimes very old ladies can be seen completely bare-chested, sweeping their little gardens. In Wakayama City the City Hall employees had found it so hot that they were constantly stepping out for a glass of draught beer or whiling away the hot hours playing mah-jong in their three-quarter-length summer underpants, known as *suteteko*. Whenever they decided to do some work in their offices, they still wore their *suteteko*. The good citizens of Wakayama complained to the mayor that they could get no attention from office workers at the City Hall who were either out drinking coffee or beer or slouched around in *suteteko* playing mah-jong or Japanese or Chinese chess. The mayor drew up new rules for 'speedy work, proper attire, punctuality and prohibiting workers from stepping out for a tea or coffee break or playing games during working hours'. These conditions, in fact, exist in most Japanese public offices, where the grossly underpaid staff have no incentive to work at all and attend to people very reluctantly; this creates quite a Kafka-like atmosphere in city halls or ward offices, where one may wait hours before even being asked what one wants.

Air-conditioning helps to defeat some of the summer sultriness, but one must be careful, because it can bring on the most awful chills and aches and neuralgias; indeed this summer I caught pleurisy from an air-conditioning machine. One of the most unique air-conditioning machines in the world is one at Tosa-Yamadamachi on Shikoku Island, where there is the great Ryûgadô Stalactite Cave which attracts great crowds in midsummer because it is so chilly, sixteen degrees. An enterprising hotel keeper installed a ten-horse-power blower in the cave, connected with a big 800-foot-long pipe that leads into his hotel, which now enjoys some of the cool air that was going to waste. It is a perfect air-conditioning system that cost only thirty pounds for the ventilator and pipes, including installation charges.

There are many other ways of keeping cool of course. There are boat trips, with music, beer and dancing, round the very smelly Tokyo Harbour and up the stinking Sumida River, starting from the Kachidoki Bridge near Asakusa Matsuya department store; or one can pick up the boat at the Higashi Ginza landing-stage near the entrance of Hama Rikyu Park. If you take a nose-mask dipped in my new scent, *Flowers of Nepenthe*, the trip is cooling and relaxing.

In Onomichi, Hiroshima Prefecture, the historic temple throws open its sliding doors to everyone who wishes to come and enjoy a rest or a siesta on its cool matted floors. Or one can join the three thousand pilgrims who daily walk up Mount Tsurugi in Tokushima Prefecture on Shikoku Island; on the top of the 6,500-foot peak is the Tsurugisan Temple where one can offer prayers, in delicious coolness, to the temple gods, asking them to cleanse your soul. There is the *ishi-buro*, or stone bath, in Sakurai, Ehime Prefecture, Shikoku Island, which is a perfect Turkish bath heated by a huge stone oven constructed by fleeing Heike-clan warriors hundreds of years ago. You are provided with a straw mat, enter the bath, lie down on your piece of *tatami* and simply sweat it out. Indeed hot baths are more than ever popular in summer time; if one *has* to sweat, the Japanese think, one might as well sweat good and proper, and in comfort, preferably with the attentions of a pretty and sympathetic masseuse.

In the hot spring resort at Ibusuki, south of Kagoshima, one can practise one's chopsticks on *somen* or stringy wheat noodles cooled in a clear, icy stream; you place a small wicker basket in the cool stream and slurp up your noodles, dipping them in sweet-flavoured sauce. Mitsukoshi department store in Tokyo advertised 'A Summer Cavalcade of Soba' where one could sample bowls of different kinds of *zaru soba* or noodles from all over Japan. The store, like all others in Japan, is delightfully cooled by immense air-conditioning plants. I had a delicious lunch composed of a chilled tin of tuna, an iced peach and a bowl of *harusame*, or iced noodles, delivered to my home with some bottles of Kirin beer chilled so well that one was frozen solid. I have discovered that Kirin beer is even more refreshing drunk from a champagne glass.

Another cool experience was watching a competition of Japanese chefs making ice-sculptures for table decorations on the roof of Odakyu department store; besides the usual motifs of fish and swans, white herons, dragons flying in the clouds and arrangements of ice-flowers, there were a number of *abusturacto* entries that were praised for their *goodo designo*. But the first prize was won by a conventional subject, symbolizing summer in Chinese and Japanese ink-paintings: a dragon-fly resting on a pumpkin.

The Day of the Ox in the *doyo* season is called *doyo-ushi-no-hi*, or eel-eating day; it falls on 26th July, in the middle of what is believed to be the hottest and most enervating period of summer, the *doyo* period which covers the eighteen days before the official start of autumn on 8th August. On this day eel restaurants are crowded with people eating *unagi*, or eels, broiled over charcoal on bamboo skewers. They are supposed to keep up one's strength and vitality during the hot season. They are eaten throughout the summer, as well as on this special day, when everyone tries to taste some eels.

Paradoxically the Japanese at the height of summer often hold contests called 'summer patience meetings' at which the competitors vie with one another in wearing as many clothes as possible. They muffle up in layer after layer of garments and then sit around roaring bonfires eating hot-spiced *yakitori* or Japanese barbecue and drinking boiling hot saké. In Yamagata City the firemen annually hold this kind of competition. 'There's nothing like fighting fire with fire,' they say as they swig their hot saké or *risshu* on the first day of autumn with a temperature of over 93° F. at noon.

At Kyoto there are many summer restaurants which have straw-matted verandas projecting out over purling streams and rivers. One can relax there in *yukata*, with one's bottles of beer or special-brew summer saké (drunk chilled), while one dangles one's hot, dusty feet in the mountain-cooled water. There are several such restaurants at Kibune, in the northern suburbs of Kyoto, set among the rapids and cascades at the foot of Mount Kibune, where the temperature is well below that of the sweltering Kinki district where Kyoto and Osaka lie. Similar restaurants can be visited in the city of Kyoto itself, particularly in the Pontocho geisha area, where they are shaded by vines and the symbol of a Japanese summer, the ghostly weeping willow. Out in the countryside many enterprising restaurateurs set their customers afloat on rafts or in tubs, with awnings and paddles and of course lots to drink, and perhaps fresh *ayu* (river trout), grilled and salted, to eat. Such enterprises can be found at Handamachi, for example, at Tokushima in Shikoku, or in Shimane Prefecture on the beautiful mountain lake, Ukinuma-ike, at the foot of Mount Sambe, where the vista of the extinct volcano has been grandiosely and fashionably named *Bakansu* (*vacances*) *Biyu* (view).

Kyoto is also famous for its canals, but the law prohibits one from bathing in these watery thoroughfares of yet another 'Venice of Japan'. Nevertheless all summer long schoolboys may be seen taking dips, and even university students in their 'jump look' or 'switch look' costumes may be seen disporting themselves in the less populated reaches of the Takano and Kamo rivers, or in lakes Mizora and Takara. If you have your Bôsô Peninsular trunks with you, jump in and join them; even if you haven't it is quite easy to cobble up a gentleman's swimsuit, as many Japanese youths do, from a simple length of blue and white cotton, a towel called a *tenugui* and a couple of bits of string; it is fashioned just like the primitive but very comfortable breech-clouts worn by Japanese working youths.

About mid July is the time when the Emperor and Empress leave Tokyo for their Imperial Villa at Hayama, a seaside resort with a good beach in Kanagawa Prefecture. Millions of ordinary people too spend their week-ends along this stretch of coast, when the temperature in Tokyo, rising well into the thirties of the centigrade scale, and the discomfort index for humidity soaring well above eighty, become almost unendurable. Hayama, Zushi, Kamakura and Enoshima beaches are always the most crowded, and traffic on the roads becomes a nightmare of broiling, fuming jams. The Japanese know this, but still they go, because the average Japanese loves more than anything else to do what everyone else is doing, and will suffer untold inconvenience and discomfort if only millions of others are suffering the same. This outstanding trait of Japanese character is what makes them so wonderful in emergencies, in national cataclysms and natural disasters, in war. But it is also a characteristic that makes them at summer, spring and winter holiday times the most boring people on earth, because they all want to look the same, do the same things and be in the same places. It is an unusual Japanese—and they do exist, fortunately—who can resist all the mass pressures to conform in the search for pleasure and so-called relaxation. A Japanese who prefers to stay quietly at home during the summer rush to the seaside is considered something of an abnormality; but it is these 'abnormal' ones who are really sane, and who are the saving grace of Japan.

Mountain-climbing is in full swing throughout July and August: thousands of people every day climb not only Mount Fuji but all the other mountains of Japan, including Mount Tanigawa in Gumma Prefecture, which has over five thousand climbers a day and a force of a hundred policemen to control the queues and deal with mountain accidents, and Kamikochi Heights in the North Japan Alps, where thousands of people toil up the slopes in a single day in order to get a brief breath of cool air on the litter-laden summits before making the sweltering descent to the plains again. The Japanese passion for nature has been subtly perverted by clever and crude advertising by travel agencies, so that visiting beaches and mountains in summer time has become a positive mania with the Japanese: it has become a sort of automatic reflex to leave home and join the mass exodus to resorts, where the prices of rooms and rents of villas have recently risen to unbelievable heights; still there are people fool enough to pay these prices for the privilege of doing what everyone else is doing. It is both a strength and a weakness in the Japanese character, this almost insane will to conform.

A more pleasant way to celebrate summer in Japan is to watch displays of fireworks. This can range from having one *yukata*-clad baby hold a sputtering 'sparkler' over a carefully provided pail of water to the great, sky-filling displays that mark the end of the Buddhist Bon festival, the season of the dead, when their souls are especially remembered, and candles, incense, lamps and fires lit for them. The annual Tokyo fireworks festival is held round 18th July on the banks of the Tama River which forms the border between Tokyo and Kanagawa Prefecture. It is a big celebration, lasting for three hours, and during all that time the summer night is starred with the great chrysanthemum blooms of Japanese rockets, with their long, slow blossoming after an ear-splitting crack, and their vivid, changing colours. The great feature of such displays is always the set piece at the end, usually representing a waterfall of white fire falling into the river. Certain firms too donate set pieces, prettily designed and coloured, which advertise their products. The ceremony at the Tama River is accompanied by a lantern-floating festival, when thousands of small lighted lanterns are set afloat on the river to guide ancestral spirits back to the other world.

Certain bugs and insects besides mosquitoes are a nuisance, and indeed a plague, in Japan during the summer. As in other countries insecticides have been widely used to try to kill them off before they can do any damage. As we have been warned by Rachel Carson, these insecticides are also killing off birds, and factory wastes are killing fish, while human beings' lives are threatened by eating the birds, fish and cattle which have been poisoned by man-made chemicals. According to scientific researchers in Japan, the amount of mercury in rice, the staple diet, has slowly been increasing, as organic mercury chemicals have been increasingly employed by Japanese farmers since 1955. One often sees farmers spreading the white mercury powder over their fields. Among birds, swallows and crows have greatly decreased, and so have other wild birds. But the greatest sorrow in Japan is that insecticides have been killing off fireflies, one of the symbols of summer, and the delight of both parents and children. The poisoned paddy-field water is apparently killing a grub called *kawanina* which is the fireflies' food. Anti-flood construction is slowly eliminating the paddy-fields along the rivers, the insects' favoured hatching-places. The Chinzan-so Restaurant in Mejiro promotes business during the summer season by releasing millions of fireflies in its landscape gardens; the insects live only two weeks, so that fresh supplies must constantly be obtained, and collectors of the fireflies say that now they have to go farther and farther into the mountains in order to find their catches. The Japanese word for firefly is *hotaru*.

Fireflies are also released along the moat of the Imperial Castle every summer, to the great delight of children, who run after them waving their *uchiwa* fans and singing;

Ho-ho-hotaru,
Achi-no mizu-wa
Nigaiso
Kochi-no mizu-wa
Amaiso.

This pretty little chant may be heard everywhere on a summer evening where there are fireflies; it means: 'Please come over here, firefly! That side of the water is bitter, but this side of the water is sweet! Please come over here, firefly!' The children catch the fireflies and put them in little cages, or sometimes they hang them inside their green mosquito-net or *kaya* to 'light their summer dreams'. It is lovely to see a Japanese child asleep under one of these deep green nets with the dark red silk borders, his firefly shining in the dark, his singing cricket chirrupping in its little bamboo cage.

These singing crickets that so impressed Loti as he approached the shores of Japan are called *suzumushi*, and are as popular as wind-bells in Japanese homes during the hot weather. They are also known as the first harbingers of autumn, so they are doubly popular. The *suzumushi*'s official Latin name is *Homoeogryllus japonicus*. During the last two weeks of July there are many itinerant street vendors of these sweetly piping insects; they are sold in beautifully made but very cheap little bamboo cages representing all kinds of things—temples, boats, lanterns, houses, shrines and palanquins—but the cheapest kind of all is just a small, plain cage of delicately split bamboos. The vendors carry their wares, both living and inanimate, on push-carts or on two prettily decorated long, rectangular bamboo frames slung across the shoulder on a stout bamboo pole. Children come running when they hear the jolly vendor calling 'Suzumushi-i-i-i'. (As Loti noted, the Japanese, when calling a name aloud, prolong the final syllable in a curious nasal, complaining drawl, rather Cantonese in sound.)

Travellers this summer who used the waiting-rooms of stations in Nagano Prefecture were treated to the singing of *suzumushi*, whose bell-like voice is noted for its cooling effect. One hundred and fifty of these insects, in cages, were distributed along the Nagano lines. At Ueno station I noticed that the National Railway provided huge blocks of ice on which exhausted travellers could chill their towels and so cool their foreheads during or after a long, hot train journey. In Ginza many stores had blocks of ice outside or inside for the benefit of customers and passers-by. Indeed one beer firm put on the pavements big blocks of ice in which bottles of beer were embedded; one simply had to wait until the ice melted in order to get a free bottle of ice-cold beer: one or two Ginza hippies, I noticed, had not the patience to wait for the ice to melt but were helping along the process with their cigarette lighters, until one of the yellow-helmeted workmen on a new office block brought along a blowlamp, while another used an automatic drill.

However, there is one insect that has defied all insecticides so far, and this is an infamous beetle that chews up the orange crops; in Japanese it is called a *tengyu*. It is a large, spotted beetle with large feelers, and I have not been able to find out its Latin name. Farmers pay children ten yen for each of these beetles brought in. The largest number, 4,000-odd, were caught this year in Yawatahama, a place in Shikoku noted for its orange production.

Terebi (television) has a 'cool' look with its blue screen, and so the sales go up in the hot weather. Among the programmes offered was one of popular, lanky-legged Yujiro Ishihara singing Hawaiian melodies in the pool of the Prince Hotel at Takanawa, Tokyo, accompanied by the American beauties from Sam Snyder's Water Follies. In the garden of the same hotel it was astonishing to see the flowers of an agave in full bloom for the first time in seventy-five years. (Agave flowers are said to blossom once a century.) The great leaning tower of orange-red bloom was a most remarkable summer sight.

One startling headline ran: 'Five hurt in Osaka in Stampede of Philatelists'. Two thousand frantic Japanese philatelists had stampeded when three new kinds of Russian stamps, commemorating the boy-girl twin space-flight, were put on general sale at the Nanshin department store. The stamps each depicted Balery Bykovsky on Vostok-5 and Valentina Tereshkova on Vostok-6, two Russians who that summer became the hero and heroine of every Japanese boy and girl. 'Final Summations in Ward Vice Trial', another news item that had absorbed Japanese scandal-loving readers stood next to a headline saying: 'Softly-silhouetted Sex in Newest Paris styles'. The article went on to say:

> Dior revealed some of the most seductive bosoms ever shown in public for cocktail and evening dresses . . .

In the Japanese fashion world television showed some *goodo designo* in 'New Mode' from an Asakusa shop that makes kimono for bar and cabaret hostesses, the new style being a kimono with the side slit of a Chinese cheongsam and made of old Kihachijo weave with a broad check pattern. A man killed a fellow worker—this is always happening—in an argument about which programme to watch on the television set in their construction workers' dormitory. A junior high-school girl committed suicide shortly after she was caught shoplifting. She was only fifteen, and she hanged herself in the barn attached to her home, leaving this pathetic note: 'Please forgive my egoism, I am sorry.' She had lifted about six shillings' worth of sweets and *sarami* sausage. Then a drunken Tokyo confectioner who said his family held him in contempt sprayed his wife and two sleeping sons with petrol, set it alight and then locked all the doors before leaving the burning house. In the Ginza a length of iron piping fell from a building—this too is always happening—and seriously injured a man walking along the street. A man, committing suicide by leaping off a tall office building, killed a student walking in the street below when he fell right on top of him. 'Della Coming, Elaine Spawned', is an inscrutable headline, until one realizes it refers to the coming typhoon season. A ferry boat, the *Midori Maru*, was overturned in a storm off Okinawa, and 112 persons were drowned. Boat accidents like this are very frequent in Japan, due mainly to overcrowding. The Japanese Government paid out £60 in relief funds to the families of each of the deceased persons. The head of one family, Ansho Uezu, whose fourteen-year-old daughter had been drowned, returned the money to the Government, all except twenty cents, with this note: 'I am keeping twenty cents so as not to appear ungrateful to everyone who donated the money to us survivors. This I am happy to accept.' He asked that the money be given to a more deserving family, as his had no financial problems. I was deeply touched by this man's act, and by his fineness of feeling displayed in the little note. It was the sort of thing my father would have done.

Meanwhile the summer heats were beguiled by the information that the Tokyo Metropolitan Government's sewerage office will sponsor a nationwide 'Sewerage Work Promotion Day', which would include various activities, among them the opening of sewerage facilities in Tokyo to the public and the 'inspection of a drainage and sewage disposal centre now under construction by Governor Ryotaro Azuma with visiting housewives'. Most of Tokyo's sewage is dumped in the Sumida River or on a small island in Tokyo Harbour call 'Dream Island'; no wonder dysentery is rife in Japan.

There were more cases of bars swindling customers; there was one of a bar demanding that a customer pay a bill of 19,000 yen (twenty pounds sterling) for two bottles of beer. Contrary to the customer's order for only two bottles, employees of the bar and hostess girls served him fruit juice and whisky, and when he complained the bartender took him by the neck and forced him to drink the whisky. The bar, the Biwako in the Shimbashi geisha and amusement quarter, had its operating permit cancelled.

Beer halls were doing a roaring business, and provided special hygienic tanks in which customers could vomit to their hearts' content before proceeding to down more *nama* or draught beer. One day I saw the little white statue of *Mannequin Pisse* at the end of the central platform at Hamamatsucho station dressed in its seasonal garb of summer *yukata*; some drunk had placed a bottle (empty, of course) of Sapporo beer in its arms.

While we are waiting for the Government to make the expected change in the law prohibiting skyscrapers—and plans for scores of these buildings are already drawn up—we learn that Tokyo is slowly sinking into the sea, and that about one half of Tokyo's twenty-three wards would be flooded should a summer typhoon as great as the Ise Bay typhoon strike the capital. About one half of Tokyo has sunk between two and eight inches during the past year. The sinking is largely caused by the dense concentration of factories and housing apartments incessantly pumping water out of the ground. A highly sensational movie has already been made showing enormous seas sweeping down the Ginza where strippers are cowering in the nude on the steps of the Nichigeki Theatre. A typical toll of one day's traffic accidents, published in all the newspapers and posted in large figures outside every police box, gives, for Tokyo alone, seven dead, 160 injured and seven fires. These figures are moderate, for an average day; often they are much larger. And only 55 per cent of telephone calls get through because the lines are so busy. If you should want to call the Japan National Railway inquiry office at Ueno station, your chances of getting through are one in ten. All these difficulties increase, and the dangers to life and limb pile up, in summer time.

In an attempt to escape from it all for an hour or so the Japanese have a custom, alas almost dead in Tokyo, called *yusuzumi*, which means just strolling about aimlessly enjoying the cool of evening, wearing fresh cotton *yukata* and clip-clopping geta. During an evening's *yusuzumi*, men often tuck up the skirts of their *yukata* into their black *crêpe* silk belt or *obi*, and pull the wide sleeves up to the shoulder, so that legs and arms can feel any cool breeze that passes. The stroller may stop at a stall to eat a big slice of strawberry pink water-melon with its glossy black pips, or to suck a dish of shaved ice topped with synthetic and highly coloured flavourings.

Almost the only place in Tokyo where one can enjoy a real *yusuzumi* is round the Shinobazu Pond in Ueno Park, where every summer a wondrous Plant Fair is held. Lanterns are hung along the lakeside paths, the five-storeyed pagoda is floodlit, and *O-bon* musicians bang their drums and shrill their fifes in the *bon-odori* tower, lantern-hung, on the little island in the middle of the lake called Benzaiten, where stands the pretty, illuminated temple to Benten, goddess of beauty.

I have often watched, on the long summer evenings, the self-forgetfulness and gentle gaiety of dancers, both young and old, round the *bon-odori* tower: the gravity and grace of strapping young workmen in blue-patterned white *yukata*, their natural elegance and simplicity and deep, smiling absorption in the dance. Old ladies and gentlemen too dance lissomly and joyfully the complex rhythmical movements of the ancient folk dances. Young men and women on the tower's lower platform are teams of amateur folk-dancers who make the correct movements which are copied and learned by those down on the ground. There is an intensity of pleased concentration in performing correctly the steps and movements of the arms and hands, a deeply rapt yet happy, not fanatical, look on the faces. It is sweet to stand watching them in the light strands of swaying shadow made by weeping willows. They invite me to join them, and, though I am not wearing *yukata* (some of the Japanese dancers are in ordinary clothes too), I move into the ring and follow the movements, those movements that are like the actions of fishermen casting and drawing nets, of peasants in the fields reaping, scything, binding, lifting, sowing, all done with a flowing formality that pleases and instructs the city-wearied body.

Shinobazu Pond is surrounded by stalls selling all kinds of plants—flowers, shrubs, dwarfed trees, rocks for 'dry gardens', stone lanterns, mosses, ferns and sometimes entire trees, well swaddled in straw and hempen rope, their roots in canvas bags filled with water. At some plant stalls there is the chilly tinkle of glass wind-bells hanging from rustic, moss-covered wooden frames with ferns sprouting from them; the wind-bells have a pretty name in Japan—*furin*, which is slightly onomatopoeic. If a customer buys a big, leaning pine tree, cleverly twisted, for his garden, the plant seller will plant it and tend it and trim and torture it for a year without extra charge. Such a tree costs about three hundred pounds. The wind-bell frames of bark and moss and branches, sometimes formed to resemble houses or boats or lanterns, are much cheaper, only about half a crown. I bought one, and carried it round the park with me, while the little bell went *furin-furin-furin*.

There were other stalls, near the Buddhist temple to Benten, selling those artificial flowers concealed inside small shells that open out when they are dropped in a glass of water; they are sometimes made with artificial angel-fish attached to them too. But there are lots of tanks of real tropical fish; at some of the low, white tanks laid on the ground, where tiny black, red and gold fish are wriggling, crowds of small children are crouched with small hoops covered with rice-paper; each hoop costs ten yen, and the trick is to be quick enough to scoop up a fish and get it into the little bowl of water provided before the paper breaks. The children are sometimes successful, and then they proudly carry their prize home in a small polythene bag filled with water.

The plant sellers do not seem to be doing much business; there are other plant fairs in Tokyo that are even livelier, like the one at Asakusa, held on 31st May and 1st June, 30th June and 1st July, and which is called *ueki-ichi*, meaning, roughly, 'those things which are sold during a certain period only'. These periods are believed by the Japanese to be the best time for buying and transplanting shrubs and trees. It is connected with the *yama-biriki* period, which is the annual period of summer when it is considered safe to climb Mount Fuji. (*Yama-biriki* means 'open mountain', and need not only apply to Fujiyama.)

But Ueno Park tonight is lively enough with dancers, 'avec' couples seeking a darkish, retired place (impossible) and children eating fish fritters, lollipop ices, 'electric candy'; children with toys, ballons, tiny turtles crawling up bamboo ladderkins, baby chicks in brown paper bags and fistfuls of fireworks.

A few roman candles are let off at the far side of the pond, sending up rather irregularly their red, blue, green and white globes of fire like a drunken juggler practising with balls too hot to hold. The whole eccentric performance is doubled in the inverting lake.

No one walks alone here tonight, except a few old people, a tramp or two and myself, the solitary 'person from outside'. My melancholy is like the big, rhubarb leaves of the giant lotus plants that rise on stiff stalks above the lantern-lit waters of the pond. I am like the old, half-sunken rowboat marooned among them, its paint now faded blue, making a sharp, interesting shape on the dark-lit waters. But I cheered up when I picked up a lost pocket comb called Fine Sister.

I saw here two or three Japanese country youths standing rigidly immobile in the lamplit dark, as if posing for photographs. I couldn't think what they were doing until I saw some 'artists' making rapid pencil sketches of them, only 200 yen a portrait. The ancient *samurai* attitude came out strongly in those country boys as they posed with an almost supernatural stillness amid the swarming throngs.

A large number of young men this summer have bandaged thumbs, fingers, wrists, toes, feet: the Japanese seem to be more accident-prone in this season.

The dim cinemas, packed to suffocation, are a-flimmer with the audience's scented, coloured paper fans. 'Cooling' films—spine-chilling horror movies—are being screened. There are green and blue 'cooling' lights in bars. Some bars play twelve-tone music or *musique concrète*—Japanese composers, needless to say, have outdone Schoenberg and Webern, Stockhausen, Dallapiccola and John Cage—because this type of music is thought to be weirdly chilling. Rooftop beer-halls have waterfalls and revolting 'ethereal' quavering electric organ music, often played with the usual unashamed amateurishness of self-taught performers. Hawaiian bands are everywhere, until one is quite sick of the sound of those bilious electric guitars.

Screens made of thin green plastic rods hang outside open doors and windows and bars have swinging half-doors like those in Westerns. On the counters the ash-trays are filled with water to prevent the ash from blowing about under the blue-bladed electric fan that moves ponderously from side to side with the deliberate graciousness of an ambassadress greeting guests at a garden party, imparting to all and sundry the dispassioned blast of a freezing, cordial official smile. Cold and scented, tightly rolled *o-shibori* (hand towels), iced tea, iced coffee. Kabuki, also, puts on its 'light' summer shows with plays about ghosts and ghouls among weeping willows.

Girls returning home from the local hairdresser have their new permanents or old-fashioned pompadours wrapped in gauze scarves: a custom imitated from America. I saw a young woman, dripping blood, being carried unconscious into a maternity hospital from a taxi: a suitable subject for a tale to 'chill the blood' in this hot weather fanned by the long, languorous, delicate, ravelled shadows of weeping willow leaves, the very essence of summer, and of the supernatural that haunts us with the spirits of the dead in this season.

Some men can be seen, in the heat of the day, unbelting their trousers and undoing the front, heedless of the crowds around them. They are not exposing themselves: they are merely tucking their shirts well in again; some of them have a rubber band round their waists to keep their shirts down and their pants up. I have seen tough workmen, in oily breeches, *jikatabi* and stained sweat-shirts, sporting a pink or green chiffon scarf loosely knotted round the throat. It does not look absurd, but brings out touchingly the essential maleness of the wearer. He wears such a scarf because in this stifling weather all gauzy materials are held to be cool or cooling. Little girls are arrayed in the lightest and airiest of frocks and little straw bonnets: how elegant are small children's clothes in Japan!

This summer business girls (known as BG's) are wearing sleeveless white blouses composed of layer upon layer of row upon vertical row of gauzy frills. Men's sports shirts are of a sort of lacy open-work material, grey or black or brown, under which a sherbet-toned sweat-shirt is worn. *Mambo* boys wear white pants and Hawaiian shirts, straw trilbies or boaters. Priests wear white cotton robes covered with a long black gauze outer garment like a duster coat, and invariably wear a panama hat on their shaven polls.

It is curious that only this afternoon I should have been wondering again about the significance of those gigantic straw pilgrim's sandals hung on the sides of a small wayside shrine near my wine shop in Sendagaya. Because I started reading Lowes Dickinson's *Appearances* and in his essay on Nikko found this enchanting passage:

> Here in a ravine is another [shrine] where men who want to develop their calves hang up sandals to a once athletic saint. 'The Lord', our Scripture says, 'delighteth not in any man's legs.' How pleasant, then, it must be to have a saint who does! Especially for the Japanese, whose legs are so finely made, and who display them so delightfully. Such, all over the world, is the religion of the people, when they have any religion at all. And how human it is, and how much nearer to life than the austerities and abstractions of a creed!

Another example of giant sandals is the one carried every year to the Asakusa Kwannon shrine in the belief that everyone in the procession will enjoy good fortune during the coming year. In the mountain districts of Ibaraki Prefecture school children make giant straw sandals which they transport, with great difficulty, to the shrine of the Great Buddha at Kamakura. These sandals are called *zori*, a word which is written with two characters meaning 'grass footwear'. They are made of rice stalks or a kind of reed. On summer days, *zori* of a specially fine quality, made of bamboo sheaths, may be used for strolling in the garden after the *chano-yu* ceremony in the tea arbour. In recent times plastic imitations of these *zori* are often seen. They are in a sense a symbol of long journeys, and Colonel John Glenn was presented with a pair of straw *zori* by an old Japanese man before making his historic space flight. Another kind of straw sandal, with long straps that are wound round the ankles and calves, are called *waraji*, but these are not generally worn today. These sandals, sometimes seen worn by characters in Kabuki plays (for example, in 'Kanjincho'), and in costume, or *chanbara*, sword-fight films, are also symbols of arduous travel. In Asakusa an enormous *waraji* hangs near the Nio-mon Gate. It was offered to the god Nio who is the guardian spirit of Asakusa. *Waraji* are offered to him because it is believed he has the magic power of overthrowing evil spirits and curing illnesses, especially of the feet and legs, which are so important to travellers. In many resort places small pairs of straw *zori* are sold, and small pairs of *waraji* made of plastic are on sale as souvenirs in Nagano Prefecture. At Morioka, in Iwate Prefecture, I even remember that at a sandal-maker's house he presented me with a crude, strong pair of *zori* specially made to be

Shop selling decorated thongs for *geta* and *zori*

Kakemono

Japanese um

For a Japanese meal: chopsticks, with box and china chopstick holder, toothpicks and rice spoon

Lacquer lunch box containing pickled beans, seaweed and lotus root

Saké bottle and cups

New Year rice cakes offered to priests

(*Right*) New Year kites

Fine faces: papier-mâché *daruma* dolls and their vendor

Dwarf trees, or *bonsai*, for sale. On the salesman's head in the foreground is the white cotton towel said to aid mental concentration and to indicate hard work

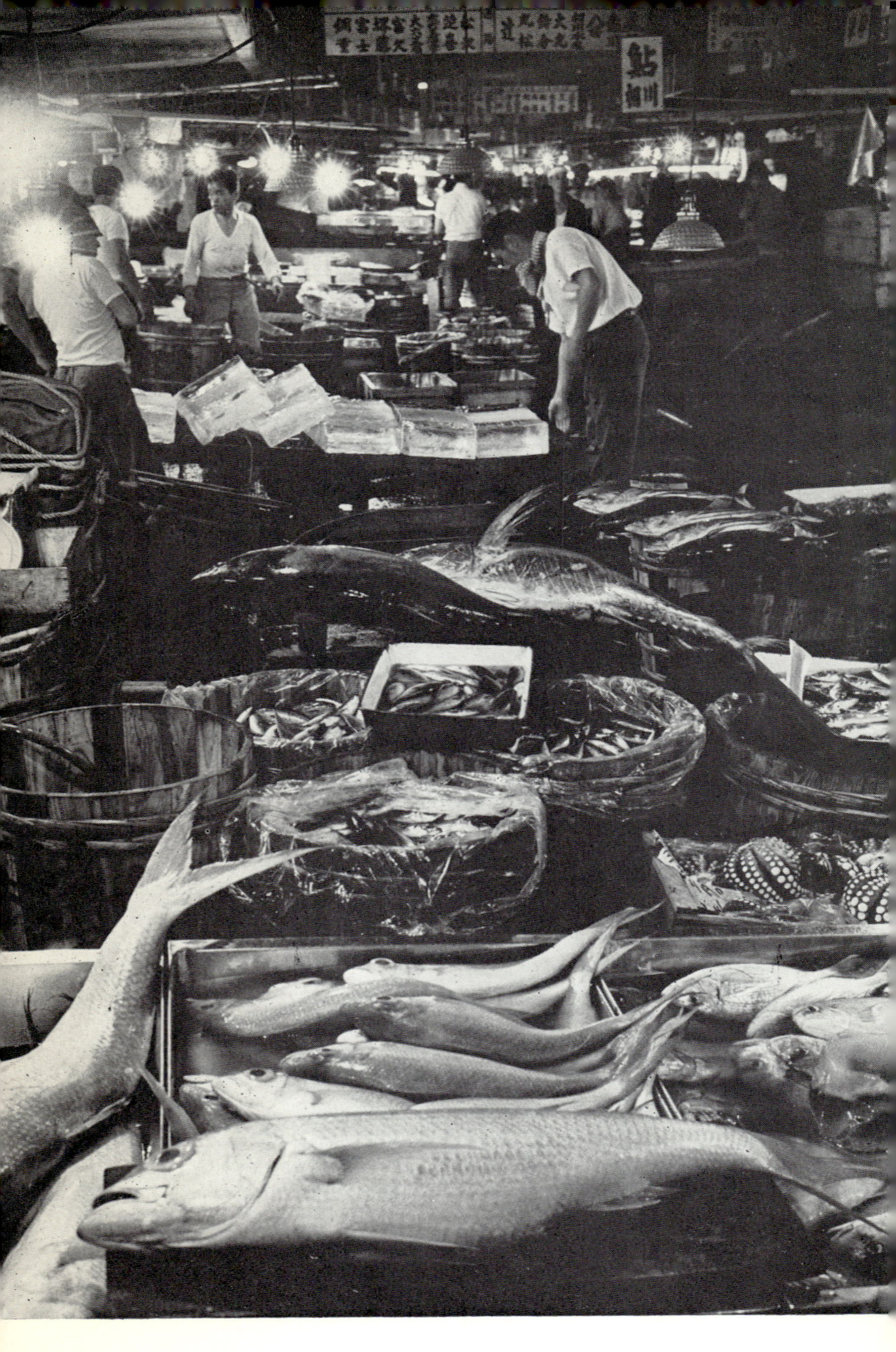

Fish market

worn by cattle. A foreigner should not wear *zori* in the street in Japan, as it will attract perhaps unwelcome comment and attention; but it is pleasant, in summer and autumn, to use these cool sandals in one's little garden. As the thong between the great toe and the next may chafe and burn feet unused to this type of footwear, one should begin by using a wad of cotton wool wrapped round the thong. The only place in Japan where I remember seeing *waraji* worn was at Ohara, a small, pretty village outside Tokyo, where the *Oharame* or country women of the Ohara district wear dainty *waraji* with one loop on each side as they walk along the country roads carrying bundles of rice or flowers or bamboo on their white-kerchiefed heads. They are also said to be worn in certain parts of the Tohoku district, but I never saw them when I lived there.

There is a special kind of plant which the Japanese love to have in their homes in summer; one also sees it on the counters of shops and in sub post offices. It is called *yatsugashira*, or yam, and stands in its thickly matted, bulbous root clumps in the water of a shallow dish. The stems are a slender, fleshy, dusky pink, its heart-shaped leaves rather like those of a cyclamen but a little narrower; they are of a deep, matt green colour, and when they first appear they are neatly rolled up. But they soon open out, for the plant responds very eagerly to light, though with infinite slowness; one has to keep turning it, frustrating its yearnings, to keep its small forest of leggy stems vertical. It is a kind of stagnant mobile, only just moving, but silently and ceaselessly alive, as long as it has water. Why does it give such an impression of coolness and calm, with its jungle-like tangle of fleshy stems? I think the impression comes from one's sense that the plant is constantly absorbing moisture, and constantly, with the utmost languor, moving and turning in the effortless slowness one longs to attain oneself in the wet summer heat.

I came upon this very appropriate quotation about the Japanese summer in David Stacton's remarkable novel about medieval Japan, *Segaki*: 'It was now the middle of July, a month when one's mind runs in somewhat thoughtful and hazardous channels.' About this time we learned that the Emperor had shaken hands by mistake:

> An official of the Prime Minister's Office has a distinction unique in all Japanese history—he has shaken hands with the Emperor. It later turned out that the Imperial handshake was a mistake.
>
> Jitsuzo Tokuyasu, director of Administrative Affairs in the Prime Minister's office, was standing near the line of foreign diplomats at the

> beginning of the Imperial banquet given by Their Majesties the Emperor and Empress on Tuesday for King Bhumibol Adulyadej and Queen Sirikit of Thailand. Their Majesties, in accordance with traditional procedure, went down the line, shaking hands with members of the diplomatic corps.
>
> They then came to Mr Tokuyasu. He was deeply tanned after a summer vacation and was wearing a Thai medal on his chest. The Emperor and Empress evidently thought he was a foreign diplomat and shook hands with him. Since the Emperor Jimmu, no Japanese has ever before shaken hands with the Emperor. Mr Tokuyasu was greatly reassured when protocol experts told him that to have refused a proffered hand would have been a much more flagrant impropriety than his breach of centuries of Imperial tradition by shaking hands with the Emperor.
>
> In the olden days no Japanese was permitted to touch the body of the Emperor. It was also forbidden to stand at any spot where a person would look down upon the Emperor during a public appearance. It is said that when the Emperor Meiji was measured for Western-style suits, his tailor was required to take the measurements without touching him. Postwar changes have ended these traditions.

This would have provided material for several hilarious scenes in a Firbank novel. Perhaps now that the first Japanese has shaken hands with the Emperor the privilege will be extended to others as one more proof of Japan's oft-protested democratization or democracy, which word the Japanese have adopted into their language under the form of a deliciously atrocious pun, *demo-kurushi*, which means 'suffering from democracy'.

I spent all the summer of 1962 in Japan looking for a job, but failed to find anything suitable. I even tried the English conversation schools that everywhere in Japan are cashing in on the frantic Japanese craze to learn English conversation. I made long trips to remote suburbs, to Asagaya (where there was a nice little Tanabata Festival), to Ogikubo, Nishiogikubo, Higashi-hachioji and even to Kôfu, visiting shabby little shacks where a few foreign tramps and birds of passage, totally without any kind of teaching qualification or experience, jawed away at dumb Japanese students about their travel experiences and their sexual life. The fees paid to such teachers were ludicrously small, something like four shillings for a ninety-minute chat. Many of them had pirated textbooks or duplicated copies; I noticed at one school, for example, a duplicated copy of Clarke's Conversation Model Course. What infuriated me was that the Japanese, so eager to learn, should be duped in this way, and done out of their hard-earned money which they had saved carefully, to pay for a series of useless courses. The profits for the Japanese and foreign promoters of such mushroom 'language laboratories' were enormous; the profits for the pupils were nil.

That autumn I lived from hand to mouth in Tokyo, never knowing where my next yen or my next meal was coming from. This is certainly the way to get to know Japan; but it is a terrifying and heartbreaking experience, this encounter with merciless struggle for survival that is the lot of most Japanese every day of their lives. It is really a fight to keep alive: if one has no privileges and no job and no status, one might as well kill oneself, which is what many Japanese do every day in their deep unhappiness, loneliness and despair, griefs they keep to them-themselves and hide under pleasant smiles, so as not to afflict or affront others. I too learned to smile as they do in adversity and hardship, and found in that lesson a cure for the soul: to maintain a proper attitude, whatever happens, helps the Japanese to survive, and helped me to survive too.

PART FIVE

AUTUMN

I

JOURNEY INTO AUTUMN LIGHT

THE light in Japan is always slightly peculiar, different from the light in any other country I know. It has the strange, oblique intensity that often lends objects a tranced look and gives landscapes momentarily the appearance of being immobilized under glass. I like to think that this quality of the light that both animates and hypnotizes Japanese scenes is due to Japan's curious, slanting position on the globe: certainly the fact that in Japan the land is never far from seas, lakes and rivers must contribute to these impressions of luminous clarity. Indeed it might be said that Japan is more water than air, more sea than land.

It is in autumn that the light in Japan reaches its perfection of queerness: it has qualities both limpid and piercing, and in October and November the sun in clear, crystal blue skies has a sharp, poignant brilliance that both rejoices and rends the heart: it seems like the ultimate expression of some indefinable and unfulfilled yearning, and the vast, still sunrises and sunsets over the great cities and plains and mountains at this time of the year are like suspended sighs of sadness and regret for the passing of mortal time. To my mind, an autumn sunrise or sunset in Japan, over the Pacific, the Japan Sea or any of her countless lakes and waterways, expresses the essence of true Japanese sensibility and the height of her natural beauty: the light, both vivid and evanescent, makes the eyes and the heart ache with an even more refined melancholy of unshed tears than anything experienced in spring at the sight of falling cherry flowers.

For me, the symbol of autumn in Japan is not the gorgeous arrays of the Imperial chrysanthemum and the valleys of scarlet maple or the city streets and country lanes paved with the golden-yellow, fan-shaped leaves of the ginkgo tree. In autumn I love most of all the sight of deep orange persimmons, chandeliered like random lights or lanterns among the bare, dark brown, down-curving branches of a lone persimmon tree whose fruit glows richly against calm, blue autumn skies or is silhouetted against a rust-coloured dawn or the long shawls of vermilion, amber, lilac, grey and pink mist rising into a deep azure sunset sky already studded with icy stars or stunned into breathless silence by the low, full, ascending harvest moon. At such times I feel a sad hilarity that makes my lonelinesses even more acute and comic.

I experienced this utmost refinement of loneliness and melancholy in an autumn journey I made through the Inland Sea from Kōbe to Takamatsu and Beppu on the magnificent new passenger ship of the Kansai Steamship Company, the *Sumire Maru*, one of the several luxuriously appointed vessels that ply the routes among the pine islands of the Inland Sea. I was pleased to be travelling on the *Sumire Maru* because *sumire* is the Japanese word for a violet which, after the dandelion, *tampopo*, is my favourite flower.

The morning light over the Inland Sea as we sailed across to Shikoku was pearly with mist, through which the strange outlines of islands and solitary fishing boats drifted like slow dreams. Before leaving Kōbe I had consulted an ancient, white-bearded sage of a fortune-teller in the gateway of the Ikudama Shrine in Osaka. His name is Omboro Yashao, he charges only two hundred yen for a ten-minute consultation, and though he looks so decrepit and ragged it is said that he is a millionaire. The first thing he told me was that I was going on a pleasant voyage. An extraordinary sensation came over me as he began palping and kneading my palms and fingers in a very workmanlike, practical way. I felt myself floating in amber and golden light, and a keen, irrational happiness seemed to vibrate in every fibre and nerve of my body. The fortune-teller informed me that I was not yet married, and that though I was already a 'success' I should become even more successful with the help of some good Japanese girl as my loyal spouse. He also advised me to have the gap between my front teeth filled with gold, for 'gold attracts gold', he said. He exclaimed at the length and clarity of the lines on my palms and on the edges of my hands and fingers, and said he had never seen two such perfect palms before. With absorbed deliberation, hardly breathing, he bent his wrinkled old face over them, feeling and pinching their full, sensuous pads and mounts, and reverently traced the main lines with dright red pencil. Again I experienced a strange sensation: as I gazed at those vivid red lines, they seemed to come alive, to glow and move, and their candid, open pattern seemed to dance with a new meaning that flooded my whole being with calm security and bliss ineffable. It was the sort of feeling I had always hoped religion would give me and never did—a feeling of faith in myself, in my destiny on earth and beyond it.

I was reminded of this feeling of blissful security as the *Sumire Maru* softly swam, with deliciously gentle vibrations like those the fortune-teller had sensed in my palms, through the misty pine islands on the Inland Sea. I wandered round the ship's charmingly decorated public rooms and radiant decks and felt I was being transported into a fairyland of light and leisure.

Dazed with my happy dream, I visited the captain on his spacious glassed-in bridge, all calm and order and scientific luxury. Up there, high above the grey-blue waves, it was like drifting through space in a crystal globe. Amid all this ethereal yet practical wonder of white paint a-glitter with golden brass I noticed the blue teapot and cups of pale green tea for the captain and his two assistants on the bridge, and the pigeon-holes stuffed with many-coloured, rolled-up flags. There was a small Shinto shrine of plain wood on a shelf above the table bearing the charts and the weather-map: before it there had been reverently placed some simple flowers and offerings of rice and fruit and tea. Two small electric candles glowed with a mystic radiance on either side of the sacred shrine, dedicated to the safety of mariners. The bridge was both factory and temple, both scientific and mystical, both engine and altar.

We passed the experimental soundings that are being made for a great bridge to be built between Honshu and Awaji, that island of puppets operated in their leisure by artist farmers on primitive but gorgeously dressed stages set up in the harvested rice fields.

The Japanese, with what I think is a mistaken passion for attributive comparisons, call the Inland Sea 'the Aegean of Japan'. If comparisons must be made, I should call it rather 'the Mediterranean of Japan', because there are some parts of it quite empty of islands, and because, like the Mediterranean, it is 'in the middle' of the earth of Japan.

After a perfectly cooked lunch, served very nicely by the kind, handsome young stewards, we arrived at Takamatsu, where I transferred to a hydrofoil boat, a modern innovation recently introduced by the Kansai Steamship Company to facilitate travel between islands. This was my first experience of travel by a hydrofoil vessel, which was like a huge speedboat that skimmed effortlessly over the waves now dancing with sharp autumn sunlight, and enabled me to make the trip to the romantic island of Shodoshima in only twenty minutes. At the little port of Tonosho I saw a strange sight—many high racks of wet rice-straw: sea water is pumped over these to make salt.

I took the 'skyline course' round the island in a car, though comfortable touring buses are available. Perhaps it was because of the grey-green olive plants growing everywhere that Shodoshima reminded me of Tuscany. (Shodoshima is the only place in Japan with a climate in which olives have been successfully domesticated. Charming souvenirs of the island are in the form of glass paperweights in which a spray of olive leaves and a few black olives are enshrined. The flag of Shodoshima displays a white olive wreath surrounding a dove of peace.) I was also reminded of southern and central Italy and of Sicily by the winding, dusty, pale brown roads on the rocky hillsides terraced with olive groves. There were also high stacks of brown leaves covering piles of new seed potatoes, another of the island's unusual crops, which are grown on terraces of stepped stones and are exported in cylindrical straw containers similar to those used for bagging rice to all parts of Japan.

At many points along the thrilling bends of the mountain roads there were bands of stone-breakers, descendants of those men who had quarried the gigantic blocks that had been conveyed—no one knows how—to the shore and shipped across to Honshu for the construction of the great castles at Himeji and Osaka. Some of these massive blocks, quarried centuries ago, still lie near the site of Toyotomi's shipyard on Shodoshima.

There is a scarcity of water on this island, as on many of the islands of the Inland Sea, and so a number of artificial lakes have been created which that afternoon lay white and still among the misty brown hills. The prospect of the Mito Peninsula, that appeared to be floating on cloud and water into the first lavender shadows of approaching twilight, was unforgettably beautiful and poetic. At the famous Kankakei Gorge, with its eccentric rock formations, the maples were in all their hectic glory of crimson, orange, vermilion and gold, and under the yellow and lavender lights of sunset these seemed the very colours of Japan.

The return to Takamatsu by hydrofoil at dusk was also an indescribably lovely adventure. A dark light had fallen over the straits between Shodoshima and Shikoku, but the waves, a blackish green, were illuminated by uncanny reflections of the long, pale rose and amber sash of sunset that irradiated the nocturnal, islanded horizon under a pall of elaborately magnificent storm-clouds. In the distance, the level-roofed plateaus of Yashima glided, their shapes the black of ebony, against the sky's narrowing *obi* of dying crimsons. The voyage back to Takamatsu, though swift and smooth, was a spectral one, made hauntingly wild by that autumn sunset with its strange gusts of wind and its keen but ghostly glimmerings on the darkling waves.

In Takamatsu I took the autumn chill out of my bones with flask after flask of hot rice-wine at the delightful *tempura* restaurant called Tenyasu, which means something like 'Abode of Fried Fish Peace'. Here the chief cook-master was an elderly, jolly man with a blue and white cotton towel rolled tightly and knotted like a fillet round his shaven head; he is famous in Shikoku for his remarkable resemblance to Winston Churchill. We had some briny titbits with our saké as we waited for his deep, round pan of fresh cottonseed oil to heat to a temperature of 150 degrees. He tested its temperature by casting in a few drops of carefully prepared batter. Then we were served, on wire mesh trays covered with folded white paper, with eel, shrimp, devil-fish, green peppers, quarters of small onions, stems of ginger and slices of delicious lotus-root. Then came bowls of *o-misu-shiru* soup or *o-mi-o-tsuke*, which means, literally, 'most honourable and revered and great soup'. It was rich and hot and had a true tang of the sea with its handful of small mussels at the bottom of the lacquer bowl. One drinks the soup, slurping appreciatively, from the bowl, holding back the mussels with one's chopsticks, that afterwards can be used to pick the boiled meat out of the pretty little blue shells. A bowl of rice. A cup of green tea. It was all so delicious I had two 'sets' or helpings of everything.

In the main street of Takamatsu I saw another fortune-teller, a numerologist, who oddly enough told me exactly the same things as the fortune-teller at the Ikudama Shrine in Osaka. He arrived at his result by computing the numbers derived from my name, spelt in *katakana*, and from my Japanese name, Flourishing Tree of Dew-drops, and from my age, reckoned in Showa, the name of the present era in Japan. After complicated calculations, he established a figure 'radiant with luck and joy' and looked it up in a kind of breviary, where my happy fate was printed. He said it was the first time he had ever read a fortune from that fortunate page. He was wearing autumn kimono and a hat like a *songkok*; he had the face of an ascetic actor, and his final smile, as I departed, was faint but miraculous. I believed implicitly in everything he told me, as it was so wonderful.

I sailed that night from Takamatsu to Beppu, again on the *Sumire Maru*. There were many happy honeymoon couples on board. It was touching to see those youthful pairs, so quiet and self-conscious, so touchingly young and hopeful, so perfectly well-behaved: no clutchings and kissings in public, not even the touch of hands. They all wore what was almost a regulation uniform for autumn newly weds on their honeymoon: the girl in a neat suit and smart little cloche hat, the boy in his Western-style business suit of grey or sober blue, with rather wide trousers and generous turn-ups. In a Japanese male, this type of suit marks the beginning of respectability and responsibility after the student uniforms, jeans and sweaters of bachelor freedom. His new apparel is a rather sad garb, distressingly shapeless on his still firm and athletic body; he looks better wearing the traditional kimono and *haori*, or in *tanzen* and *geta*, or in the ship's *yukata*, returning rosy cheeked from the bathroom before retiring for an early night of wedded bliss.

We arrived in Beppu after a comfortable night's sleep and a delicious breakfast eaten in the golden clarity of a perfect sunrise. There was great agitation on the quayside at Beppu, as always when a boat arrives. Swarms of buses, taxis, tourists, children on school excursions and hotel guides carrying brightly coloured hotel flags. I took a taxi for a few hours' rest and relaxation and an excellent barbecue lunch at the splendid new Kijima Kanko Hotel, high in the lovely hills outside Beppu Spa. One of the attractive novelties of this hotel is the Swedish-style farm, with its plump porkers, fine Holstein cattle and a flock of Merino sheep. These animals are rather rare in non-pastoral Japan—except in the northermost island of Hokkaido—so the Japanese find them interestingly exotic. One of the 'exotic' features of the farm is a brick silo tower with a conical red roof.

After lunch a 'skyline drive' by car down into Beppu, passing a large sitting Buddha, much finer, I thought, than the Buddha of Kamakura, and very Chinese, or perhaps Korean, in style.

From the heliport at Beppu I was wafted aloft in a K.A.K. helicopter of the Kanki Airlines. It was one of the 'Vertol' type. Its rapid vertical take-off was something quite new to me, as was the only moderate racket of the blades fore and aft. The hostess on the twenty-minute flight from Beppu to Aso was dressed like a typical Japanese bus girl, in blue uniform and forage cap and white nylon gloves. She spoke pleasant English and was so kind to me, giving me nice smiles, fastening my seat-belt for me and offering me exquisite boiled sweets with very persuasive gestures, that I could not resist.

But I soon turned my attention from her to the landscape of Kyushu below—the terraced ricefields, freshly harvested, patterned with round stacks and long, straight rows of sheaves hung out to dry on bamboo racks. (We were flying at only 500 feet.) There were here and there black patches left by bonfires of burning straw. The afternoon sun shafted low over this golden and green landscape tinged with brown and yellow, all the colours of ripeness: it has been a bumper rice harvest this year.

Then we were flying over the outer rim, the original crater of the vast volcanic formation of Mount Aso, the largest in the world. It is about eighty kilometres across and it contains many subsidiary volcanoes and craters, most of them dead, like old boils on a great round face; but Mount Aso itself is still smoking, and today there is a soft plume of white smoke rising from its crater. Inside the ancient crater walls the earth is visibly darker and richer, the grass lusher and greener. In the fat fields there are rows of newly reaped rice laid out to dry before binding and stacking. I stared in admiration at the neat patterns of the fields: some were covered with blond squares of matting on which the freshly thrashed rice was laid out to dry in the sun of this volcanic 'Land of Fire'. Rows of long, plump white *daikon* or giant radish (more like our parsnip in shape); rows and rows of corn-cobs. Under thatched farmhouse eaves long fringes of orange corn-cobs drying, or strings of dark persimmons, a fruit, when dried, that is delicious in autumn and winter. In some gorge-like glens there were dark blue-grey and white streams rushing over rocks under autumn-tinted trees. The harvest landscape of Mount Aso, so mellow and rich under the late afternoon autumn light, was one of the most satisfying, pictorially, that I have ever seen from the air.

The smoking crater of Mount Aso itself: a most impressive grey-green pit of growling steam, grey and white; long, bare skylines on which even the immense parties of school excursionists, silhouetted in their black uniforms against the boiling clouds, look dwarfed and lost, and their endless chatter is extinguished. A few groups of 'company men' in depressing business suitings stand here and there in stiff, noble attitudes, being photographed by the professional photographers with their heads under funeral black hoods of cameras. The nicest souvenirs here are postcards on which local wild alpine flowers are pressed; their Latin and Japanese names are given, the former sometimes inaccurately: *gentian*, *pteridophyllum*, *anaphalis*, *gnaphalium multicena Well*, *gentiana Thunbergii Griseb*, *gentiana Scabra Bunge* var. *Buergeri*, *paederia scandens merrill* var., *Cinna Momum Camphora*, *Hydyahgeoideae*, *Davallia Mariesii Moorei*, *Shortia Soldanelloidesrar Genuina Makino* (a pretty bell-flower known to the Japanese as *iwakagami*), *Climacium japonicum Limas*, *Schigocodon Soldanelloides Sieb*, *Solidago Urgameel*, *Narlinearifolia Saustier* and *Majamthemum bibloium D.C.*

In the pleasant gardens of the Aso Kanko Hotel, a Swiss chalet style place on a very large scale, I noticed white camellia, vividly blue gentians, sorrel and cosmos.

From Mount Aso I took the helicopter again on to Kumamoto, my favourite city in Kyushu where, at night, I wandered round the deserted, floodlit castle and, with a suddenly discovered friend, drove in his car to some heights outside the city to gaze down on its street lamps and neon towers. This time I had the impression that Kumamoto, more than any other Japanese city, was a city of bicycles. Everywhere there were racks for them, across the pavements, outside *pachinko* parlours and restaurants, and at all the cinemas there were special attendants who issued parking tickets for customers' machines.

My day in Kumamoto was a happy one. I am always happy in that city whatever the weather or the season. Autumn and the light of autumn are lovely there. My last recollection of Kumamoto as I trudged round some fields outside the city: dark crimson dwarf maple trees against the deep grey of a tiled roof. Ripe persimmons scattered like constellations of orange stars across the bare brown tree branches, and glowing against the intense blueness of the light in the autumn skies above the dark-tiled roof of a wooden farmhouse. In the early radiance of dawn, thc new moon of November, flat on its back and glittering like a well-used sickle, worn and sharpened by many hands, many harvests.

'Autumn Leaf Fields'—someone on the train from Kumamoto to Moji told me that this was the meaning of 'Akihabara', the name of a district in Tokyo not far from Ueno station, which is celebrated nowadays for its fantastic jumble of small shops selling every imaginable kind of electrical equipment, all brand new, at considerably reduced prices. Most of my household goods were bought there, considerably cheaper than I would have got them in department stores. Akihabara is a most exhilarating place, with its little warrens and arcades of dazzlingly lit, wide-open booths piled from floor to ceiling with churning washing-machines, walls of television sets, all showing different pictures, blaring radios, all on different stations, meckering tape recorders and throbbing refrigerators icy under banks of electric fires glowing that particular gold-vermilion colour that is also the colour of charcoal radiant in a *hibachi* or stone household brazier, the colour of autumn maples.

North of the big city of Hakata, famed for its coloured plaster figurines (I prefer not to dignify such slick and expensive products with the name of 'doll'), the train enters one of the greatest regions of industrial Japan: the forests of tall chimney-stacks with foliage of brown smoke at Kirosaki. The great new city of Kitakyushu, combination of five already existing factory towns. At Tobata, one of these towns, there is the magnificent sight of an immense vermilion suspension bridge over brown wooden and grey-tiled roofs of workers' humble houses. Against the blue autumn sky, this bridge has a splendour typical of the season.

At Moji station, the cries of the sellers of *o-bento* or boxed lunches of cold rice and fish and pickles, the calls of the sellers of green tea with their baskets of little earthenware or plastic teapots and their huge aluminium kettles of boiling water were like the chantings of priests in a busy temple.

It is the first time I have travelled along the west coast of Japan, the Japan Sea coast that faces China and Korea. Shimonoseki, site of the Dan-no-ura Temple, where the Heike clan made their last stand, and the setting of Hearn's famous story of Mimi-Nashi-Hoichi in his collection of supernatural tales, *Kwaidan*. On the beach at Dan-no-ura there are to be found small crabs called *Heike-gani*, because the markings on their shells are thought by the Japanese to resemble the infuriated faces of the defeated Heike warriors. The west coast shore scenery and contorted off-shore pine islands are very like those of the Kii Peninsula. But of course the light here is different, for we are facing mainly west; from this side of Japan the long, deep ginger and pale violet sunsets over the black seas plated with dull gold reminded me very much of some of the skies in the coloured wood-block prints of Hiroshige and Hokusai. On this side of Honshu, I was surprised to notice, nearly all the roofs of houses and temples have brown or rust-red tiles instead of the blue-grey ones seen in every other part of Japan. They are brilliantly burnished by the fiercely squinting autumn sun in bays and glens of dark red and orange maple, fiery foliage already falling into shadows of blue and lilac this late autumn afternoon. A row of leaning pines all yearning the same way, black against the blue sea at Nagatoshi, followed by sandy beaches of pale yellow, an unusual sight in Japan, where beaches are mostly coarse and stony. In the blue-violet light, the tree fountains of suspended persimmons are exactly the vibrant orange colour of the small wooden boundary markers in the fine sand at the edge of marine fields. Little rustic thatched barns and huts of reed and wood stand all along the sandy dunes.

Round Tsuda this beautiful coastline seems to reach the height of wild perfection. Hagi is a perfectly lovely, unspoilt medieval port town with its fine *shoin* shrine, dedicated to Yoshida Torajiro, a famous loyalist, who taught here. The charming, cosy little harbour of Kamate. At Mihomisumi there is a magnificent rocky coast of a type the Japanese characterize as 'male' in its beauty. Hamada: a fair-sized, bustling port. Great brown-tiled temple roofs swoop down on the small lanes and streets round the station. At Yunotsu a fine wooded hillside is completely covered, and ruined, by the grossest of advertising signs in horrid colours. It is a spa town with radioactive waters, and these signs are advertisements for inns and baths. At five-thirty a pearly pink and dove grey sunset over the gently foaming waves on the dusky sands.

I spent a few days at the enchanting little city of Matsue (yet another 'Venice of Japan'), one of the pleasantest and most interesting provincial towns in all Japan. It was untouched by bombing during the war, and so it still preserves a clear, calm feeling of the Japan of a bygone age, the Japan of only thirty years ago. Many old houses are still standing, the most picturesque ones of grey, weathered wood being along the autumn-tinted moat of the ancient castle donjon, and near the site of the house once occupied by Lafcadio Hearn when he taught here at the Shimane Middle School. In Shiroyama or Castle Hill Park the donjon itself appears to be completely authentic: no poured-concrete castle this, but an imposing edifice of massive square wooden pillars and beams, steep, solid wood stairs, their treads and balustrades smoothed with the steps and hands of countless millions. The worn wooden handrails, worm-eaten, moved me when I thought of the millions of hands that had polished them to such a fine patina. The interior is fairly dark, for the only lighting comes from the bell-shaped paper windows in each wall of the three storeys. So, as in most Japanese castle museums of this type, it is rather difficult to see the exhibits of ancient swords, armour and historical relics of the Shimane Peninsula. The view from the top floor of Lake Shinji and the peaks of Mount Yakumo (Peak of Eight Clouds, Crane Peak and Tortoise Peak) is most lovely, and is one of the best in the San-in district.

Everywhere in the donjon I was impressed by the very sound and skilful woodwork; it is this woodwork which gives all the dignity and character to the old houses of Matsue. These have Kyoto-type, wood-barred windows, and on the oldest there is a lot of plain flat board forming sliding shutters over the upper windows, the wood weathered to a silvery grey that is most subtle and poetic in tone.

Several times I walked over the famous 'Great Bridge' of Matsue, *Matsue O-hashi* of a celebrated folk-song. From it can be had fine views of Lake Shinji, especially at twilight and dawn when the 'feminine' character of the lake is most pronounced, according to nature-viewing connoisseurs. In Hearn's day the bridge was a typical strutted Japanese wooden structure, but now it is built of steel and concrete, though still following the ancient curved line of the original. Its balustrades are now of pink granite with the usual domed metal caps. The two 'viewing platforms' of the earlier bridge have been retained at the centre of each side of the bridge; it is pleasant to lean here at sunset and gaze upon the lighted lake with its small island of Yome-ga-shima. One can hire a boat to visit the little shrine, called the Bridal shrine, on this islet, much patronized by this autumn's newly weds, who also make trips to the Yaegaki shrine, about four miles away, whose guardian deities are said to look favourably on those who have wedded for love, something still rather uncommon in modern Japan. But there are still quite a number of the old-style wooden bridges, extremely graceful, with their long, gentle arch, and still bearing traces of crimson paint.

Beside the moat, opposite their stonemason's shop, a young man and his father were packing a big stone garden lantern, wrapping each part carefully in woven straw and tying them up very thoroughly with straw rope.

I was in Matsue on 15th November, which is the popular festival known as *Shichi-go-san*, literally 'Seven-five-three', a happy day for three-year-old children of either sex, five-year-old boys and seven-year-old girls. Their parents, if they can afford it, dress them in traditional finery or in smart new Western-style clothes and take them, in car or taxi or even a truck or a van if possible, to local shrines and temples to pray for their future. One of the best places to see a really traditional observance of this festival is at the Nanzenji Temple in Higashiyama-ku, Kyoto, or at the great Izumo Taisha shrine in Matsue. This venerable and extremely beautiful and sacred shrine lies at the foot of Mount Yakumo, about one mile from the centre of town and is reached through an avenue of magnificent pine trees. It is dedicated to Okuni-nushi-no-Mikoto, a Shinto god who is traditionally associated with medicine, sericulture and halieutics. After the sacred shrines of Ise, whose style that of Taisha resembles, the Izumo Taisha shrine is regarded as the most purely Japanese, and is the most venerated in Japan. All the Shinto gods from all over Japan are popularly believed to meet at this shrine every October; therefore October receives the appellation *Kannazuki* or 'Month with no Gods' everywhere in Japan but at Izumo, where it is called *Kami-arizuki* or 'Month with Gods'.

November 15th at Matsue was a rainy day, but fortunately many children and their parents braved the weather to visit the Izumo shrine. Nearly all the boys were very fashionably and stylishly dressed in the latest Western styles for five-year-olds, and nearly all the girls, especially the three-year-old ones, wore truly gorgeous array, the gold and scarlet kimono with vermilion sash. Enchantingly excited, their eyebrows shaved and faces powdered white, these miniature geisha clutched fans and gold-brocaded purses. Many seemed overawed by the grandeur of the occasion as they imitated their parents by clapping their hands and bowing their bobbed heads before the shrine.

However, not all little boys and girls of the ages of three, five and seven were participating in the festival. Some had parents too poor to dress them in antiquated finery or in new clothes.

My impression is that the people of Matsue are enchantingly sweet-natured, as original and authentically Japanese as the district they live in. Smiles from everyone. In the excellent Yamagoya Bar, one of the Suntory chain beside the river near the Great Bridge, I met many interesting people, including students and their teachers or *sensei* from Shimane University and the local director of the N.H.K. broadcasting station. The girls at the beautiful and comfortable Minami-kan inn where I stayed were utterly sweet and kind to me. One afternoon, as I was sheltering from the rain near a tea shop, the young master of the shop called me in for a chat and some tea-ceremony tea, made by whipping up powdered green tea with a small bamboo whisk in freshly boiled water. It is thick and rather bitter, but refreshing. It is somehow a very sobering drink, possibly because of the formality one associates with the tea ceremony. It may take hours to perform, but it is so full of interest and charm and true spiritual restoration that one comes away feeling refreshed and purified, as after a perfect performance of Noh, with which *cha-no-yu* is allied in temper and purpose. The Minami-kan had a small teahouse in its stone garden on Lake Shinji.

There are some surprising examples of Western-style architecture in Matsue: a château-style bank, a newspaper office like a wooden Swedish farmhouse or villa and, in Shiroyama Park, an extraordinary, half-dilapidated, wooden, Western-colonial-style mansion with a vast *porte-cochère*, verandas, balconies and pillars. I opened a side door, hoping to be able to explore it all on my own, but a little old woman immediately leapt out of a cubby-hole to tell me the place was uninhabited and visitors not allowed. It would have been quite useless to try to get in by giving her a tip, as such things are not done in Japan. I was unable to find out what the place was, but it had perhaps been some sort of official residence, or an hotel or a restaurant.

Alas, the majority of the Japanese are not as kind to animals as one would wish. There is the immense popularity of such ignoble films as *Mondo Cane* and *Mondo Infame*, at showings of which a large part of the audiences gape with bated breath and greet the most horrible mutilations with shrieks of laughter. Everywhere there are zoos to entertain tourists and the kiddies, and in these enclosures, often at the most celebrated beauty spots, the kings of the jungle and forest lead a life of bored degradation and cruel discomfort. Even the 'natural' zoos like those vast monkey kingdoms on Takasakiyama at Beppu and at Choshikei on Shodoshima are distasteful to me: I dislike the sight of those wild monkeys, with crimson faces and backsides, squabbling among each other, to the great amusement of tourists, over the handfuls of dried peas and nuts the human visitors see fit to scatter about. In Shiroyama Park at Matsue there is a miserable cage like a large parrot's just below the gracious donjon, centuries old, that the newly weds visit with ceremony and respect. As soon as they have visited the castle and taken numerous snapshots of themselves in newly wedded bliss they betake themselves to the monkey cage where crouch six poor, bored baboons, enduring the human taunts and laughter with a resigned indifference that is something like genius—it has to be, as it is their only defence. There is nowhere for them to hide, only a couple of sawn-off boughs, slippery with scrambling. The newly weds, relieved of the necessity of being awestruck by the castle, rattle the cage bars, throw balls of the paper they carry round in secret wads for all sorts of purposes, try to poke the poor creatures into entertaining life with bits of bamboo or tease them with the lovely autumn horse-tail grass, *suzuki*. The monkeys just sit and endure it all. Sometimes when they hear a child approaching they rise on their hind legs and look with rather hopeless expectancy above the wall round the bottom of the cage: children, unlike adults, nearly always have something to eat. I gave one of the monkeys a banana, and at first he didn't know what it was—he thought it was just another joke. The discovery that it was a *banana*, a *real* one, produced such demented screams that I had to hold my ears, and I realized that the poor beasts were mad, stricken incurably with melancholia and the utmost despair. It was like a mad scene from Hogarth. The screams were greeted with loud laughter by the newly weds and they smiled and bowed at me for having provided them with such fun and with subjects for more snaps. In return I bowed to them more deeply than they had bowed to me, which is a refined insult, especially coming from me, and gave them my special 'meaningless' smile as I walked away. I think all politicians should be put in cages and fed uneatable rubbish instead of being installed in white houses all with modern paintings. Only the *very* sincere would then wish to run for election, and it would mean an end to politics and nuclear deterrents and 'working lunches' and 'briefing breakfasts' at which the world is slowly being pushed, with every semblance of rationality, into total extinction. I do not understand the world that takes such savage delight in cruelty, nor do I understand human beings who do nothing about it.

The Lafcadio Hearn Memorial Hall: a cold little museum, badly lit, badly arranged, with items poorly selected. The photographs of Hearn with his Japanese family and school groups are the most interesting things. I did not care for the character revealed in the rather precious and curly handwriting, so dreadfully even, like one plain two purl: he must have been rather pompous, self-satisfied, and yet furiously frustrated and a crashing bore to talk to. Glass cases contain some of his clothes done up in plastic bags. A complete library of books written by or translated by Hearn, including some Loti scraps, not very well done. I felt sadness for Hearn, for his difficult life, increasingly poor sight and growing dissatisfaction with the Japanese at the end of his life. This dissatisfaction, I have noticed, affects many foreigners who live for any length of time in Japan. Hearn felt he was not sufficiently loved and appreciated by the Japanese. But after all, why should one be? If one makes oneself an outcast, whether in one's native country or in a foreign land, one should not expect sympathy.

A delightful train ride, lasting seven hours, from Matsue to Osaka, passing many quaint little hot springs and Mount Daisen, the pseudo-Fuji, and its great National Park on the right. Round Tottori the mountains and river gorges are superb at this time of the year, the wet, red fires of maple foliage sparkling in the air's rainy light. The sandy dunes which form a feature of the coast at Hamamura are unique in Japan. The train is crowded with drunks—mostly farm hands who have just finished the rice-harvest; their great red moon-faces keep looming over me and I find my pale, frail hands shaken in their colossal mitts, hard and brown as wood, while they attempt to force me to drink from bottles of beer or saké. I notice that on Japanese trains drunken men seem to think it is their right to invade the first-class compartments and refuse to pay the conductor the extra money due on their second-class tickets. There was one drunken priest, his thin, ascetic face luridly flushed round the small, mean eyes. When he smiled at me he showed a mouthful of ruined teeth plastered together with gold and silver, and a tongue purple with an indelible pencil which he was sucking with every sign of enjoyment between swigs of saké from an enormous bottle.

At every station there are displays of big, mop-headed chrysanthemums. Over mountains brilliant with autumn-tinted light, the sunny skies have a few swansdown clouds. The maples are like great sheaves of paintbrushes dipped in hot colours. Splendid cliffs and little bays near Yoroi and Kasumi. Kasumi is the station for the Daijoji Temple which contains many paintings by the eighteenth-century artist Maruyama Okyo and his disciples. Okyo with his realistic landscapes founded a new school of painting which was named after him. Many of the paintings are classified as 'Important Cultural Properties', while Kasumi itself has been awarded the Government title of 'Outstanding Scenic Place'. Soon after leaving Yoroi station the very informative conductor on the train announced that we were crossing the highest steel bridge in Japan; it is 132 feet high and 1,015 feet in length. On leaving the bridge we entered the Momomi Tunnel, six thousand feet in length and the longest on the San-in line.

A terrific uproar of drunken men in the first-class compartment, where they interrupt the billings and cooings of the young newly weds. The conductor does nothing about it. This is always the case on Japanese trains. Nor do the other Japanese passengers give me any help when three of them start amiably but boringly pestering me to drink and eat *o-bento*. In Japan a man is almost allowed to get away with murder, provided he is drunk. Inebriation provides the most fitting of extenuating circumstances for those Japanese who from time to time feel they simply have to kick over the traces.

Kinosaki: one of the oldest and most popular spas on the spa-lined San-in railway. Outside the station a long row of hotel guides carrying their eye-catching, gaily coloured banners, greeting bashful newly weds with frank but courteous smiles. It is a popular stop on honeymoon holidays. Television does not appear to have reached this part of Japan's west coast yet; it is odd to see a town with no aerials or 'antennae', as the Japanese call them.

Toyo-oka: noted for the manufacture of wicker trunks. A curious little red bridge, high in the air on a rocky eminence that also bears a pillar with a long, needle-like metal shaft stuck upright in it, one of the most pointless memorials I have seen.

It is good to reach Osaka again, and a rather low geisha party, attended by some self-styled 'literary geisha' who seem to me to be idiocy incarnate. *Shamisen* music, singing, dancing with fans and sheaves of autumn leaves, many flasks of hot saké. At dawn I found myself in the amusement district of Namba, in a low-class house overlooking the canal that runs beside Dotombori, playing blind man's buff with no clothes on.

Next evening, at the staggeringly dull O.S. Revue theatre for a depressing Japanese leg-show amid plastic maple leaves. This might have been spectacularly pretty, like the Autumn Dance at the Nichigeki in Tokyo, had it not been for the semi-nude Japanese girls with their surgically improved eyes and busts, their modern plastic faces and the hideous pock-like scars of countless inoculations pitting their upper arms.

Scenes on the new Tokaido express from Shin Osaka to Tokyo: leaving Shin Osaka station by the first Hikari express at 6 a.m., I went to the buffet car for some coffee as soon as the train had left the station and was surprised to find some Japanese business men already drinking bottles of Asahi beer with their breakfasts of curry rice. I regularly saw this kind of breakfast being enjoyed on the train at 6 a.m. It was quite Elizabethan to me, for Queen Elizabeth I always used to drink a quart of ale at breakfast. But not, I think, as early as 6 a.m.

I much admired the decorous behaviour of a party of about forty elderly countrywomen, gold-toothed, deeply tanned from their work in the ricefields and farms, now with neat hair styles, imposingly and elegantly attired in best kimono of a sober shade, wearing coat (*haori*) and stole of dark silk. They had on spotless white *tabi* and prettily decorated *zori*. In their hair were tortoiseshell and metal combs. They were clean, modest, quiet in demeanour. Their leader, an elderly lady similarly attired, collected from time to time in a large polythene sack her charges' rubbish—orange peel, paper, empty *bento* boxes and the plastic teapots and cups now so revoltingly used for serving *o-cha* (tea). So often on Japanese trains and in Japanese streets people just throw their trash anywhere: it was refreshing to see these simple old ladies displaying such admirable social consciousness and doing their bit to keep the train clean.

A very plain-looking middle-aged business man was sitting next to me. He had obviously learnt his English at some conversation school, for he was anxious simply to show off his acquired textbook phrases, and paid no attention at all to my replies. For example, he asked: 'Are you a tourist?' I answered 'No.' But he did not take this in, and went on: 'Have you seen Mount Fuji?' 'Yes.' 'You come to Japan to see cherry blossom?' 'No.' 'You like geisha girl?' No answer. 'Is this the first time you travel on New Tokaido line?' 'This is the twentieth time, to be precise.' But he did not notice this, and continued: 'Hope you will enjoy cherry blossom and geisha girl during your business trip in Japan.' No answer. 'What is your business in Japan?' No answer. 'I think you are not an American, you have no wife and kids with you.' At this point I got up and went to the buffet car. It was my only means of escape from this exceedingly boring stereotyped conversation.

One of the great delights of train travel in Japan is that one is able to sample, at almost every stop, local foods and delicacies. Even on the new Tokaido line super-express one can enjoy these station lunchboxes or *o-bento*—charcoal-broiled eels with soy sauce and sweet saké from Hamamatsu; Shizuoka chopped sea-bream with rice in round earthenware pots, accompanied by Izu mushrooms and *wasabizuke*, a kind of horseradish; at Maibara, rainbow trout marinated in sweet vinegar; at Nagoya, minced chicken with chopped boiled egg, seaweed, cucumber and broiled chicken liver all in separate sections of the little wooden lunchbox (chopsticks and paper napkin provided free of charge); at Yokohama one can get *shumai*, a Chinese minced pork delicacy that also includes ground ligaments from Hokkaido shellfish, green peas and onion, each portion wrapped in a thin pastry skin, and served, of course, with rice and soy sauce.

2

LIFE IN SUITA

When I lived in Suita, I was always interested in the sparkling white dustcart that came round every week collecting the rubbish. It played a tinkling little tune, like an air from some elegant antique music-box, to warn residents of its approach. The tune was *O-Edo Nihonbashi*, originally a seventeenth-century children's song and now apparently very popular, for I hear it everywhere. I liked the men who worked so hard to collect the rubbish: they were always cheerful and smiled happily at my piles of paper and bottles. 'Oss!' they would say, greeting me in Osaka dialect, and I soon learned to answer them in the same way. Just before Christmas I tried to offer them a small tip, but they refused it: they are forbidden to accept tips or gifts. In this respect they were very unlike the Tokyo dustmen, who rather expect a little money present now and then. I shall always remember the willingness and honesty of those cheerful Osaka dustmen. They are my brothers.

As I was wandering in a back alley of Suita City I met a group of inebriated workmen, all very jolly, wreathed in rosy smiles, perfumed with saké and *shochu* and prodigal with handshakes. As I passed on to the self-service store to buy my daily ration of spinach I was touched when one of the young workmen, rapturously waving, called after my departing form: 'Abebe! Abebe!' It was the only foreign name he knew and because I am a foreigner he called me by it. I was also immensely pleased to be associated, however remotely, with that noble human being, the Tokyo Olympics marathon winner, whose monumental triumph I had happened to witness on the television screen of the Inuyama restaurant in Shinjuku (where I had ordered my usual 'Baby Lunch' because it is cheap and because I was dieting).

The pleasure I felt at being called 'Abebe' reminded me of the happiness that suddenly struck my heart when a bar boy in Sendai informed me that my students at Tohoku University, who were unable to pronounce my name correctly, had given me the charming nickname 'Kawa Kappa', an inspired Japanese bastardization of 'Kirkup'.

My little wooden house, purely Japanese in style, situated in this working-class suburb of Osaka, is just a few minutes' walk from the site of the great Japan World Exposition to be held in this place in 1970. It will bring great prosperity to this modest satellite town of the Kansai megapolis. Already farmers in Yamada Village, where most of the ground for the exhibition site has been bought, have become millionaires overnight. For them it has been a sudden transposition from poverty and hard work to wealth and ease. They hardly know what to do with their money and their time, an enviable dilemma. The great feature of Expo '70 is to be a 1,300-foot tower, the highest in the world of course, designed by Japan's leading architect Kenzo Tange. There will be splendid modern gardens and lakes, and a 'moving road' four miles in length. Sanyo Electric Company's special pavilion, called the Electropia, will show the ideal life we are all supposed to be going to lead in the electronics age of the near future. I hope it all comes true. How far away it all seems from this humble, humdrum little suburb of Suita!

The priest of Sozenji Temple in Higashiyodogawa is Nishioka Sogaku, a distinguished-looking man of great simplicity, kindness and good humour. When I lived in Suita I often visited his small but lovely temple.

On my first visit I sat with him in the main room of his charming house, sipping green tea and looking across the polished boards of the long veranda at a small, rectangular, walled rock-garden. I felt there was some special quality in this typical formal garden, with its cleverly arranged stones, tea bushes and neatly raked white gravel. It was the wall that first drew my attention, and I learnt from Priest Nishioka that he had made it himself from stones, bricks, tiles and rubble left lying around the district after the Second World War. On 7th July 1945 Sozenji had been burnt to the ground by fire bombs, but Nishioka Sogaku managed to save all the treasures and sacred relics of the place. The next year he rebuilt the temple with his own hands.

The formal garden of tea bushes, rocks and finely raked gravel is in the *hichi-go-san* style—a subtle arrangement of seven rocks, five tea bushes and three more stones—and was created by Kato Kumakichi. Priest Nishioka is proud of Sozenji, and well he may be, for it is a place of some importance in Japanese culture and history. It was founded in 1441, and contains the tomb of one of Japan's early converts to Christianity, Lady Gratia Hosokawa, and the tomb of the Enjo brothers who were massacred there in a bloody sword-fight. Today their grave is still a place of pilgrimage, and every year on 3rd and 4th November a ceremony of remembrance is held for them.

I was invited to attend one of these ceremonies in 1965. There were long scarlet and white banners on tall bamboo poles round the entrance and courtyard of the temple. The service was conducted by a high-ranking priest of the Soto sect of Zen Buddhism, to which Sozenji belongs. He was wearing splendid crimson and white robes, a gold and black brocade cape worn in such a way as to leave the right shoulder uncovered, and a hexagonal brocade hat like a crown. He was assisted by a rosy-cheeked, shaven-pated young nun in black, grey and dark blue robes.

The priest banged a drum and a gong. Four young priests were sitting on either side of the altar, kneeling on flat square cushions in front of chests containing copies of the sutras which they began to chant to the accompaniment of drum and gong. Each priest would take up a volume of the sacred writings and let the folded pages ripple swiftly through the air like an accordion or a paper waterfall. This method of reading the sutras is called *tendoku* or 'moving reading' and the young novices performed it most gracefully. Only once did I remark a slight clumsiness, a quickly corrected faltering in the smooth 'waterfalling' of volume after volume.

The service was followed by a tea ceremony in the garden. The associations of the temple with such devotees of the tea ceremony as Oda Nobunaga and the Ashikaga and Hosokawa families make it natural that Sozenji should be an important centre of the tea cult in the Kansai region. Priest Nishioka's mother, whose tea name is Koshiga Soei, is a master of the Rikyu tea-ceremony school. She trains many young people in this exquisite and complicated art, including Keiko, her teenage grand-daughter, who is already quite an expert in tea ceremony and classical dancing.

The tea cult, known as *cha-no-yu*, is a highly refined and polite form of aestheticism and is said to promote, in the strict discipline of its training and observance, spiritual enlightenment and mental composure. At the same time the cultist is able to enter a state of mind in which he can appreciate the finest subtleties of Japanese painting and pottery and flower arrangement as he gradually becomes more and more sensitive to the almost imperceptibly delicate aroma of the frothy, whipped, green tea powder. At its best, the tea ceremony is always observed in a small but perfectly constructed and decorated teahouse or *sukiya*, whose main room will be extremely restrained and *shibui* in style and atmosphere; it should be designed to accommodate only five people. There is also a *mizuya*, a kind of pantry where the tea-service utensils—the often priceless though rough-looking bowls, the bamboo whisk, spatula for measuring out the tea powder and ladle for taking the hot water out of the iron pot or kettle—are washed and arranged. The guests wait in the *yoritsuki* or waiting-room until they are invited to enter the tea room proper by walking slowly and quietly and meditatively along the *roji* or formal garden path or stepping-stones connecting the *yoritsuki* and the *sukiya*. There are separate entrances for host and guests, but both are made very small and low, so that all have to enter this abode of spiritual enlightenment by creeping on their hands and knees, a symbol of their willing humility.

The guests, after bowing to the host, must in a prescribed order kneel one by one on the mat in front of the alcove, or *tokonoma*, and contemplate first the hanging scroll, or *kakemono*, and then the incense holder, which must always be held or placed on the mats in a special small square of silk named the *fukusa*. A small collation follows, known as the *kaiseki*, and etiquette demands that no guest should leave a dish unfinished, for the host brings in everything himself and it would be considered the gravest discourtesy not to eat everything he offered. The meal ends with the presentation of sweets. This is the first part of the tea ceremony, governed by the most elaborate rules of etiquette that take years to learn properly. After it, the guests retire to the waiting-room until soft strokes of a gong summon them to the tea ceremony proper. The five or seven strokes on the gong indicate that the host is ready to serve his guests with the *koi-cha*, or thick tea. When they re-enter the tea room they find that the hanging scroll has been removed and a flower arrangement placed in the alcove.

Koshiga Soei, a lady who always seems to be bubbling with happiness and vitality, takes my hand and conducts me to the tea-ceremony area, where some *tatami* has been spread between two huge oiled-paper umbrellas. I sit with some other guests on a bench in front of a low table and observe the preparation of the tea. A few autumn maple leaves keep drifting down from the clear, still sky and fall gently on the *tatami*.

Part of the pleasure of the ceremony is watching the controlled but relaxed grace of Koshiga Soei and her grand-daughter. I like the serious and sincerely interested way the guests admire the simple utensils—bowls, bamboo spatulas, the black lacquer tea caddy. I like the way Keiko, in her splendid kimono and *obi*, handles so gravely and quietly, so easily and yet with great precision, this most elaborate of ceremonies. I could watch her for ever as she slowly poses the spatula on the *tatami* and gives it a long look. It is of very dark wood, with a lovely knot in the middle of the slender handle, and the slightly curved spoon part is still stained pale green with a little of the powdered tea Keiko has just measured into an ancient tea-bowl. Then she raises the simple bamboo ladle for hot water, and with a gravity beyond her years holds it before her a moment, considering it as if it were some perfect flower, before smoothly dipping it into the kettle and pouring the hot water over the tea in the bowl. A brief pause: then she extends her frail hand and elevates the bamboo whisk: with a subtle acceleration of circular movements she gently whips the mixture into a froth and gracefully presents the bowl, with a bow, to each guest. We all bow our thanks for the tea and also for her youthful grace, her preternatural dignity, quietness and complete self-possession. Despite the formality we feel relaxed, for we realize we are in the hands of someone in full control of her art.

I was served with a rustic-looking bowl of thick, bitter tea, its green froth the delicate colour of a stagnant pond. I have never been able to get used to the peculiar taste and thick texture of this tea, and it always gives me indigestion. Nevertheless I am willing to suffer a little discomfort to experience the sense of cleansing and spiritual calm that *cha-no-yu* sometimes inexplicably brings me.

The bowl must be held in the palm of the left hand and steadied by the right, which gives it three turns in a clockwise direction so that the design and texture of the bowl may be properly appreciated. Then the guest takes a sharp slurp and commends the host on its perfect flavour, airy froth, delicate consistency and admirable colour. He takes another two slurps before passing the bowl to the next guest who, after going through the same complicated procedure, passes it on to his neighbour, and so on. The prescribed etiquette requires that the place on the lip of the bowl from which a guest has drunk must be wiped with a special piece of white paper called *kaishi*. When the last guest has taken a sip the bowl is returned to the host by the chief guest. All guests then pass round the tea caddy and the spatula for delicate admiration, after which, in a less formal atmosphere, it is usual to serve thin tea or *usu-cha*.

On another occasion I was privileged to attend a tea ceremony at night at Sozenji. This is a most unusual event, performed exactly as in Rikyu's time, and it is limited always to only a few intimate family friends. There were about six guests that night. It had rained all day, but now the night was clear and starry. The whole dim garden gave off muted sparkles of wet light reflected from dripping stones, leaves, roof-tiles.

Old-fashioned square lanterns called *andon* were placed in the garden and in the house, lit by wicks dipped in rape-seed oil. Additional soft illumination was provided by wicks dipped in small teacups of oil standing on rough pottery saucers, and by slim tallow candles fixed by spikes on tall dark wooden candlesticks. Lamps were suspended along the eaves of the shrine for the war dead of Higashi-yodogawa in the outer garden. The dim light was mysteriously romantic on the pale grey paper windows, on which from time to time silhouettes of figures wearing kimono would profile themselves in the formal attitudes of a wood-block print.

The sound of a mallet on a wooden gong—a quick *pan-pan-pan-pan*—gave notice of the start of the ceremony. The oldest guest, an elderly lady in fine autumn kimono and *obi*, bearing before her a lighted candle, leads us out into the twilit, lamplit garden, over stepping-stones laid across gravel and lawn. We are all wearing big flat *geta* made of *sugi* (cryptomeria) and whose loops and thongs are of strips of twisted bamboo leaf. We are guided to a lamplit seat where we must wait to be called to the tea room. We sit on round straw cushions and warm our hands at a *hibachi*. Our hostess, Koshiga Soei, comes quietly out of the house and, after washing her hands and mouth at a little trough, comes to meet us with a candle. She opens a bamboo lattice gate, and exchanges her candle with that of our leader. No words are spoken at this stage of the ceremony, but bows are exchanged. The hostess goes away, leaving the gate open. Our leader places her candle beside the washing-place. We purify our hands and mouths, using a cedarwood ladle. The last guest to wash takes the candle and closes the gate behind her.

The tea-ceremony house or *cha-seki* at Sozenji is called *Ryo-sho-tei*, and is constructed in exactly the same style as that of Rikyu, the great sixteenth-century tea master. It is very plain and small—the main room is only four and a half mats—but it is a place of unusual refinement and peace. The entrance door is low, so that we are compelled to enter with bowed heads, in proper humility.

First of all, two bowls of very 'light' (not 'thick') tea were shared by four people. Koshiga Soei and Keiko were again exquisite in their calm performance of this unique private ceremony for a few friends. I was spellbound by the virtuosity with which Koshiga Soei carried out the fire-repairing ceremony which followed the preparation of this first tea. She is a fairly elderly lady, but looks remarkably youthful: her good humour and gravity go well together. She was wearing a subdued autumn kimono which showed her perfect taste: it was dark brown, and plain, decorated only with a few pine needles of gold thread. As I watched her mending the fire, I thought it was no wonder she looked so agile and youthful, for she had to do so much kneeling, rising, turning and bowing, all executed perfectly, without a hint of strain. It was like an abstract ballet.

It would be impossible here to describe every detail of her performance. First she brought in small lumps of charcoal in a lacquered bamboo-leaf basket and some incense called *matsuga*, made from pine tree leaves.

Then she rose and went out and came back with a bowl of specially fine ash. There were also some small twigs of charcoal, painted white. All these objects were carried ceremoniously into the room, held at the height of the *obi*, and placed carefully on the mats in precisely ordained positions. Nevertheless an easy, light conversation arose between the master and her guests: this is called *yobanashi*, or 'night talk'. She used a large crane's feather to sweep some faint traces of ash from the polished wooden edges of the square brazier sunk in the centre of the mats. Next she carefully placed an iron ring on each of the hooks on either side of the hot-water pot, which she then slowly lifted, like a chalice, and set on a pad of folded white papers which she had previously produced from the folds in the neck of her kimono. We all admired the sober loveliness and simplicity of the pieces of charcoal as she laid them one by one in the brazier and then sprinkled and raked ash around them.

Then we tasted *amazake*, a thick, sweet rice wine served in small blue-and-white cups, which we stirred with dark wooden chopsticks: this is made only on special occasions, for intimate friends. This was followed by a most delicious, delicate meal prepared and arranged by Priest Nishioka's gifted wife, who is an expert in this very tasteful style of Japanese cooking.

After this fairy banquet of tiny vegetables, herbs, ferns, pickles, flowers, clear soup and bean-paste sweets, there was a short interval before the next tea, which would be strong and rich. I enjoyed strolling round the cool garden, my *geta* chiming on the stones. The quietness and the fresh-scented air among the rain-washed leaves was something very rare so close to the heart of industrial Osaka. A jet aircraft passed overhead on its way to Itami airport, but could not ruffle the essential tranquillity of my mood. In the distance the new Tokaido line express train, like a long string of luminous pearls or crystal beads, was drawing slowly into Shin Osaka's great glassy cathedral of a station. In the lamplit garden the old ladies were murmuring and crowing to each other, recalling the wonders they had seen, and from time to time giving notes of gentle, sighing laughter.

When we went back into the teahouse we found some changes had been made in the setting. The *kakemono* had been removed from the alcove and a new flower arrangement was on display. The fresh flowers were supposed to clear the air of fumes from the previous ceremony and dinner.

The new tea was made by Koshiga Soei. After ceremoniously admiring the bamboo hot-water ladle, she laid its plain cylindrical wooden cup on a china stand and let the end of the handle drop with a slight tap on the *tatami*: at the sound of that tap everyone bowed. The tea was made in a rather large, very ancient, bowl, which was passed from one guest to another: the tea's curious mild bitterness was still strange to my untutored palate. Then, passing the candle round, each of us examined the empty, pale brown bowl and uttered an admiring word or two on its sober perfection. Its inside was still lacquered with traces of the thick green tea—a superb, vibrant green.

After some ethereal sweets shaped like ginkgo leaves and candied blades of grass, it was time to go. Still kneeling, we bowed low to our hostess and to Keiko, and they bowed in return. Then we bowed to the *tokonoma*, to the cold-water container, to the brazier and to the kettle. My last memory is of Koshiga Soei kneeling at the little door of the teahouse bowing and smiling her good nights to the bowing guests slowly drifting away into the lamplit shadows of the small garden which that evening had seemed to contain the universe.

3
TWENTY YEARS AFTER

It is twenty years since the war with Japan came to an end, shortly after the dropping of the two atom bombs on Hiroshima and Nagasaki. Memorial services for the war dead—those in Tokyo attended by the Emperor and Empress—have this year been particularly solemn and laden with memories.

Very few people know that services are also held for the dead of Japan's former enemies at a Jodo Buddhist temple on the outskirts of the great industrial city of Osaka. Memorial services called *Segaki* are held for the repose of ghosts and spirits and the souls of the dead at the Ju-ganji temple on the slopes of Mount Ikoma, green with pines, shrill with cicadas.

I was invited to attend a *Segaki* service and to visit the various buildings of the temple by its priest, Shinkai Yamaguchi, a friendly, jovial and high-spirited man. The name of his temple means something like 'Double Hopeful Wish'.

During the Second World War there were enshrined at Ju-ganji the ashes of 1,086 prisoners of war captured by the Japanese. Priest Shinkai entrusted his precious lists of names to me. These show that the ashes were those of 379 British, 482 Americans, 163 Dutch, 30 Australians, 23 Canadians, 7 Indians, 1 Italian and 1 Norwegian. How did these ashes come into the hands of Shinkai Yamaguchi, and why did he preserve them with such careful reverence?

The story begins in 1943, when a number of Japanese troop transport ships began to arrive in Osaka Harbour carrying prisoners of war from Singapore and Hong Kong. Many of the prisoners had died on the voyage, from wounds, malnutrition or various diseases including dysentery and beri-beri. Among those from Singapore alone, 255 were dead on arrival. They were immediately cremated at Osaka. Priest Shinkai heard about this and went to the military headquarters to ask for the prisoners' ashes, which the authorities finally allowed him to collect from the prison camp. However, everyone was against having anything to do with the ashes of these dead enemies.

Priest Shinai collected the ashes of the dead prisoners, blessed them and enshrined them in his temple, where he conducted services for the repose of their souls. Many of the young priest's parishioners condemned this act of compassion, and he had much trouble because of the hostility it aroused. But the priest believed it was his sacred duty to tend the souls of these dead human beings who had died without any kind of spiritual comfort.

Despite great opposition on all sides, Shinkai Yamaguchi went on gathering the ashes of prisoners who died in the prison camps of Osaka. No one would tell him their names, only their nationality. He went on holding services for them.

After the war, in the first days of the American Occupation, Juganji temple was visited by American Military Police, who came to take the ashes away. There is a photograph of Shinkai Yamaguchi standing in his Buddhist robes in front of the altar with its precious Buddhas; his neatly boxed and labelled collections of ashes are piled before him as he offers his prayers for the men's souls before the ashes are sent back to their respective countries. On the priest's right is a young American soldier, on guard duty. I was shocked to see that this soldier was wearing his battle helmet and military boots inside the sacred place. Priest Shinkai told me, smiling, that he had been unable to make the young soldier understand that he must take off his boots before entering a Buddhist temple. The soldier had acted in all innocence.

Though the ashes were removed from his keeping, Shinkai Yamaguchi held a memorial service for the dead men every year. Eventually he received a complete list of names of those whose ashes had been in his care. He went to the American Army Headquarters in 1953, and the lists were handed to him. In 1955, after a special solemn memorial service for the souls of the dead prisoners, he sent out letters describing the ceremony to all the next-of-kin. These letters were sent out with the assistance of Japanese officials at the American Cultural Centre in Osaka, who formed a committee that included some of the priest's own parishioners to deal with this complicated task. In his letters the priest added that a special memorial service for these dead persons would be held every October, and that if the correspondents would send photographs of their dead relatives he would display them on the altar.

The priest received about three hundred replies and fifty-two photographs. These letters were very moving. He showed me some from England and America. Without exception, they expressed gratitude for the Japanese priest's thoughtfulness and humanity. There was no resentment, no bitterness.

Shinkai Yamaguchi had the photographs framed in a dignified way and displayed them on his altar. I saw these photographs, surrounded by bowls of smouldering incense, by lighted candles, by offerings of fruit, flowers, cakes and vegetables that included one giant tomato on its own exquisitely gilded and lacquered stand.

Behind the photographs stood all the lovely but confusing paraphernalia of a Buddhist altar: numerous unusual small Chinese statues of holy men and saints, fierce-looking guardian deities, gilded lotus leaves and buds, gongs, lacquer trays. The front of the altar's slightly raised floor was spread with a pure white cloth.

The main central image is a dark, impressive Buddha shrined in a golden niche. Beside him stand a smaller, brighter image of Amida Nyorai and a fine Kanzeon Bosatsu, Buddha of love. The statues are important Cultural Treasures.

On the left of the altar was a sheaf of tall, thin wooden planks inscribed with names of the dead: they stood in a tub of water, which is supposed to give refreshment to parched souls. On the other side of the altar was a box containing hundreds of small white stones, each inscribed by worshippers with a single holy word from the sutras. These stones would later be used in the foundations of the new temple which Shinkai Yamaguchi will start constructing soon. Already he has built a pagoda which, when the interior decorations are completed, will be used solely to enshrine the photographs of the dead prisoners and their sacred memory. The Kanzeon Bosatsu, Buddha of love, will also be placed here to watch over them. Regular memorial services are now conducted, and began with a special opening ceremony in the spring of 1966.

I knelt on the sedge mats in front of the quiet altar, among some of the local people who were praying there, and bowed to the Buddha.

After making my prayers, I looked at those photographs of my dead compatriots. Some of them had been inscribed by their relatives. Among the names I noticed those of Staff Sergeant Samuel Brown (of Walker Estate, Newcastle upon Tyne); James W. Hooker, Royal Navy (of Hartley Wintney); Ernest Edward Manley, A.R.C.M., Bandmaster, 2nd Battalion the East Surrey Regiment, died 15th

January 1945 (of Shalford, Surrey); they all looked young, healthy, cheerful, photographed mostly in uniform at cheap studios in Portsmouth, Plymouth, Newcastle upon Tyne, Aberdeen, Cardiff, Belfast, Glasgow, Liverpool, Manchester. Looking at those typically Western faces with their broad, lively smiles, it seemed strange that they should be dead, and even stranger that their memory should be perpetuated here in this small Japanese temple.

It is the only temple in Japan where the memory of our soldiers, sailors and airmen is kept green, 'in the cause of world peace', which Shinkai Yamaguchi gives as the reason for his devotion.

4

TEMPLE VISIT

WHENEVER I feel too depressed and exhausted by the daily grind of life in Tokyo I go off wandering alone in the mountains of northern Japan for a few days, or spend some time at a temple. I am not a Christian, and indeed before I started visiting Japanese temples I felt I was incapable of any kind of religious belief. Now, though I am far from understanding the religion of Buddha, I am beginning to sense within me the stirrings of a strange faith which is partly Buddhist and partly something poetic and humorous devised by my own imagination.

My contacts with Buddhism have been mostly through the Zen Soto sect of the religion; I have stayed at the sect's two main temples, both of them enormous and rambling and beautiful as the sutras themselves, Eiheiji in Fukui Prefecture and Sojiji at Tsurumi, near Yokohama. I am absolutely useless at Zen, which I simply cannot understand and which means nothing to me at all. The spiritual peace which I always hope to find at such temples always evades me: just as I begin to meditate, lounging on the matted floor with a bottle of champagne for company, a telephone rings in the corridor and a hefty young priest comes scampering along the reverberating wooden floor to answer it in an extremely loud voice. Or a message is loudly relayed by a female voice over the public address system, turning the whole place into a railway station. In fact temples are among the noisiest places in Japan: only the Japanese, who seem to be impervious to noise, could possibly manage to meditate successfully there.

I was amused, when I first visited Eiheiji, to find my name written up in white letters on the vertical black boards at the entrance which list the names of visitors: my name was given as 'Shames Kirkup'. It was dusk, towards the end of a brilliant October day. The whole temple was shrouded in faint mist, through which I could see the green, velvet-mossed roofs hanging among the tall pines, as in a Chinese painting.

I was conducted by a shaven-pated young priest along miles of shining wooden corridors and up flights of steep wooden stairs to what seemed to be the topmost rooms in the vast complex of buildings spread all over a mountainside. There was a lift, but this was apparently used only for transporting food and mattresses. The young priest took me at a spanking pace, and as my feet shuffled along in a pair of skimpy slippers my calves began to ache and I began to feel out of breath, for I am not in training for marathon races. As we dashed round a corner I was very nearly hit on the head by a mallet wielded by another young priest who started to bang it on a wooden gong shaped like a fish—a flat but oddly carrying sound. It was 5 p.m.

Just as I was thinking I could go no farther, we scampered up a final steep flight of slippery wooden stairs and I found myself left in a large, well-appointed Western room with the usual hard-stuffed Japanese Western-style furniture in frilled, stiff white covers. The room had a name, which I was told later meant 'Glorious Cloud', and it was reserved for the reception of foreigners.

A handsome, dignified young priest served me with pale green tea which had a flavour of the sea, and with three small white-and-pink sugar cakes. On the table stood a cigarette box containing 'Peace' cigarettes: there was a cumbersome standing lamp, and a stale atmosphere as of a place long unused and unheated. It was very like the reception rooms which one finds in most Japanese factories and company offices.

After some polite, meaningless chatter, I was escorted to two large Japanese rooms. On the way there I was shocked to see some women in the distance: I had thought Eiheiji was an entirely male preserve, and I felt a keen sense of disappointment when I was told that female tourists are now admitted to this sanctuary once sacred to men only.

My rooms had huge *tokonoma* (alcoves), big enough to sleep in if I had so wanted, and they were adorned with *kakemono* (scrolls) the size of bedsheets on which a few bold black characters had been painted. Sticks of incense were burning in grotesquely carved wooden bowls on little lacquer tables in each *tokonoma*. In the blue *hibachi* there was a pair of metal chopsticks for arranging the rosy glowing lumps of charcoal in the ashen sand. A little rake was also supplied with which I raked wave-patterns in the sand around the hot charcoal, creating a miniature landscape garden whose restrained beauty was carelessly destroyed by a visiting priest who stuck the butts of his cigarettes and his used matches into the sand with scant regard for my sensitive arrangement.

For a while I was left alone. I drifted into the dusky corridor and gazed out of a window at the beautiful blue-grey of the sloping, twilight roofs and listened to the sound of fountains junketing from two large, flower-shaped metal basins in the dusky courtyard far below. My dreamy gaze was arrested by a number of quick, twitching movements across the nearby roofs: they were made by small animals with pale, bushy tails—*musasabi* or flying squirrels. The sky was already darkening, but in the courtyards it was night, for dense shadows lay under the magnificent, venerable cedars. Most of the gigantic pillars of the temple and the unpainted woodwork of the rooms were made of this noble timber.

My young priest guide came trotting back to tell me that supper was ready. It was then 6 p.m., and the usual bedlam of the temple was increased by the clangorous plangencies of an importunate bell whose throbbing note seemed to well up out of a distant chasm like the slow ripples of a flung stone in a spectral lake.

The dining-room had about forty mats. On two sides of the room, small red and gold lacquer tables were arranged in long rows, and in front of each was a small flat square cushion to kneel on. The tables were about one foot high and one foot square, and, as they were so small, there were two tables to each guest. On them stood tiny red lacquer soup bowls on whose red lacquer lids the temple crest was stamped in gold. Beside the bowls were laid plain wooden chopsticks in a paper sheath on the back of which prayers were helpfully printed. A young priest who was as good-looking as a film star sat at another table slightly apart: he had no food before him. He explained that he would read prayers for grace, and urged us to enjoy our food, which was all vegetarian and made by monks. We join in the priest's chanting of prayers as our soup slowly grows cold in the bowls. Beside soup, we have small dishes of pickled lotus root, radish, carrot, spinach, chrysanthemum leaves. When we begin to eat I discover there are two kinds of soup: in one bowl the ingredients include fresh, tasty sliced phallic mushrooms (*matsutake*) and chestnuts; the other has small cubes of bean-curd paste (*tofu*) bobbing in it. The meal is exquisite, delicious to taste and refined in appearance.

From time to time there is an *accelerando* of gongs and drums in the distance, where some kind of service must be going on in the main hall. The other guests at the meal eat in silence. Outside, in the corridors, priests are running about with small bells and clappers. One of the guests, a schoolboy of sixteen who is staying with his grandfather in the next room to mine, obviously cannot follow the text of the prayers or read some of the characters on the printed chopstick sheath, and a fleeting smile keeps jerking across his plump lips when he is not avidly gobbling rice from the bowl held close to his mouth. For dessert we are served with a segment of pear (*nashi*), my favourite fruit, and some sort of gluey jelly together with strange baked seaweed that is curiously plaited and smells like caramel cream: it is as crisp as a biscuit.

We are given a small paper bag of presents: two diminutive sugar cakes, a handkerchief printed with the temple's name and a packet of vividly coloured postcards showing views of the main buildings. The priest pours green tea into the empty soup bowls; we drink the tea with restrained slurpings of approval. The meal is over, but now we have another prayer from the back of the chopstick sheath. Then the priest tells us to put the chopsticks back in the sheath and use them the next day at breakfast. The atmosphere has been one of refined frugality which I always associate with traditional Japanese arts, particularly with poetry and painting.

It is only 7 p.m., but it is bedtime. In my room the beds are made up on the floor, but I have no wish to sleep at the moment and so I go wandering round the chill, darkened corridors and great waterfalls of mountainside stairs. More than once, drawn by curiosity, I opened doors and screens and glided like a ghost through mysterious rooms and great halls. In Japan I often feel I am not really myself, but a ghost of some ancient warrior, or a creature possessed by the spirit of a mystical fox or snake: that evening, as I tramped the corridors and grounds of the temple, I felt distinctly that I was the reincarnation of a mountain priest, for everything, though strange, seemed so familiar to me. At times I knew that I was possessed by the spirit of a horse, and heard echoes of melancholy neighings from the mountains. As I walked I found my head nodding with the motions of a noble, bridled steed, and my feet kicked sparks from the gravel of a deserted path.

As I was thus prancing silently and slowly along a wide corridor that led I knew not where, I encountered a tall European woman with grey hair and long skirts walking in meditation, with eyes lowered in the correct manner. I thought she was some ghost, and because of this, and also because I realized that she was British, I gave no sign, and we floated silently past one another without a word. Later I heard that she was no ghost, but a woman from England who was studying Zen.

On the walls of this dimly lit corridor were photographs of the great snowfall at Eiheiji in 1960. The whole temple had been buried under snow. The snowy roofs were house-high waves of frozen whiteness. Avalanches of snow had burst through the wood and glass walls of the corridors and flights of stairs had become sheer, smooth slopes, like ski-runs. It took an army of villagers and priests over a week to shovel it all away.

My priest companion looked disapprovingly at me when I blew my nose, because I used only one hand: one should always use both hands when blowing one's nose on a piece of paper. (Put the used paper in kimono sleeve and take it home to be disposed of.)

I lay awake all night, listening to heavy rain running like fountains from the roofs that are great tents of scrolled grey tiles muffed with moss; the tiles gleam with odd reflections from rare courtyard lamps. It was very cold, but in my bed on the floor I was very warm and comfortable, because before retiring I had taken a marvellously hot bath in a very plain, cavernous bathroom with a little shrine and a wooden notice saying: 'A god lives here, so do not speak or laugh while you are bathing, or he will be offended.' It was good to bathe thus with the priests in utter silence: Japanese public baths are usually so noisy! Indeed that bathroom was the quietest place in the temple.

Priests began running with bells along the corridors about 4 a.m. A gong began sounding an urgent summons to morning meditations. The gongs were joined by drums. The rain, dripping from various heights upon a variety of surfaces, both soft and hard, also plays its liquid percussion. A vast, wet wind from the mountains lurched into the room when I opened the sliding glass windows, and blew in a storm of dead leaves and a blizzard of pine needles. My priest and I shuffled sleepily along tunnels of roofed corridors and along open verandas, roofed and unroofed, up and down flights and flights of stairs to the main hall of worship, where I knelt through the long, incomprehensible service in dazed discomfort. Just when I thought I could bear the torture of kneeling no longer, a strange thing happened: I took leave of my body and forgot its pain, and found myself floating, still in the kneeling position, far above my body, upon which I looked down with satisfaction and amusement when I saw it was holding its pose in a trance of perfect immobility. Then someone up at the altar bashed a gong and I was back in my pain-racked body again, but determined to endure everything.

After a spartan breakfast of green tea and pickles I went to visit the temple's great hall, a huge affair with the most wonderful coffered ceiling I have seen in Japan: each square is different, exquisitely painted with a clear-tinted design of birds or flowers. In the grave, dark Zendo, or Hall of Zen Meditation, I found only one young priest who was sweeping the floor with a ragged home-made broom. I asked him if I might take a photograph of him in the pose of Zen meditation, and he obligingly got up on the raised platform running round the hall. The platform was covered with *tatami*, and there were rows of round, black and very hard-looking cushions. The young novice took one of these, on which his name was printed on a white tag, and settled firmly on it as he knelt to take his pose. He folded his hands in his lap in the approved manner and then at once seemed to become impregnated with deep inner stillness. Fortunately he was sitting in a pale shaft of sunlight that came through the open door, so I was able to take a dramatic shot of him in those austere and rather gloomy surroundings. As I took my leave a very old and cantankerous priest came running up and crossly asked the novice if I'd taken a picture of him. He upbraided the young man, saying the taking of such pictures was not allowed, and giving me baleful looks: I think he was just jealous because I hadn't taken *his* picture, something I had no desire to do.

I shimmered through the shaft of sunshine and out into the garden. A deep-toned gong struck and made autumn leaves fall and pine needles snow upon a large metal lantern. I left the young priest to his busy life of eating, sleeping, bathing, meditating, studying, cleaning the garden, worshipping, washing floors and bowls, serving visitors, banging gongs.

Later I had a brief interview with a head priest. I had to sit composedly on my heels on a square flat cushion outside a pair of sliding doors; in the kneeling position, I waited about ten minutes before the doors were opened to reveal my host. He was a massive man with a big, hearty laugh who reminded me very much of Dr Ramsey, the Archbishop of Canterbury, or Dr Samuel Johnson. His nose and smile were big, but he had very tiny ears on his shaven skull. His big hands with one long nail on the little finger of the right hand moved delicately as he showed me examples of calligraphy. He said that the character of the complete priest may be summed up in the phrase *un-sui*, which I gathered meant 'cloud-water'. He said that young priests who graduated from a Buddhist university like Komazawa were trained intellectually; what they lacked was physical training in the hard life of the temple: *un-sui* is the perfect combination of intellectual, physical and spiritual qualities that make a 'complete' priest. He certainly seemed to me to be one of the completest persons I have met.

Once when I was staying at Sojiji Temple in Tsurumi I wandered into the young priests' dormitory and spent a pleasant hour there chatting to them as one of their number shaved their heads with a cut-throat razor. When it was his turn to have his head shaved, each priest would kneel on a *zabuton* and hold a sheet of old newspaper in front of him after bowing to the shaver. The young priest with the razor then moistened the bristles on the other novice's head and began a careful scratching and scraping. It took about twenty minutes to shave an entire head, and all the while the priest being shaved kept his head bowed over the sheet of newspaper on which the clusters of tiny black bristles fell like scatterings of iron filings. When the operation was completed the shaver would run an appreciative hand over the greeny-blue, glassy smoothness of the shining pate, then bowed low in return as the shaved one bowed low in gratitude.

The young novices all seemed to be healthy, apple-cheeked country lads, and I wondered why they had chosen to study for the monkhood. In them I sensed what I had sensed in many young Zen Buddhists, a kind of repressed energy and violence that emerged in their manner of speaking and moving, which, though controlled, seemed to come from a deep well of inexhaustible vitality. They had none of the profound tranquillity of some of the older priests; in their archaic robes, they seemed to be bursting with life and energy. It is the physical training of the hard temple life that helps them to harness such forces for correct ends. There was something impressive about those youths, even when they sprawled on the matted floor reading newspapers or sat crosslegged in front of the television set that stood in one corner of their quarters. I wanted to live life their way, but did not know how to begin.

After I had watched several young men have their heads shaved, word came to me that a high-ranking priest had been informed about my visit and was concerned because I had not seen the head-shaving ceremony done in the correct manner. This made me realize how public life in a temple is, and how gossipy: like all Japanese people, monks love gossip, and so my unofficial visit to the young monks had provided an ideal opportunity for the exercise of this boundless faculty. When various messengers and informants had come and gone, running between the priest's chamber and the dormitory with succulent tit-bits of chatter, I finally received an invitation to visit the older priest and to observe the formal method of shaving the head. I went to his room, drank tea with him and admired his paintings, while an acolyte prepared the various bowls and cloths for the operation. He bowed to the priest, who bowed in return and lowered his head, holding some folded, pure white paper in front of him as the shaver set to work. It was not nearly as interesting as watching the young men being shaved in the dormitory, and I was bored by the stiff formality of the proceedings. I was glad I had first seen the operation in more relaxed surroundings and under less stringent rules. Rules there are in Japan, in temples as everywhere else; but the Japanese invent complicated rules for the sheer pleasure of breaking them. I had broken the rules at Sojiji, but I felt that, instead of being angry with me, everyone was excited and interested by my infringement of a code that was made to be broken, for Buddhism is, if nothing else, permissive and all-inclusive, which is perhaps why I, an outsider, feel so very much at home in the temples of Japan.

At the beginning of this chapter I said that I was beginning to have some glimmerings of a peculiar kind of religious belief. I can best illustrate these glimmerings in the following way: when I moved into my house on the campus of Japan Women's University I discovered a group of ancient stone Buddha figures and *o-jizo-sama* in a corner of the garden. They had been overgrown and neglected, and so I cut away some of the tree branches concealing them and swept them with a broom. To my surprise, this simple action filled me suddenly with tremendous happiness and peace, and I found myself instinctively clapping my hands twice in front of the statues and bowing my head in not very articulate prayer. Now I frequently place offerings of incense, fruit, wine, vegetables and sweets before the statues. Two of them are memorials of small children, and I just know they love me to leave a dish of chewing-gum or Batman toys in front of them. Every morning, at dawn, when I make my first cup of tea, I also take cups of tea to the figures in the garden, clap my hands twice, bow my head and talk to them for a few moments. It has become a ritual, like having a bath: if I don't do it, I feel unsatisfied, unclean, unhappy. Just to share my morning tea with those statues brings peace and happiness into my life, and I feel sure they look forward to my visits. They have become my guardian spirits. Can this, I wonder, be the beginnings of faith? It is a feeling I have never had before, and one I could never have known if I had not come to spend my life here in Japan, and to take tea at temples.

Index